Narrativity in Cognition

Brook Miller

Narrativity in Cognition

palgrave
macmillan

Brook Miller
Center for Humanities and Digital Research
University of Central Florida
Orlando, FL, USA

ISBN 978-3-031-40348-4   ISBN 978-3-031-40349-1   (eBook)
https://doi.org/10.1007/978-3-031-40349-1

This Palgrave Macmillan imprint is published by the registered company Springer Nature
Switzerland AG.
The registered company address is: Gewerbestrasse 11, 6330 Cham, Switzerland

Paper in this product is recyclable.

To Ellis, Sam, and Chrissy, with love and thanks

ACKNOWLEDGMENTS

and critiques
re much
gues
r

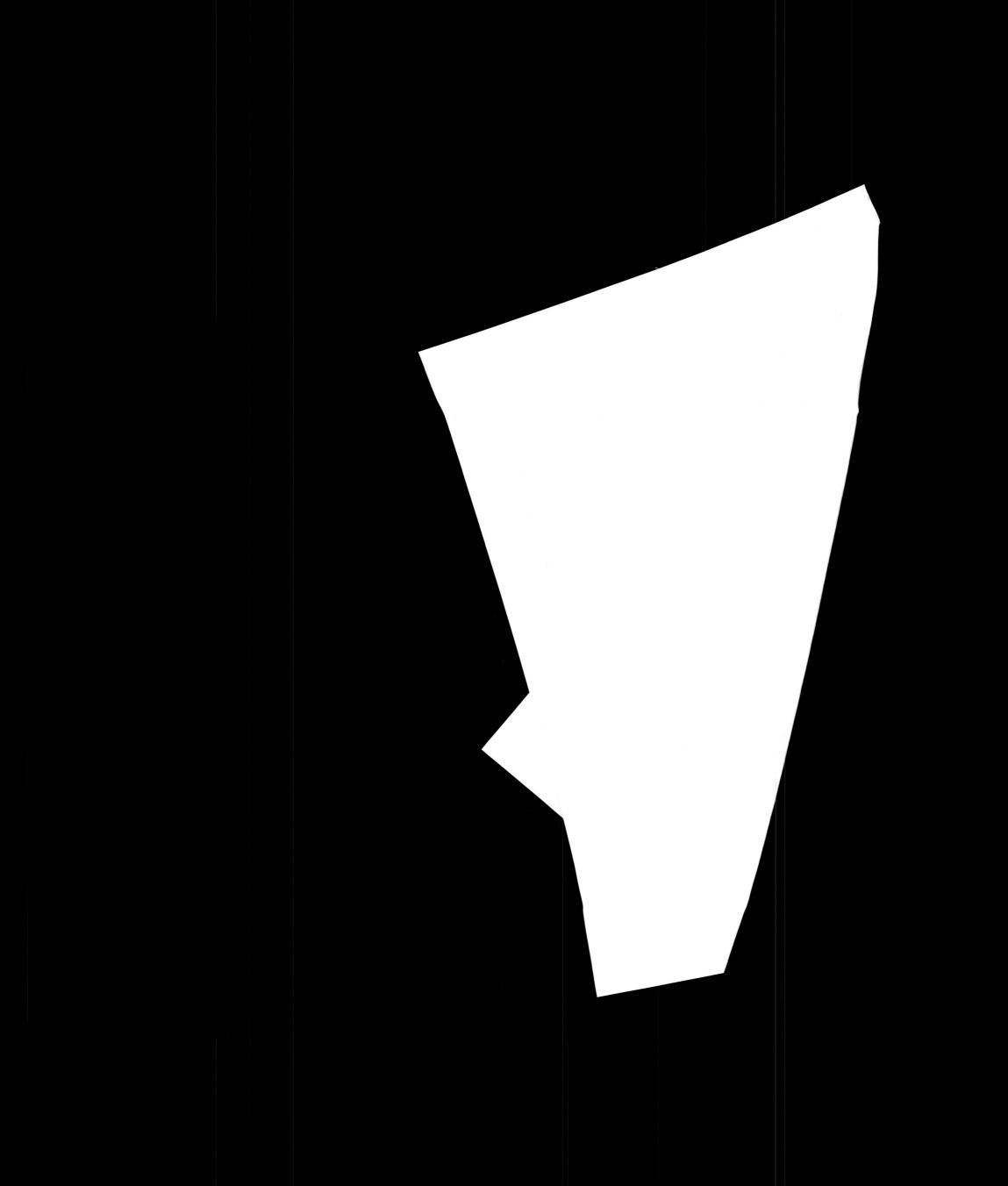

To Ellis, Sam, and Chrissy, with love and thanks

ACKNOWLEDGMENTS

Many people provided outstanding feedback, suggestions, and critiques during conferences and manuscript reviews. The ideas here are much improved by these efforts. Specifically, thanks to my friends and colleagues Dr. Don Wehrs, Dr. Marco Caracciolo, and Dr. Mike Sinding for their generosity and support.

Thank you to the Hanse-Wissenschaftskolleg (Delmenhorst, Germany) for supporting this work with a 2020 fellowship in the "Fiction Meets Science" program, and particularly to Susan Gaines, Dr. Dorothe Poggel, and the rector of the HWK, Professor Kerstin Schill, for their generosity and collegiality. Thanks to the University of Minnesota, Morris, especially Dr. Julie Eckerle and Dr. Michael Lackey for their friendship and support. Thank you to the University of Central Florida's College of Arts and Humanities and the Center for Humanities and Digital Research, especially Dr. Bruce Janz, Dr. Mark Kamrath, Dr. Amy Giroux, Executive Associate Dean Lyman Brodie, and Dean Jeffrey Moore for support and opportunities for growth. Thank you to Bob Bergman and Sue Strommer, proprietors of the Wesley Heights and Grand Atlantic writers retreats, for their hospitality.

Thanks to Sam Miller for help with illustrations.

My love and thanks to my family and friends.

CONTENTS

1 Introduction   1

2 Approaches to Narrative   9

3 Narrativity and Intention   33

4 Narrativity and Reading Narratives   59

5 Cognition: Contemporary Views and Debates   95

6 Events and Weak Narrativity   119

7 Affect and Weak Narrativity   155

8 Narrativity in Higher Order Cognition   197

9 Conclusion   229

Index   235

LIST OF FIGURES

Fig. 2.1   Narrative features, experience, and narrative reconfiguration   10
Fig. 3.1   Authors, readers, intention, and narrativity   36
Fig. 3.2   Author, reader, narrativity, and intention: artifactual and
           processing views   37
Fig. 7.1   From Bakker and de Boon: Pleasure, Arousal, and Harmony   174
Fig. 7.2   From Bakker and de Boon: order and variation   175
Fig. 8.1   Mapping of component processes to cognitive functions (rpt.
           from Hassabis and Maguire 2007)   198
Fig. 8.2   Necessary features of scheme structure (rpt. from Ghosh and
           Gilboa 2014)   208
Fig. 8.3   Hypothetical Functional Neuroanatomical Model of Memory
           Schemas (rpt. from Gilboa Marlatte, p. 620; note: a brain
           diagram at the top of this figure is not included)   210

List of Tables

Table 4.1   A Taxonomy of Relationalities   75
Table 4.2   Processing structures in narrative reading and ordinary
             experiences   77

Introduction

Narrative is at once ubiquitous and difficult to define clearly. In part, this is because there are so many varieties of narrative: fictional narratives, journalistic narratives, some poems ('narrative poems'), histories, and the like forms of (usually) written communication. Then there are primarily oral forms, like recounted stories from friends and loved ones. Film and television programming is full of narratives, and one could plausibly claim that films with little or no language (such as Michael Dudok De Wit's *The Red Turtle*) are nevertheless narratives. In our heads, we may hold narratives of various kinds—an autobiographical story (or stories) of who we are, stories that characterize and even define others, stories we are formulating (for various purposes), and episodic memories may qualify. These may be communicated, intentionally conceived for communication, or generated in the course of reflective thought.

There are many borderline cases—for example, can intuitions, observations, fantasies, fear responses, and the like have narrative features? If so, should they be considered narratives? If they do have narrative features but shouldn't be considered narratives, what accounts for the origins of their narrative features (since they aren't rendered through a formal process of narrative construction)?

How might all of these entities with narrative features relate to how we think, act, and communicate? Take a fictional example to illustrate these complexities. Rachael goes to her book club one night, prepared to discuss

B. Miller, *Narrativity in Cognition*, https://doi.org/10.1007/978-3-031-40349-1_1

a well-regarded novel about several attempted prison escapes from the penal colony Devil's Island in French Guiana in the nineteenth and twentieth centuries. On the drive to the book club host's house, Rachael thinks about her assessment of the book—it was so packed with historical detail that there wasn't enough character development. However, she learned a lot from the book about the history of French occupation and about the atmosphere of the period. On the way, she passes the county penitentiary and notices a group of men in prison jumpsuits gathering garbage at the perimeter of the high chain-link fence. One of the men looks up and stares at her as her car zooms past. When Rachael arrives at the book club host's home, she finds that the host (and Rachael's longtime rival), Elizabeth, has switched the book (telling the other members, but not Rachael) and has set up a video interview with the author of the new book (a vampire romance), which Rachael hasn't read. The author is charming and smart, and the book sounds more like something Rachael would connect to emotionally. The author appears on Elizabeth's large screen monitor and appears to be in a luxurious hotel room.

From this small set of details, narratives or entities like narratives might intertwine in any number of ways—Rachael might fantasize about the luxurious life of the author on the monitor, imagining a scene from her life (a part of her *life-story*). Rachael might feel Elizabeth's behavior is part of an effort to marginalize her (Rachael), and to become the leader of the book club (say Rachael had started the book club with some friends). This might be understood as an 'ongoing story' of Elizabeth's desire for control. More complexly, Rachael might respond to her marginalization by reframing her evaluation of the book about Devil's Island—whereas the Devil's Island book was substantive, the new book reflected a pure entertainment with little of value. This contributes to a larger trend, and perhaps a story, about the direction of the reading group, and about Rachael's own changing interests as a reader. In a humorous thought, she might compare Elizabeth to the brutal French authorities in the Devil's Island book and graft the situation in the book club onto the plot of the book. Moreover, the gaze from the prisoner on her drive over sticks with her, and she finds herself thinking up a story, inspired by events in the two books, in which he is plotting escape and needs to prey upon a lone driver.

This makes her instinctively not want to drive back past the prison on the way home, but she does so anyways, forcing herself to do something brave and feeling she has achieved something as a result. Her sense of overcoming fear may have narrative dimensions, and may be linked to how she has viewed her responses to fear in the past.

In this example, narratives are not lone entities to which the subject relates in an attitude of judgment (as Rachael begins the anecdote in relation to the book about Devil's Island). Instead, they are combinatorial, used for 'making sense' of the world (as a world of social interaction, for example), for self-evaluation, and perhaps for other purposes. They also shape, sometimes unconsciously, how a particular experience feels. Responses to narratives are shaped by experiences, but narratives also shape experiences on many levels—from long-term interpersonal dynamics (Rachael's relationship to Elizabeth) to processing of immediate experience (the high danger associated with the prisoners, a feeling Rachael may not have previously felt).

Indeed, narratives and experiences intertwine in feedback loops, as the final detail of Rachael 'triumphing' over her fear of the prison, and its potential linkages to her reading, her earlier experience in the car, and her disaffection at the book club illustrate.

Rachael's story points to how cognitive processes shape our experiences.[1] Rachael's various thoughts and responses over the course of the anecdote range from 'higher order' or 'second order' cognition—specifically, thoughts about Rachael's identity and status over long time spans—to immediate cognition of perceptual data. The question is, how does narrative fit in? In all cases, narratives might be understood to 'prime,' 'frame,' or otherwise contribute to particular evaluations, and particular perceptions can be understood to have similar effects on narratives.

Additionally, narratives seem to be retrospective configurations of experiences, and they seem to reshape one another. Finally, Rachael seems to imagine undisclosed details and anticipate future events based on a narrative logic. For example, as she passes the penitentiary on her way home she may imagine what she'd do if a man stepped into the road in front of her approaching vehicle.

Since this is only a fictional anecdote, we can't assume the truth or falsity of whether any of the kinds of dynamics described actually exist. In all likelihood, and by convention, as you read this you may nevertheless evaluate all, some, or none as plausible. The intuitive confidence you may feel reading and evaluating narrative content and narrative structure and function before considering empirical evidence may also point to peculiarities in our thinking about experiences.

The concepts 'narrative' and 'cognition' can be related in several ways. If understanding narrative is the priority, then understanding cognition can help illuminate how human readers process narratives. Another arrangement is to consider how particular types of narratives—novels in particular—'imagine minds,' as one book puts it. That is, the narratives offer direct or implied commentary on how certain parts of cognition operate. Third, and most prominently, scholarship has focused on how narratives are part of human social experience, and therefore affect and are shaped by beliefs. That is, what role might narratives play in setting the terms for or functioning as the subjects of social intercourse?

Each of these three basic approaches has a large number of subsidiary approaches. They are characteristic of the humanities, the third in particular being dominant. In this area, social cognition is often a framework for explaining the contents or impact of particular narratives.

Analyses of novels, myths, plays, and other narrative artifacts often reflect theories of how stories are shaped by and shape social beliefs. In addition, these three basic approaches are frequently employed in analyses that concern other factors internal and external to the contents of narrative. For example, an approach to understanding what happens to readers processing narratives (the first approach mentioned above) would likely be shaped by ideas about developmental, sociocultural, and historical contexts.

However, these approaches are not pursued only in the humanities. Narrative is analyzed in numerous disciplines, as well as in several sub-disciplinary approaches in psychology. Within these fields, the kinds of narratives studied, the assumptions grounding analyses of them, and the contexts in which they consider the functioning of narrative all shape disciplinary understandings of what narratives are and how they work.

This diversity reflects an ongoing lack of consensus about what is necessary and sufficient for a given text, idea, or sequence to qualify as a narrative. It may be best to think of given texts, ideas, and sequences as 'more or less' narratives, or as having more or fewer, in higher or lower concentration and consistency, of the features that we can generally agree are 'narrative' features. This is problematic, however, if we want to think in precise philosophical terms, and it's even worse if we want to conduct empirical research on how narrative intersects with cognition.

To begin addressing these challenges, the first half of this book considers questions about narrative. It begins with what specialists in narrative form from a variety of fields have to say about narrative and the concept 'narrativity.' It considers how we process narratives and how narrativity emerges in ordinary cognition.

The second half of the book focuses upon the temporal and semantic structuring intrinsic to these ordinary cognitions. It argues that a range of processes, from perception to long-term conceptualizations of identity, history, and goals, involve narrative qualities. It proposes to call these qualities 'weak narrativity,' with the goal of providing an explanation of emergent, provisional, sense-making dynamics involved in perception that can be considered complementarily with innovative research into the emergent, provisional, and sense-making role narrative and storytelling plays in social discourse, higher order thinking, and other fields.

To do so may seem at odds with how we understand the operations of cognition and 'consciousness.' Older models have not typically engaged narrative as a topic of study. However, emerging ideas in cognitive psychology and neuroscience might help us understand whether the features of cognition we associate with narrative and narrativity exist empirically, and if they do, how they fit in with a general understanding of cognition.

The processes associated with 'weak narrativity,' within the context of this new research, might help address some difficult questions, such as: What cognitive processes seem to automatically or unconsciously delimit event boundaries that are subsequently accessible in memory? What processes underlie detail selection for the present experience or recall of temporality? What mechanisms facilitate the experience of salience when we experience narrative texts, and do those same salience mechanisms apply to non-textual, ordinary 'situations'? How are experiences enchained into meaningful sequences? What is the 'stuff' of identity, and how is it generated, consolidated, deployed, and altered in varied contexts and over time?

The thesis developed in this book is that we can make inroads into describing and understanding how narrative figures into our thinking by emphasizing narrative processing. Consider the 'ready to hand' nature of stories we communicate to others. When we retell a story, we may be simply drawing on our memory of an artifact to create a new communicative artifact, modifying it by thinking about, as the story is elaborated, how the audience might perceive it. However, what about our ability to give narrative form to experiences that we've never communicated or heard communicated on the spot?

For example, let's return to Rachael—she arrives at home, and her part-ner asks her about her evening at the book club. As she recounts the eve-ning, she offers several narratives of all that happened—the odd coincidence of seeing the prisoner and the book she'd read, Elizabeth's power play and the video interview with the author, and the fear she overcame on the drive home. In each case, as is evident from the description above, Rachael's stories involve evaluative assertions that either place a particular observation of or experience of an event within contexts that anchor a particular value relation to Rachael (in the sense that she generates an analytic or emotional evaluation of agents in the event, often in relation to how she values herself or believes she is valued by others).

The fact that Rachael comes home ready to communicate these stories probably reflects a process of silent rehearsal conducted on the drive home, but the materials for such rehearsal themselves may seem available without much conscious reflection. Who or what the agents are, how they relate, and what spatial and temporal boundaries the story falls within may seem like givens, while Rachael may give more conscious attention to framing her stories within larger narrative or non-narrative contexts. The struc-tures of the stories themselves culminate with the emergence of evaluative claims—in a sense, the stories are processing systems for arriving at those claims.

Rachael's experiences—and I believe experience generally—are under-stood narratively for the sake of, or *toward*, evaluative claims. I use the term 'valuative' because 'evaluative' tends to involve epistemological clo-sure, usually offered in an analytical framework, whereas 'valuative' can designate valuations that emerge from experience and post-experiential processing, and that maintain combinatorial freedoms that 'evalua-tions' do not.

This claim about the importance of narrative to cognition rests on a view of narrative as a particularly malleable form of processing that com-bines emotional and analytical features, automatic and reflective cogni-tion, and that produces and continually revises narrative concepts of self and experience. As such, narrative processing, while it draws upon cate-gorical, analytical thinking and understanding, can also be its supporting architecture, a point illustrated through the complex relations between episodic and semantic memory. Narrative processing is a profoundly flex-ible, self-relevant form of particularistic concatenation that draws upon and supports our temporal sense, salience-seeking systems, and social understanding. More simply it is, as narrative theorist David Herman puts the matter, a basic strategy for human understanding that links automatic, unconscious phenomena such as how we delimit experiences in the world to higher order thinking processes, such as the elusive search for personal meaning (2003).

These concepts will be developed in the chapters to come. Conceptually, it builds upon insights from discourse theory and narrative hermeneutics that conceptualizing of narrative as a form of processing helps scholars explore its elusive, iterative, contextual nature. As Hanna Meretoja (2022) writes about narrative identity, "'narrative' should be understood less as a noun than as an activity: as the temporal, interactional process of narrative reinterpretation that is constitutive of identity" (p. 281). This book extends Meretoja's insight into individual perceptual cognition, albeit 'weakly.' Weakly narrative processes align well with some of the most promising models of cognition emerging in the empirical research, and they warrant the hypothesis that the role of narrative in higher order cognition can be more fully understood through attention to the emergent narrative features of lower order cognition.

Or, for now, consider the following coda to Rachael's story: after her partner goes to bed, Rachael puts on the local news. The first story is breaking news—within the past hour, a criminal broke out of the county prison and car-jacked a commuter traveling along the adjacent highway. Imagine the narrative processing in Rachael's head as she goes to awaken her partner.

NOTE

1. The distinction between 'cognition' and 'experience' is relevant to this discussion. Cognition refers to structures and processes of perception, memory, reflective thought, intuition, and other means by which we acquire knowledge and understanding. 'Experience' draws from the phenomenological tradition. It refers to first-person conscious experience characterized by meaning and the feeling, or 'what it is like-ness,' of happening. The thesis of this book via these definitions is that experience is constituted in part by cognitive processing that employs a narrative logic. Also, narrative thoughts that emerge in the course of ordinary cognition are linked to a feature of ordinary cognition: narrative forms help render the stream of phenomena meaningful. I've preferred the language of cognition here in anticipation of the chapters that explore theories of cognitive processing in the second half of the book.

References

Herman, D. (2003). Stories as a tool for thinking. In D. Herman (Ed.), *Narrative theory and the cognitive sciences* (pp. 163–192). Center for the Study of Language and Information.

Meretoja, H. (2022). Life and narrative. *The Routledge Companion to Narrative Theory*, 273–285. https://doi.org/10.4324/9781003100157-26.

CHAPTER 2

Approaches to Narrative

How is narrative related to experience?[1] There's a relatively old debate about the relation of narrative to real life: Are narrative features part of experience *and* retrospective configurations of experience, or simply the latter?[2]

The question can be represented graphically. In Fig. 2.1, there are three options: either narrative reconfigures non-narrative experiences, as in A, or narrative features inhere in experience (B), or both A and B are the case (C). It seems self-evident that narratives as commonly understood are reconfigurations of experiences. For example, you might say to a junior colleague, 'let me tell you the story of how I decided to support Elba as the new manager of our department.' In your subsequent telling, you'd likely select and organize experiences that ultimately make your reasons for supporting Elba understandable, and even persuasive. Perhaps you'd present circumstances that at first made you support another candidate, and a set of events that convinced you Elba was the right choice. Perhaps you regret this support, and your report makes it seem reasonable that you held the view you did at the time, perhaps with some explanation of the subsequent events that made you withdraw that support. Simply put, your view of Elba's appropriateness for the post is explained via a configuring of experiences. So A describes a necessary characterization of narrative, which means that B is not fully explanatory.

B. Miller, *Narrativity in Cognition,*
https://doi.org/10.1007/978-3-031-40349-1_2

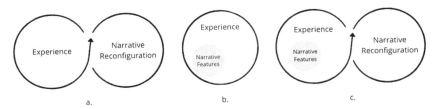

Fig. 2.1   Narrative features, experience, and narrative reconfiguration

This book argues that C is, in fact, an appropriate way to view the situation. Before we begin making the case for this, let's consider a series of subsidiary questions that emerge from comparing A and C.

1. Is narrative somehow *intrinsic to* the reality that humans experience?
2. Is narrative an *intrinsic process or property of* how we experience reality?
3. Is narrative a *vehicle for* imbuing our experiences with meaning?
4. Is narrative *exclusively a means of communicating*, sometimes about what we've experienced?
5. Are narratives *exclusively artifacts* that we employ to communicate about past, present, future, and hypothetical experiences?

For each, if the answer is yes, then how and why?

These questions indicate a variety of potential relationships between narrative and experience. While affirmative answers to questions 1 and 2 would seem to support model C, negative answers would suggest model A is correct. Affirmative answers to questions 4 and 5 would suggest a strong version of model A. An affirmative answer to question 3 raises interesting possibilities for understanding either model A or model C. In terms of the latter, the way in which narrative is a 'vehicle' might have a fuzzy boundary with the idea presented in question 2, that narrative is an intrinsic process or property of how we experience reality.

In this chapter we'll survey the variety of ways narrative has been implicated in experience, beginning with approaches to the relationship, followed by a review of how narrative has been used to collect data about and make sense of human experience across a range of academic disciplines. The goal is to introduce the variety of approaches to the issue, rather than to offer exhaustive analyses. Chapters 3 and 4 consider many of the issues raised here in greater detail.

2.1   Definitions of Narrative

What are the necessary and sufficient properties of narrative? 'Narrative' functions as an umbrella term, including objects and phenomena that individual theorists do not group together. This has implications for taxonomies of the general characteristics of narrative, as well as narrative's inner structural relations. For example, a prominent debate regarding narrative in relation to history contrasts 'narratives' to sequences of events, such as those that comprise an 'annal.'[3] The difference is generally understood to involve a stronger emphasis on causality and context in narrative, as well as a structural sequence featuring beginnings, middles, and ends.

Minimalists, like Peter Lamarque, require only temporal extension and certain kinds of sequential relations, especially causality. Lamarque's thesis is that "at least two events must be depicted in a narrative and there must be some more or less loose, albeit non-logical relation between the events. Crucially, there is a temporal dimension in narrative" (Lamarque, p. 394). Catriona Mackenzie (2009) believes causality, as well as sequentiality, is necessary to minimal narrative definitions.[4]

While minimalists focus on the features and logic that comprise narrative, others insist on the integral nature of perspectives or knowledge outside of the narrative proper to any constitutive features. For example, Peter Goldie (2012) argues that "narratives have narrative structure to a greater or lesser degree: coherence, meaningfulness, and evaluative and emotional import" (p. 13). Yet he believes narrative requires a narrating perspective with encompassing knowledge. So, for Goldie narrative cannot emerge *in situ* without reflective construction.

Katherine Nelson (2003) describes "three essential components of narrative": "temporal perspective, the mental as well as physical perspective of self and of different others, and essential cultural knowledge of the unexperienced world" (p. 28). Her insistence on these attributes reflects a developmental model of the emergence of narrative capacities in children.

Minimalist theories risk making 'narrative' indistinguishable from perception and causal inference. More robust theories, by contrast, can preclude the possibility that narrative is inextricably part of experience. Also, maximalist theories struggle to clarify rather blurry lines between what's narrative and what's not narrative, and end up deploying concepts like 'narrativity' and 'proto-narrative' to acknowledge that non-narrative texts, and even non-textual features of cognition, can have narrative features.

Some thinkers address this problem head-on. Kintsch and Van Dijk (1978) propose an influential model of narrative composed of "micro-structure," "macrostructure," and "superstructure," separating minimal narrative elements while maintaining a robust view of narrative as a whole. Marie-Laure Ryan describes narrative as a "gradient" concept and supports a "fuzzy-set" definition of narrative, which helps "eliminate[ ] bad stories." For Ryan (2007), this criterion for narrative is related to "context and the interests of the participants" (i.e., the audience and author/story-teller) (p. 30). However, this position opens the door for some ambiguity, as Ryan insists on a distinction between "being a narrative" and "possessing narrativity" (p. 30).

This ambiguity is addressed by David Herman, who describes narrative as a combination of gradience for certain features and strict requirement for others. For readers who'd like to delve into definitional debates about narrative in more detail, Herman's 2009 *Basic Elements of Narrative* provides an insightful discussion of the different positions. In defining narrative, Herman invokes three key threads in narrative research that will subsequently be described in this chapter: first, discourse context, communication, and interpreters; second, a history of attempts to link narrative to experience in philosophy and psychology; and third, the range of roles narrative plays in the study of particular topics in psychology.

2.2   Narrative as a Form of Social Discourse

Narratives have long been viewed as special forms of social discourse conveying cultural values, conflicts, and models of development. Folklorist Vladimir Propp (2010), for example, identifies generic narrative functions in folk tales. His model suggests the existence of persistent genres transmitted through culturally determined narrative traditions, which themselves become important reference points for assigning meaning to experiences, agents, and the like.

In the late 1960s, Labov and Waletzky pioneered an influential model that positioned narrative as integral to ordinary social discourse. In so doing, Labov and Waletzky highlight everyday narrative discourse as a vital area for study. Narrative discourse analysis explores the semantic grammar of narrative to make sense of its social function.

Ideas about narrative and history have had a complex relationship, stemming from the tendency of historians to employ narrative forms in history-writing. In the 1980s, a number of historians theorized about the necessity and priority of narrative in relation to the past, weighing in on whether narrative is imposed upon past experience or inherent (or inchoate) within it. Louis Mink views narrative as a mode of comprehension, while Hayden White (1980) critiques narrative versions of history because they reflect a fundamental human desire for meaning.[5] White's view reflects strong suspicion toward narratives as sources of biased meaning in postmodern thought. Mink offers some pro-narrative views but expresses a Sartrean skepticism toward seeing meaning in experience. Mink (1970) argues that "life has no beginnings, middles, or ends; there are meetings, but the start of an affair belongs to the story we tell ourselves later, and there are partings, but final partings only in the story" (p. 557). Within critical theory, Jean-Francois Lyotard argues that the sustaining sociocultural 'meta-narratives' of post-Enlightenment modernity were in crisis in a post-modern age.

2.3   Narrative as Integral to Various Kinds of Experience

A variety of thinkers have considered narrative as inseparable from how we experience time and ourselves. Philosophical discussions of time have long implicated features common to narrative and ordinary experience. Aristotle is often credited as the first Western thinker to argue that narrative arts emerge from how humans experience time, including the view that narrative consists of beginnings, middles, and ends that track the disruption of an order, followed by resolution.

St. Augustine of Hippo offers an early version of the view that our experiences of the present are penetrated by anticipation of the future and memory of the past, a theme elaborated by Edmund Husserl in his theory of temporal 'protention' and 'retention' in presence, and developed by Martin Heidegger. In these views time is a human production, in which befores and afters (in the form of memory and anticipation, in particular) mediate the experience of the present so that it is a rich and evolving thread rather than a succession of discrete instants. Paul Ricœur (1983/2009), in *Time and Narrative*, links this tripartite temporality explicitly to narrative, seeing in it inchoate structures of beginning, middle, and end, though he ultimately views narrative as a phenomenon proper to a different modality, and sees the experience of temporality as pre-narrative.

In contrast to theories defining narrative as a *post hoc*, ideologically sus-pect way of making sense of personal and social history, Alasdair MacIntyre claims that our lives take on narrative forms embedded in larger historical stories, even in a context of postmodern crisis about the failures of some of the grand theories of modernity. So, for MacIntyre "narrative history of a certain kind turns out to be the basic and essential genre for the charac-terization of human actions" (p. 42).[6]

MacIntyre's view rests upon the hypothesis that narrative is "constitu-tive of human identity, not imposed *a posteriori* on a non-narrative thing-in-itself" (Hinchman and Hinchman, p. xxiii). This theory has several later iterations, such as Miller Mair's belief that stories are "habitations" which so dominate our thinking that we have no other way of knowing the world than through them (p. 4).[7]

This view shifts the debate from communications about history into the interior, subjective experience of consciousness. Theories about the role of narrative in consciousness have been described, collectively, as the "narra-tive hypothesis" or "Narrative Practice Hypothesis." Variations focus upon the elements of consciousness in which narrative is important: for example, episodic memory, the notion of selfhood, and the internalization and application of social norms.

The narrative hypothesis is, broadly, that humans are uniquely devoted to storytelling. Psychologist Jerome Bruner (1991) offers the most influ-ential early formulation: "We organize our experience and our memory of human happenings mainly in the form of narrative…Narratives, then, are a version of reality whose acceptability is governed by convention and 'narrative necessity' rather than by empirical verification and logical requiredness" (pp. 4–5). Bruner sees narrative first as part of 'folk psychol-ogy'—narrative is a means of understanding what motivates others, and therefore a key to understanding social events (based upon prior familiar-ity with narratives that offer normative versions of social events). Second, narrative is the stuff of autobiography—a central feature of consciousness is the continual construction of a coherent life story (and this reflexive process 'codes' life events in relation to normative values).

The role of perspective is important in discussions of the narrative hypothesis (cf. Goldie, above). Phillip Lewin (1992), for example, sees narrative structures as essential to apprehending the intentionality of oth-ers. That is, narratives have built in points-of-view that insinuate meaning into temporal sequences through forms of reference to sociocultural val-ues. Narrative perspective is important for two reasons—first, it illuminates the behaviors of others; and second, it fosters a sense of distance from one's own experience. These views of perspective take narrative as a 'second order' configuration of experience and understand 'perspective' as 'narrative perspective' rather than the implicit subjectivity of immediate presence.

Following the identity-orientation of these branches of the narrative hypothesis, successors of Bruner have considered how the narrative hypothesis might help us understand the elusive experience of self. For these thinkers, selfhood either *is* narrative or is a synthesis, nodal point, or distillation of narratives. Narrative accounts seek to explain the self for whom subjective experience appears to be curated. Scholars such as Daniel Dennett have written influential accounts of how self is an illusion, the 'center of gravity' in narratives fabricated in the brain, and Marya Schectman views autobiography as constitutive of selfhood. There has been significant resistance to these views, perhaps best exemplified in Galen Strawson's 2004 argument "Against Narrativity."

Versions of the narrative hypothesis offer models for how subjects internalize social values into their mechanisms for coping with social experience and into their self-images. For some of these thinkers (cf. Paul Eakin), narrative perspective has an inchoate irony that is experienced subjectively as the difference between the self as a 'teller' or moderating consciousness and the self as an actor in the world.

Others focus upon narrative's role in Theory of Mind, providing a logic for folk psychological intuitions of the motivations and perceptions of other subjects. Folk psychological and autobiographical approaches to narrative as part of consciousness generally operate at a relatively high 'level' of cognition, in which reflection and deliberation play key roles.

Philosophers Daniel Hutto and Patrick McGivern argue that narrative figures into thinking about the past and future as "mental time travel." Narrative allows us to organize important elements of experience into concatenated wholes while accounting for the thoughts and actions of others. The capacity to synthesize heterogenous elements of experience into time-extended simulations makes narrative a particularly flexible and powerful processing "tool for thinking" (Herman 2003).

In literary studies, reader response criticism has been supplemented by increased interest in cognition through the emergence of cognitive literary studies. Taken together, scholars of narrative and psychologists have explored the experience of consuming received narrative. Whereas for literature, film, and other humanities scholars, this emphasis has tended to illuminate how readers (and viewers, and listeners) of narrative have participated in constructing the meanings of the narratives, psychologists have investigated the psychological mechanisms through which readers, viewers, and listeners consume narratives, as well as the near and long-term impacts of this consumption (cf. Richard Gerrig). In pursuit of a meta-explanation of the themes reviewed in the last several paragraphs, there has been a tendency to describe storytelling as an evolutionarily advantageous activity, and storytelling as a 'bio-cultural' practice. This group, which includes Joseph Carroll, Brian Boyd, Dennis Dutton, and Nancy Easterlin, tends, along with Paul Hernadi, to view narratives as adaptive mechanisms that reflect evolutionary group imperatives, rather than immediate individual advantage.

Some recent narratologists, including Monika Fludernik and David Herman, have reassessed the nature and function of narrative by considering how narrativity derives from "cognitive ('natural') parameters" (Fludernik 1996, p. xi), or by viewing narrative as a basic strategy for human understanding (Herman 2003). Each model offers relatively brisk assessments of how properties of narrative figure into cognitive functioning, and ultimately locate narrativity in post-experiential cognitive processing. However, each offers suggestive ideas about how narrativity emerges in relation to goal-directed cognition and allostatic cognition, and in the uniqueness of narrative's representation of human experience (for more, see Chap. 3, Sect. 3.3).

Recent work in discourse studies (Bamberg and Georgakolpolou 2008) has argued for recentering discussions of narrative around the 'small stories' evoked in everyday communication and discourse. Alexandra Georgakopoulou (2007) describes this 'small stories' approach as seeking a "reconceptualization of [narrative] structure…directed towards":

- A study of structure as sequential and emergent, that … hinges on a view of narrative as talk-in-interaction.
- A study of structure as temporalized, that hinges on a view of narrative as dialogic, intertextual, and recontextualizable.
- A pluralized view of structure as variable and potentially fragmented that hinges on a view of narrative as consisting of a multitude of genres. (p. 86)

2.4   Narrative as Methodology

Scholars from numerous fields regularly employ narrative methods in their research. As Morgan and Wise (2017) argue, "narrative provides a natural format for describing development and change through time, with later states unfolding from earlier ones in sometimes convoluted paths" (p. 2). Narrative is particularly useful for explaining complex systems and offers a logic that helps expose evidentiary gaps and suture different forms of evidence together. Morgan, Wise, and Beatty cite examples from Darwinian theory, paleoanthropology, political science, and medicine.

Yet narrative has occupied, and continues to occupy, a subordinate position in many fields. In sociocultural theory, for example, "narrative, especially first-person singular narrative, has been very much marginalized by the social sciences until recently because the social scientists have used the empirical scientific paradigm as a model" (Watkins-Goffman p. 4).[8]

Most fields that have adopted the concept have fashioned it from a commonplace, and perhaps parochial, understanding of the term, and have "reinterpreted the idea of narrative" to suit their disciplinary assumptions (Hatavara et al. 2013, p. 248). Hatavara et al. describe a series of turns toward narrative, which moves interest away from literary fictional narratives to non-fictional forms. Inspired by the "narrative turn in literature, with its structuralist program and scientific rhetoric" in the 1960s and 1970s, historiography experienced a narrative turn in the 1970s, followed more broadly in the 1980s and thereafter in fields like psychology and other social sciences, education, and media and communication studies (pp. 14–15).

Van Peer and Chatman catalog how disciplines including anthropology, ethics, psychology, sociology, history, and historiography studied narrative before the turn of the century (pp. 2–3).[9]

In the face of this diversity, they suggest focusing on types of narratives, rather than grouping them all together, and accepting the incompatibility of research deploying different types.

Kreiswirth sees narrative as ubiquitous in the social and natural sciences. While he shares Lyotard's view of narrative as "the quintessential form of customary knowledge," he believes its traveling and usage are overextended (p. 38). Brockmeier notes that because of the vast range of narratives and applications, the concept 'narrative' itself has been treated as a baggy, unhelpful metaphor (p. 101).[10]

Behind this wide range of uses of the term 'narrative' are the needs of individual disciplines, which include accumulated histories of research assumptions and practices within which narrative-based research must be reconciled. Additionally, however, the metaphorical character of the concept 'narrative' relates to the divisive nature of the concept itself. While fields like psychology *may* be open to the charge that they haven't attended carefully to the scholarship in narratology, there is no consensus even about the definition of the object narratologists purport to study.

2.5   Narrativity in Perceptual Cognition

A number of theories suggest inchoate narrativity is part of perception. The groundwork for these ideas was done in the 1930s, when Frederic Bartlett pioneered the idea of 'schemas' as central to perceptual experience, challenging contemporary notions of memory based upon static capture and recall of past events. Instead, Bartlett describes processes of construction and reconstruction.

Schemas provide a way of explaining our facility for narrating our experiences. In the late 1970s, Schank and Abelson pioneered "frame theory," which described "holistic situation schema … of a prototype nature" (Fludernik 1996, p. 17). Mark Johnson and George Lakoff described 'image schemas' as embodied, pre-linguistic concepts. Successors of this work have developed the idea to emphasize the analog relationship between sensorimotor activity and image schemas, and to see inchoate small stories built from them in experience (Lakoff 1997; Johnson 2013). For example, Johnson (1993) described the "PATH" schema (following a trajectory of 'source,' 'path,' and 'goal') as analogous to one of the archetypal narrative structures of Western storytelling, the 'journey.'

While schemas may provide a key link between perceptions and our ability to retroactively configure them into narratives, a number of thinkers believe narrative is a practical strategy for negotiating experience. David Carr (1986) offers an early, emblematic statement of this view: "Far from being a formal distortion of the events it relates, a narrative account is an extension of one of their primary features. While others argue for the radical discontinuity between narrative and reality, I shall maintain not only their continuity but also their community of form" (p. 117). He notes that during practical negotiations of the present, the "means-end structure   of   action   displays   some   of   the   features   of   the beginning-middle-end structure" characteristic of narrative (p. 122). Others include Mark Turner, who describes "narrative imagining" as integral to human cognition (p. 9). His view that "narrative imagining is our fundamental form of predicting" is explored in Chap. 6 (p. 20). Jongepier offers key conceptual groundwork for the thesis of this book in her argument that "implicit narrativity" structures experiences (p. 51). Some scholars consider narrative to be for making inferences about targeted social agents' beliefs, motivations, and values as a component of folk psychology (Zunshine 2006).

Recent scholarship in narrative hermeneutics aligned with the 'small stories' approach summarized earlier seeks to relocate the study of narrative in cognition to the "countless processes of everyday understanding that we typically realize in passing, mostly without noticing. When we are asked, say, what time it is or what is our address, the interpretive charge mostly goes without being noticed. This is not to maintain that everyday interactions and 'small stories' do not have a wider, existential significance. In fact they do have" (Brockmeier and Meretoja, p. 7).

2.6   Narrative and Selfhood

Narrative and its building blocks are implicated in a variety of theories of identity, identity development, and the development of autobiographical memory. Dan McAdams and others have theorized the importance of a developing 'life story' or 'narrative identity' in identity construction (McAdams 1993). Daniel Dennett views the self as "a center of narrative gravity," or as Susan Schneider puts it, "a kind of program that has a persistent narrative" (Dennett 1992, p. 416; Schneider 2017). Naomi Eilan (1995) offers a model of "perspectival awareness" in 'low level' cognitive experiences: "such awareness is not yet 'the capacity for detached reflection on oneself' that develops along with language and conceptual thinking, but it is enough to suggest a kind of ladder or continuum between bodily interaction with the world and developed reflectivity" (p. 20).

Richard Menary (2008) insists that the "minimal self" is an embodied, "pre-narrative" subject and agent: "our embodied experiences, perceptions, and actions are all prior to the narrative sense of self, indeed our narratives are structured by the sequence of embodied experiences" (p. 75). These experiences are "taken up into inner dialogue," generating a new component of self—a narrator-function—which "emerges in terms of narratives as anchored in the pre-narrative sequence of experiences of an embodied subject" (p. 79). For Menary, the interposition of a discourse-based narrator is key to explaining the "intersubjective" nature of self-hood. He sees inner speech as key to generating self-awareness and self, and discredits the idea that self is "an independent substance with intrinsic properties or a functional object" (p. 79).

The implication of narrative in selfhood is complex, however, because of the elusiveness of both narrative and selfhood as concepts. Markowitsch and Stanilou (2011) review how research into selfhood involves many different notions of self: "narrative self," "self as containing conceptual knowledge of one's own personality traits," "self as... agent," "core self," "proto-self," and "feeling self" (p. 22). 'Narrative self' operates at a higher level of cognitive processing than the 'core self.' Amid this multiplicity, they seem to agree with Northoff's et al. (2006) assessment that it is unclear whether these are simply relevant within particular cognitive functions or whether there can be a unified theory of self.

Keith Oatley (2007) proposes that people possess "narrative consciousness" in the form of a "unified narrative agent" (p. 378). He "explore[s] [following David Velleman], the idea of a conscious unified self, based on functional properties of narrative" (p. 380). Specifically, narrative qualities including action plans based upon goals and intentions, emotions as forms of self-feedback, and coherence based upon meaning are critical to the emergence of a central organizing agency, a self (pp. 383–4). These qualities, moreover, permit communication of our own mental states with others, to receive and process like communications, and to formulate theories of others' states of mind and self while unconsciously, and sometimes consciously, refining our own (pp. 385–6). Thus, we construct a self analogously to a novelist constructing a character, but "improvising as we go along" (p. 386). This self is "embodied...[and] accomplishes things in the world and interacts with others whom we assume are constituted in a way that is much like our self" (p. 386). Oatley argues that consciousness has four aspects: "simple awareness, the stream of inner consciousness, conscious thought as it may affect decisions and actions, [and] consciousness of self-with-other." Also, Oatley proposes multiple roles for emotions: as a "primary form of Helmholzian consciousness,...[as] frames or scripts for interindividual relationships, ...[as] caused by disruptions of action or expectancy...," and as the basis, when combined with language, for "social cognition...based on narrative-like simulations" (p. 390). Third, narrative capacities are developmental. Finally, "modern narratizing consciousness" is the product of historical changes in human interaction wrought by economic, political, and technological developments.

Autobiographical memory may depend upon narrative logics for organizing principles. According to this model, autobiographical knowledge exists in a hierarchy capped by "overarching lifetime periods or themes," with an intermediate level of "repeated categories of events (i.e., every Thanksgiving) or temporally extended events (e.g., a picnic or vacation)" (Holland and Kensinger 2010, p. 4). At the base, event-specific knowledge is retained. Autobiographical memories (i.e., specific memories rather than autobiographical knowledge) are preserved because of their relevance to autobiographical knowledge and goals, as well as their emotional nature. These 'intermediate level' forms of autobiographical knowledge drive the search for 'low level' particulars: "When we are cued to retrieve an autobiographical memory, we begin our search at the intermediate, general level and then move to retrieving more specific information" (p. 4).

For Holland and Kensinger, this search strategy suggests that autobiographical memory retrieval is reconstructive, including narrative memories (p. 6). Our global "personal narratives" are likely to incorporate particularly important events—especially emotional events—through "enhanced rehearsal" (p. 19). Thus, in this self-memory system model, narratives are continuously subject to reconstruction and supplementation, particularly in relation to "intermediate level events," though sometimes individual events such as "flashbulb memories" are more directly impactful.

Global personal narratives may have a key role in retrospectively organizing experience. Milivojevic et al. (2016) hypothesize that "narratives may provide a general context, unrestricted by space and time, which can be used to organize episodic memories into networks of related events" (p. 12412).

2.7   The Development of Narrative Capacity in Human Socialization

Work on the role of narrative in psychosocial development often complements theories of the role of narrative in identity. Many theorists, such as Fivush and Haden (2003), suggest that narrative abilities are language-dependent, while others (cf. Rubin et al. (2003)) hold that narrative both plays an important role in autobiographical memory and can be non-linguistic (p. 889). In the "sociocultural model of autobiographical memory" (Merrill and Fivush 2016, p. 74), Nelson and Fivush see the developmental emergence of a capacity for narrative structure and content as vital to the development of autobiographical memory. In this model, "narrative structure and content" develops around ages 3–5, after the establishment of a "core self" and in feedback with the emergence of increasingly autonomous temporal concepts, complex language concepts, self-representation, and theory of mind. It co-develops roughly with the establishment of episodic memory and overlaps with the establishment of autobiographical memory.

Autobiographical memory and narrative capacity ultimately lead to the capacity for "phenomenological representations of the past, present, and (presumed) future," which emerge in "late adolescence and early adulthood" (McCoy and Dunlop 2016, p. 16). Waters and Fivush (2015) suggest that "coherent autobiographical narratives [could contribute to] … psychological well-being" (p. 1). Merrill and Fivush note that social psychology implicates narratives in a number of ways, including "Erikson's theory of psychosocial development, [in which] developing individuals … resolve [personal challenges] through coordinating the self of the past, present and future in ways that allow for healthy identity and functioning, and this is accomplished, at least partly, through a narrative understanding of the self through time" (Merrill and Fivush 2016, p. 73). Second, Bronfenbrenner's ecological systems approach (1979) spawned the idea of 'narrative ecologies' crucial to psychosocial development (Merrill and Fivush, p. 74). As Fivush and Haden (2003) state, "each of us creates a life narrative embedded in sociocultural frameworks that define what is appropriate to remember, how to remember it, and what it means to be a self with an autobiographical past" (cover). Merrill and Fivush suggest that "intergenerational narratives" (passed within familial groups) play important roles in familial and individual development.

This survey has not been exhaustive—as Hatavara et al. and Brockmeier both suggest, the role narrative plays in studying cognition is wide-ranging. Here we have touched on a number of ways theorists have embraced or rejected narrative as a form or techne which guides cognitive processing. But we have not considered, for example, one of the most obvious ways narratives might impact our thinking: the cognitive effects of exposure to narratives. In cognitive literary studies, researchers have examined the nature and effects of reading narrative forms in some detail. Overall, the field is wide and appears to be growing in range, depth, and influence.

Later chapters argue for a practical view of narrative as part of experience, based on recent research into how cognition, including emotion, works. Before we explore this research, we need to acknowledge the central difficulty of this kind of work: narrative, and its genesis, are complex concepts. To grapple with this, and to establish the grounds upon which we can establish an argument for narrative's roles at all levels of cognition, the next chapter examines the relationship between narrative and intention.

Notes

1. 'Experience' is a complex and contested term. See Grethlein (2018) for consideration of the term itself. Here I use 'experience' to refer to the 'seeming' of the subject's cognitive engagement of the world. In this view I am aligned with Brockmeier and Meretoja's (2014) view of narrative as a "hermeneutic practice," including the view that "meaning-making is not just about cognition, knowledge, consciousness, or the mind, but about living a life in a cultural world" (p. 2, p. 5). This project takes up their call to emphasize "countless processes of everyday understanding that we typically realize in passing, mostly without noticing" (p. 7). As I use the term, experience refers to first person, temporally extended engagement of the subject with phenomena. I am trying to maintain a relatively ordinary, commonsense view of experience, as seen in the distinction between the following statements that might represent thoughts: "I understand what body-shaming consists of" and "I am experiencing body-shaming." In the latter, the speaker reflects upon an ongoing social discourse or process that typically induces emotional responses. The engagement of the subject with this phenomenon through time is the experience. Statements such as "I have been through an experience of body-shaming" refer to memories of body-shaming, but the remembering could itself be an experience of engaging with a mental phenomenon.

2. For an earlier presentation of the conversations that make up this debate, please refer to the 2003 collection *Narrative and Consciousness: Literature, Science, and the Brain* (OUP), which tackles this relation through essays about the neural substrates of narrative, narrative and selfhood, narrative and autobiographical memory, and the workings and social functions of fiction in individual and group psychology. This essay considers these ideas,

referring to updated models of cognition published since 2003, as well as to the diverse ways narrative is studied and is a tool for research across many disciplines.

3. Carroll (2001) offers an intelligent analysis of how narratives differ from mere sequences.

4. These citations are all drawn directly from Richard Menary's formulation of 'minimalist' definitions of narrative. In addition to these, Menary also cites Mark Slors' description of how a sequence of perceptions narrating the story of our movements is continually produced: "If we go from a to b, we will pass through all intermediate places separating a and b according to the route we take, thus producing a sequence of perceptions narrating the story of this route" (the position of our bodies at different places, the position of our eyes, etc.) (Slors, 1998, p. 73). Menary offers this characterization in the service of describing an 'embodied,' rather than 'abstract,' narrator: "This minimal embodied narrative allows for a subject of experiences (the minimal, embodied, feeling and perceiving self) and, therefore, anchors narratives in the unfolding sequence of embodied and embedded perceptions of an individual. This is quite different from the self as an abstract narrator. Narratives arise directly from the lived experience of the embodied subject and these narratives can be embellished and reflected upon if we need to find a meaningful form or structure in that sequence of experiences" (76).

5. White writes that the "value attached to narrativity in the representation of real events arises out of a desire to have real events display the coherence, integrity, fullness, and closure of an image of life that is and can only be imaginary. The notion that sequences of real events possess the formal attributes of the stories we tell about imaginary events could only have its origin in wishes, daydreams, reveries" (p. 27).

6. Qtd. in Hinchman and Hinchman (1997, p. xxiii).

7. Qtd. In Hinchman and Hinchman, p. xxiii.

8. However, a range of psychologists, philosophers, literary scholars, social scientists, and neuroscientists have entered diverse discussions of the roles narrative might play in consciousness. These discussions explore social behaviors, autobiography, and cognitive functions. With the development of fields such as narrative psychology and cognitive narratology, there is growing interest in clarifying what narrative means when we think of it in relation to cognition and consciousness. As the study of consciousness gains acceptance in neuroscience and cognitive psychology, subtopics like how narrative figures into consciousness attract increased inter-, intra-, and cross-disciplinary interest among humanists (cf. Herman, Hogan, Young), social scientists (cf. Brockmeier, Sparkes), and natural scientists (cf. Schacter and Addis) alike.

9. Specifically, they note that

> the study of narrative has been undertaken in different disciplines that until recently have had little contact with each other. The range of those disciplines is impressive. In anthropology, for instance, Geertz's (1983) book contains a chapter "From the Native's Point of View," pleading for an "interpretive" anthropology in which the perspective of the other culture is thoroughly represented. In a similar vein, but with respect to a Western culture, Lavie (1990) describes the oppositions and tensions under Israeli military occupation of the West Bank through an analysis of the narratives produced by different sides in the conflict. In philosophy, there is Ricoeur's great project (1984). In ethics, Greenspan (1995) argues in favor of the "perspectival appropriateness" of moral sentiments, while Nussbaum (1990) has pleaded for an ethics informed by the various and multifaceted perspectives of narrative literature; this notion has also led her into the domain of jurisprudence (1995). In psychology, Herman (1995) has attempted to link narrative structure to Chomsky's universal grammar. William Chafe is convinced that "narratives provide evidence for the nature of the mind" (3). In sociology, Liebow (1993) constructs a description of homelessness on the basis of narratives told from the perspective of homeless women. In history, a whole new area of investigation, called "oral history," has sprung up: Josselson and Lieblich (1995) is one of the many titles that fit this category. In a similar vein, Zeldin (1994) offers a history of intimacy, based largely on a corpus of women's narratives, collected over the years. More generally, White (1973) has opened a new way of looking philosophically at history, the so-called narrativist view of historiography, which has been propagated by (among others) Canary and Kozicki (1978) and Mitchell (1981). (pp. 2–3)

10. Brockmeier writes

> the concept of narrative did not simply travel from discipline to discipline but was re-created and re-evaluated. In fact, many disciplines reinvented the narrative wheel, as Brian Schiff (2013) puts it, spreading it out as "narrative psychology," "narrative medicine," and "narrative anthropology," to name a few … the turn to narrative in the social sciences has basically been a turn to a metaphorical discourse, Hyvarinen (2010) maintains. For the most part, "narrative" and "story" have been adopted as metaphors conveying an everyday meaning that seemed to need no further specification. There are countless texts, in fact, entire textbooks, in the social sciences where "narrative" and "story" are used interchangeably with "account," "report," "description," "interview," "testimony," "information," or simply "data." (101)

References

Aristotle, and R. McKeon. (1941). *The Basic Works of Aristotle*. Random House.

St. Augustine of Hippo. Chadwick, Henry, editor. (1998). *Confessions*. Oxford Univ. Press.

Bamberg, M. G. W. (1997). *Positioning Between Structure and Performance*. 5.

Bamberg, M., and Georgakopoulou, A. (2008). Small stories as a new perspective in narrative and identity analysis, *28*(3), 377–396. https://doi.org/10.1515/TEXT.2008.018.

Bamberg, M. (2012). Narrative analysis. In H. Cooper, P. M. Camic, D. L. Long, A. T. Panter, D. Rindskopf, & K. J. Sher (Eds.), *APA handbook of research methods in psychology, Vol. 2. Research designs: Quantitative, qualitative, neuropsychological, and biological* (pp. 85–102). American Psychological Association. https://doi.org/10.1037/13620-006.

Bartlett, F. C., and Kintsch, W. (1995). *Remembering: A Study in Experimental and Social Psychology* (2nd ed.). Cambridge University Press. https://doi.org/10.1017/CBO9780511759185.

Beatty, J. (2017). Narrative possibility and narrative explanation. *Studies in History and Philosophy of Science Part A*, *62*, 31–41. https://doi.org/10.1016/j.shpsa.2017.03.001.

Boyd, B. (2010). *On the origin of stories: Evolution, cognition, and fiction* (1. paperback ed). Belknap Press of Harvard Univ. Press.

Boyd, B. (2011). *Stalking Nabokov*. Columbia University Press. http://www.jstor.org/stable/10.7312/boyd15856.

Brockmeier, J. (2009). Stories to Remember: Narrative and the Time of Memory. *Storyworlds: A Journal of Narrative Studies*, *1*, 115–132. https://doi.org/10.2307/25663011.

Brockmeier, J. (2015). *Beyond the archive: Memory, narrative, and the autobiographical process*. Oxford University Press.

Brockmeier, J., and Carbaugh, D. (2001). *Narrative and Identity: Studies in Autobiography. Self and Culture (Amsterdam and Philadelphia: John Benjamins, 2001)*. John Benjamins.

Brockmeier, J., and Harre, R. (n.d.). Problems and promises of an alternative paradigm. *Narrative and Identity*, 20.

Brockmeier, J., and Meretoja, H. (2014). Understanding narrative hermeneutics. *Storyworlds: A Journal of Narrative Studies*, *6*(2), 1–27.

Bronfenbrenner, U. (1979). *The ecology of human development: Experiments by nature and design*. Harvard University Press.

Bruner, J. S. (1997). Labov and Waletzky Thirty Years On. *Journal of Narrative and Life History*, *7*(1–4), 61–68. https://doi.org/10.1075/jnlh.7.06lab.

Bruner, J. (1991). The Narrative Construction of Reality. *Critical Inquiry*, *18*(1), 1–21. https://doi.org/10.2307/1343711.

Bruner, J. (2008). Culture and Mind: Their Fruitful Incommensurability. *Ethos*, *36*(1), 29–45. https://doi.org/10.1111/j.1548-1352.2008.00002.x.

Carr, D. (1986). Narrative and the real world: An argument for continuity. *History and Theory*, *25*(2), 117–131. https://doi.org/10.2307/2505301.

Carroll, J. *Evolution and Literary Theory*. University of Missouri Press, 1995.

Carroll, N. (2001). On the Narrative Connection. In *Beyond Aesthetics: Philosophical Essays* (pp. 118–133). Cambridge: Cambridge University Press. https://doi. org/10.1017/CBO9780511605970.009

Dennett, D. C. (1993). *Consciousness Explained*. Penguin UK.

Dennett, D. C. (1992) The Self as a Center of Narrative Gravity. In: F. Kessel, P. Cole and D. Johnson (eds.) *Self and Consciousness: Multiple Perspectives*. Hillsdale, NJ: Erlbaum.

Dutton, D. *The Art Instinct: Beauty, Pleasure, & Human Evolution*. 1st U.S. ed, Bloomsbury Press, 2009.

Eakin, P. J. (2004). What Are We Reading When We Read Autobiography? *Narrative*, *12*(2), 121–132. https://doi.org/10.2307/20107337.

Eakin, P. J. (2006). Narrative Identity and Narrative Imperialism: A Response to Galen Strawson and James Phelan. *Narrative*, *14*(2), 180–187. http://search. ebscohost.com/login.aspx?direct=true&db=mzh&AN=2006271007&site =ehost-live.

Easterlin, N. (2012). *A biocultural approach to literary theory and interpretation*. Johns Hopkins University Press.

Eilan, N. (1995, January). The first person perspective. In *Proceedings of the Aristotelian Society* (Vol. 95, pp. 51–66). Aristotelian Society, Wiley.

Fivush, R., and C. A. Haden, editors. (2003). *Autobiographical Memory and the Construction of a Narrative Self: Developmental and Cultural Perspectives*. L. Erlbaum.

Fludernik, M. (1996). *Towards a 'Natural' Narratology*, *25*(2), 97–141. https:// doi.org/10.1515/jlse.1996.25.2.97

Gallagher, S., and Hutto, D. D. (2008). 2. Understanding others through primary interaction and narrative practice. In J. Zlatev, T. P. Racine, C. Sinha, & E. Itkonen (Eds.), *Converging Evidence in Language and Communication Research* (Vol. 12, pp. 17–38). John Benjamins Publishing Company. https:// doi.org/10.1075/celcr.12.04gal.

Georgakopoulou, A. (2007). Small Stories, Interaction and Identities. https:// doi.org/10.1075/sin.8.

Gerrig, R. J. (1993). *Experiencing Narrative Worlds: On the Psychological Activities of Reading*. New Haven and London: Yale University Press.

Gerrig, R. J. (2001). "Perspective as Participation." *New Perspectives on Narrative Perspective*. Eds. Willie van Peer and Seymour Chatman. Albany: State University of New York Press, 303–323.

Gerrig, R. J. (2010). "Readers' Experiences of Narrative Gaps." *Storyworlds: A Journal of Narrative Studies* 2.1: 19–37.

Gerrig, R. J., and G. Egidi. (2003). "Cognitive Physiological Foundations of Narrative Experiences." *Narrative Theory and the Cognitive Sciences.* Ed. David Herman. Stanford, CA: CSLI. 33–55.

Goldie, P. (2002). Emotions, feelings and intentionality. *Phenomenology and the Cognitive Sciences, 1*(3), 235–254. http://link.springer.com/article/10.1023/A:1021306500055.

Goldie, P. (2012). *The Mess Inside: Narrative, Emotion, and the Mind.* OUP Oxford.

Hatavara, M., Hydén, L.-C., and Hyvärinen, M. (Eds.). (2013). *The Travelling Concepts of Narrative* (Vol. 18). John Benjamins Publishing Company. https://doi.org/10.1075/sin.18.

Herman, David (2003). "Stories as a Tool for Thinking." D. H. (ed). *Narrative Theory and the Cognitive Sciences.* Stanford: CSLI, 163–92.

Herman, D. (Ed.). (2007). *The Cambridge companion to narrative.* Cambridge University Press.

Herman, D. (2009). *Basic Elements of Narrative.* Wiley-Blackwell. https://doi.org/10.1002/9781444305920

Herman, D. (2013). *Storytelling and the Sciences of Mind.* MIT Press.

Hernadi, P., editor. *What Is Literature?* Indiana University Press, 1978.

Hinchman, L. P., & Hinchman, S. (Eds.). (1997). *Memory, identity, community: The idea of narrative in the human sciences.* Suny Press.

Holland, A. C., and Kensinger, E. A. (2010). Emotion and autobiographical memory. *Physics of Life Reviews, 7*(1), 88–131. https://doi.org/10.1016/j.plrev.2010.01.006.

Husserl, E. (1982). *Ideas Pertaining to a Pure Phenomenology and to a Phenomenological Philosophy.* Kluwer.

Hutto, D., and McGivern, P. (2016). *Updating the Story of Mental Time Travel: Narrating and Engaging with Our Possible Pasts and Futures.*

Johnson, M. (1993). *Conceptual metaphor and embodied structures of meaning: A reply to Kennedy and Vervaeke.*

Johnson, M. (2013). *The body in the mind: The bodily basis of meaning, imagination, and reason.* University of Chicago Press.

Kintsch, W., and T. A. van Dijk. (1978). "Toward a Model of Text Comprehension and Production." *Psychological Review*, vol. 85, no. 5, pp. 363–94. *Crossref*, https://doi.org/10.1037/0033-295X.85.5.363.

Kreiswirth, M. (2000). Merely telling stories? Narrative and knowledge in the human sciences. *Poetics Today*, 21(2), 293–318.

Labov, W. (n.d.). *Narrative pre-construction.* 9.

Labov, W. (1997). Some Further Steps in Narrative Analysis. *Journal of Narrative and Life History, 7*(1–4), 395–415. https://doi.org/10.1075/jnlh.7.49som.

Lakoff, G. (1997). *The internal structure of the self.* Cambridge University Press.

Lakoff, G., and Johnson, M. (2003a). *Metaphors we live by*. University of Chicago Press.

Lakoff, G., and Johnson, M. (2003b). *Metaphors we live by*. University of Chicago Press.

LaRocque, K. F., and Wagner, A. D. (2015). The Medial Temporal Lobe and Episodic Memory. In A. W. Toga (Ed.), *Brain Mapping* (pp. 537–541). Academic Press. http://www.sciencedirect.com/science/article/pii/B97801 23970251002815.

Lamarque, P. (2004). On not expecting too much from narrative. *Mind & Language*, *19*(4), 393–408.

Lewin, P. (1992). Affective Schemas in the Appropriation of Narrative Texts. *Metaphor and Symbolic Activity*, *7*(1), 11–34. https://doi.org/10.1207/ s15327868ms0701_2.

Lewin, P. (1994). "Categorization and the Narrative Structure of Science." *Philosophy & Rhetoric*, *27*(1), 35–62. www.jstor.org/stable/40237788.

MacIntyre, A. C. (2007). *After Virtue: A Study in Moral Theory*. 3rd ed, University of Notre Dame Press.

Mackenzie, C. (2009). "Personal identity, narrative integration, and embodiment." *Embodiment and agency*: 100–125.

Mair, M. (1988). Psychology as Storytelling. *International Journal of Personal Construct Psychology*, *1*(2), 125–137. https://doi.org/10.1080/1072053 8808412771.

Markowitsch, H. J., and Stanilou, A. (2011). Memory, autonoetic consciousness, and the self. *Consciousness and Cognition*, *20*(1), 16–39. https://doi. org/10.1016/j.concog.2010.09.005.

McAdams, D. P. (1993). *The stories we live by: Personal myths and the making of the self*. Guilford Press.

McAdams, D. P., and McLean, K. C. (2013). Narrative identity. *Current Directions in Psychological Science*, *22*(3), 233–238.

McCoy, T. P., & Dunlop, W. L. (2016). Contextualizing narrative identity: A consideration of assessment settings. *Journal of Research in Personality*, *65*, 16–21.

Menary, R. (2014). *Cognitive integration: Mind and cognition unbounded*. Palgrave Macmillan.

Menary, R. (2008). Embodied Narratives. *Journal of Consciousness Studies*, *15*(6), 63–84.

Menary, R. (2010). Introduction to the special issue on 4E cognition. *Phenomenology and the Cognitive Sciences*, *9*(4), 459–463. https://doi. org/10.1007/s11097-010-9187-6.

Menary, R. (2013). Cognitive integration, encultured cognition and the socially extended mind. *Cognitive Systems Research*, *25–26*, 26–34. https://doi. org/10.1016/j.cogsys.2013.05.002.

Meretoja, H. (2013). Philosophical underpinnings of the narrative turn in theory and fiction. *The Travelling Concepts of Narrative*, 93–117.

Meretoja, H. (2022). Life and narrative. *The Routledge Companion to Narrative Theory*, 273–285. https://doi.org/10.4324/9781003100157-26.

Merrill, N., and Fivush, R. (2016). Intergenerational narratives and identity across development. *Developmental Review*, 40, 72–92. https://doi.org/10.1016/j.dr.2016.03.001.

Milivojevic, B., et al. (2016). "Coding of Event Nodes and Narrative Context in the Hippocampus." *The Journal of Neuroscience*, vol. 36, no. 49, Dec., pp. 12412–24. *Crossref*, https://doi.org/10.1523/JNEUROSCI.2889-15.2016.

Mink, L. O. (1970). History and fiction as modes of comprehension. *New Literary History*, 1(3), 541–558.

Mink, L. O. (1978). "Narrative Form as a Cognitive Instrument." *The Writing of History: Literary Form and Historical Understanding*, edited by Robert Canary and Henry Kozicki, University of Wisconsin Press, pp. 129–49.

Morgan, M. S. (2017). Narrative ordering and explanation. *Studies in History and Philosophy of Science Part A*, 62, 86–97. https://doi.org/10.1016/j.shpsa.2017.03.006.

Morgan, M. S., and Wise, M. N. (2017). Narrative science and narrative knowing. Introduction to special issue on narrative science. *Studies in History and Philosophy of Science Part A*, 62, 1–5. https://doi.org/10.1016/j.shpsa.2017.03.005.

Fivush, R., and K. Nelson. (2004). "Culture and Language in the Emergence of Autobiographical Memory." *Psychological Science*, vol. 15, no. 9, Sept., pp. 573–77. *Crossref*, https://doi.org/10.1111/j.0956-7976.2004.00722.x.

Nelson, K. (2003). Narrative and the Emergence of a Consciousness of Self. Narrative and Consciousness. 17–36. https://doi.org/10.1093/acprof:oso/9780195140057.003.0002.

Northoff, G., Heinzel, A., De Greck, M., Bermpohl, F., Dobrowolny, H., and Panksepp, J. (2006). Self-referential processing in our brain—a meta-analysis of imaging studies on the self. *Neuroimage*, 31(1), 440–457.

Oatley, K. (2007). Narrative Modes of Consciousness and Selfhood. In P. D. Zelazo, M. Moscovitch, and E. Thompson (Eds.), *The Cambridge Handbook of Consciousness* (pp. 375–402). Cambridge University Press. https://doi.org/10.1017/CBO9780511816789.015.

Oatley, K., Keltner, D., and Jenkins, J. M. (2006). *Understanding emotions* (2nd ed). Blackwell Pub.

Propp, V. (2010). *Morphology of the Folktale* (Vol. 9). University of Texas Press.

Ricœur, P. (1992). *Oneself as another*. University of Chicago Press.

Ricœur, P., and K. McLaughlin. (2009). *Time and Narrative. Vol. 1*. Rpt., Univ. of Chicago Press.

Rubin, D. C., et al. (2003). "Belief and Recollection of Autobiographical Memories." *Memory & Cognition*, vol. 31, no. 6, Sept., pp. 887–901. *Crossref,* https://doi.org/10.3758/BF03196443.

Rubin, D. C. (2005). A Basic-Systems Approach to Autobiographical Memory. *Current Directions in Psychological Science*, *14*(2), 79–83. https://doi.org/10.2307/20182993.

Rubin, D. C. (2006). The Basic-Systems Model of Episodic Memory. *Perspectives on Psychological Science*, *1*(4), 277–311. https://doi.org/10.2307/40212174.

Ryan, M. (2007). Toward a definition of narrative. In D. Herman (Ed.), *The Cambridge Companion to Narrative* (Cambridge Companions to Literature, pp. 22–36). Cambridge: Cambridge University Press. https://doi.org/10.1017/CCOL0521856965.002.

Ryan, M. (2010). Narratology and Cognitive Science: A Problematic Relation. *Style*, *44*(4), 469–495. http://www.jstor.org/stable/10.5325/style.44.4.469.

Schank, R. C., and R. P. Abelson (2008). *Scripts, Plans, Goals and Understanding: An Inquiry into Human Knowledge Structures*. Rprt., Psychology Press.

Schank, R. C. (2000). *Tell Me a Story: Narrative and Intelligence*. 3. printing, Northwestern Univ. Press.

Schechtman, M. (2011). *The Narrative Self*. Oxford University Press. https://doi.org/10.1093/oxfordhb/9780199548019.003.0018.

Schneider, S. (2017). Daniel Dennett on the nature of consciousness. *The Blackwell companion to consciousness*, 314–326.

Slors, M. (1998). Two conceptions of psychological continuity. *Philosophical Explorations*, *1*(1), 61–80.

Strawson, G. (2004). Against narrativity. *Ratio*, *17*(4), 428–452.

Turner, M. *The Literary Mind: The Origins of Thought and Language*. Paperback, Oxford Univ. Press, 1998.

van Peer, W., and Chatman, S. (n.d.). *ON NARRATIVE PERSPECTIVE*. 4.

Waters, T. E., & Fivush, R. (2015). Relations between narrative coherence, identity, and psychological well-being in emerging adulthood. *Journal of personality*, *83*(4), 441–451.

White, H. (1980). The Value of Narrativity in the Representation of Reality. *Critical Inquiry*, *7*(1), 5–27. http://www.jstor.org/stable/1343174.

Zunshine, L. (2006). *Why we read fiction: theory of mind and the novel*. Ohio State University Press.

CHAPTER 3

Narrativity and Intention

Definitions of narrativity often emerge as explanatory components of theories of narratives, from classical definitions of narratives as textual artifacts to emphases on ordinary narratives and narrative as a mode of thinking. The character and conditions of emergence of narrativity are modeled in a variety of ways, but frequently as the product of intentional conscious construction. This chapter makes the case that the origins and nature of narrativity precede and exceed conventional notions of intention. That is, our intentions to construct and communicate narratives are not solely responsible for the narrative characteristics we discern in experiences. Instead, intention is shaped by intuitions of narrativity derived simultaneously from top-down (through received sociocultural values and frameworks) and bottom-up (through perceptions ready-made for narrative construction) sources.

This claim supports a larger argument that weak narrativity is emergent in cognitive processing. That is, narrativity can emerge in the apprehension of events, prior to conscious intention to construct a narrative. The view complements models of narrative as 'small,' embedded, and iterative, and is an elaboration of conversations about narrative as a mode of thinking (De Fina and Georgakopoulou 2011, p. 15).

© The Author(s), under exclusive license to Springer Nature Switzerland AG 2023
B. Miller, *Narrativity in Cognition*,
https://doi.org/10.1007/978-3-031-40349-1_3

3.1   Intention in Approaches to Narrative

Intention and narrativity are coupled concepts in a variety of approaches to narrative. Theories about narrativity usually demonstrate either explicit or implicit ideas about the relationship between cognition and narrative, and these often rely on notions of narrativity. For example, Gregory Currie views narratives as language-based "intentional-communicative artefacts" that are "distinguished from other representations by what they represent: sustained temporal-causal relations between particulars, especially agents" (2010, p. 28). Yet because there are 'non-artefactual' things with similar features, he focuses "on the graded notion of narrativity…[in terms of] the detailed representation of particulars, especially agents, in their causal and temporal relations" (p. xvii).

Design, or intention, is often described as a key threshold for narrativity. What is its nature and how does this relate to our experiences of intentionality during ordinary experiences? For Jerome Bruner, this is one of narrative's central psychological features: "narrative deals with the vicissitudes of intention" (1986, p. 17). In making sense of characters' actions and reflections in a story—and this, again, is true for literary and everyday stories—we try to understand their intentions, read their minds, and interpret the social and cultural 'habitus' through which they move (as, most likely, did the narrator who told the story).

This emphasis upon intention might surprise some readers from a literary studies background. While much of late twentieth-century literary theory was shaped by a discrediting of 'intention' as discoverable during reading, intention in narrative is of considerable interest. According to Brockmeier, intention is "a renewed focus in narrative theory…inspired by research in several areas about the human tendency 'to read for intention' (Herman 2008) or, differently put, to read for meaning (2009, p. 125). For David Herman, intention and narration are inseparable: storytelling, stories, and storyworlds are "irreducibly grounded in intentional systems," while "intentional systems are grounded in storytelling practices" (2008, pp. 240–1).

3.2   The 'When' of Intention

Some trouble for intentionalist views surfaces when the emergence and manifestation of intention are considered. For example, I may form an intention to communicate with a narrative, but thus far there is no narrativity. Alternatively, I may believe the way to explain a particular causal sequence, state, person's character, or some other dynamic or static feature of experience is through narrative. That is, I may see the narrative as an explanation, and transform elements that possess some or no narrativity above the requisite threshold into becoming a narrative. And of course, I may invent a narrative with far more obscure and complex communicative intentions in mind. In each of these examples, the idea for a narrative precedes the construction of the narrative proper (with the possible exception of the second example, in which I may believe the narrative explanation exists prior to my intention to communicate it—it is something I tell but does not seem to be something I invent).

In Fig. 3.1, please consider two possibilities. In the first, which we should consider the dominant view, that narrativity emerges during the construction of narrative artifacts. The author has an intention to make a narrative, and subsequently establishes parts of the narrative until it becomes a finished artifact. During the making of the narrative, 'narrativity' emerges.

This is a commonsense view, and it certainly seems self-evident that narrativity would be established as a narrative artifact is constructed. To give an example of this orthodox view of intention (referencing the 2013 film *Her*), if I wanted to create a story about our modern relationship to technology, I might think of a character with an interesting relationship to technology—say, both a user of and designer of technology for whom technology is particularly important. Then, I might consider how this character's relationship develops with a particularly seductive technology, complicating his ability to relate to other people by simulating an idealized human relation. Once the 'complication' is conceived, I might develop a moment of personal and ethical choice, where the character is forced to either embrace a relationship with another person or reject it in favor of an increasingly isolating relationship to technology. I might complicate it even more, giving agency unexpectedly to the technology itself, which might 'choose' to alter the relationship with the main character, creating a new crisis for the character that itself must be resolved in some manner.

However, as countless writers have experienced, building a narrative is often a messy, nonlinear process. Distorted images, overheard speech, fortuitous associations, and all manner of accidental perceptions and thoughts might inspire intention—certain recognized relationships or dynamics can precede any conscious design to make a narrative artifact. In this model, as in the example above of a narrative explanation existing prior to an

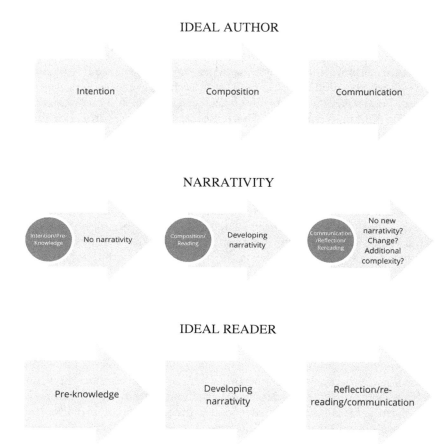

Fig. 3.1 Authors, readers, intention, and narrativity

intention or a communication, narrativity seems to precede its artifactual composition. To put this more simply, a recognition of narrative properties in a particular set of relations may precede, and perhaps spur, the emergence of an intention.

The situation becomes more complex when we place the author within the context of ordinary activity. The following diagram offers two models for how narrativity might emerge before and in conjunction with intention. I'll argue for the merits of the second, 'processing' view (Fig. 3.2).

ARTIFACTUAL VIEW

PROCESSING VIEW

Fig. 3.2 Author, reader, narrativity, and intention: artifactual and processing views

The dilemma that an 'artifactual' (as opposed to a process-focused) and 'intentional' view of narrative creates is whether the time between intention and communication involves comprehensive construction of all narrative aspects of the narrative. It precludes the possibility of inchoate or developed narrativity in the materials used in narrative prior to intention, or whether some material is somehow 'pre-narrative' or 'primed' for narrative. The case against the first option (what we can call 'comprehensive intentional narrative making') is that it requires fashioning narrative from 'raw' materials (i.e., materials with no 'narrativity') available in ordinary cognition. However, our ordinary experiences are filled with events we automatically understand narratively.

Take an example to illustrate this issue, which depends on accepting (a) the notion that narratives are *ordinarily* and *spontaneously* employed in communication, and (b) that ordinary narratives are subject to versions. Your daughter hugs you at school pick up while staring at a classmate, whose face is marked with the strains of crying, being comforted by her parent. On the way home you ask "why did Nina look upset at school pick-up today?" Your daughter explains the events that led to her friend's punishment in class, the nature of the punishment, along with an assessment of whether the punishment was fair.

If Nina's explanation qualifies as a narrative, then for an orthodox view it possesses necessary features that make it so: the implicature (intended meaning) of unfairness on the part of the authority figure, and the causal, time-extended sequence of events (primarily between her friend and the teacher) that are unfair. This narrative can be articulated on the spot, but it seems far-fetched to view it as being constructed in between the idea to tell it (perhaps in response to the question) and the actual communication. Whether or not the girl planned to make this utterance to her interlocutor (say, a parent), the narrative had clearly not just sprung forth. The girl had been thinking about what led to her friend's punishment, surely in relation to her own evaluation of whether the friend's actions merited the punishment, and whether circumstances mitigated the rightness of punishment, as well as her assessment of the characters of her friend and the teacher. In addition, this rumination likely incorporated some internal role-playing that shaped the intention (i.e., asking oneself, would I have done that in those circumstances? How would I have responded if confronted? How would it feel to receive this punishment?). Her *intention* is not separable from her attitude toward the events (and thus from the implicature—she offers a narrative, and in doing so may implicitly validate some subjects and condemn others). Her attitude evolves with a working through of the events in a narrative logic, and perhaps engaging in theory of mind and simulation for evaluative purposes.

This example of extended rumination that manifests in communication requires us to move the bar for 'intention' to the time when these ruminations commence. This occurs, at the latest, immediately after the punishment has been meted out. Arguably, though, the narrative events continue beyond the point of punishment, into the period when the narrative is already being ruminated upon. For example, the girl may speak to her friend about what happened, how she's feeling, and how the punishment will be received (and with what consequences) by the friend's parents. In this case, even once 'narrative intention' has commenced, new information could shape the implicature (for example, perhaps the subject initially views the punishment as relatively reasonable but changes her evaluation when an anticipated additional punishment from her friend's strict parents is taken into account).

In addition to new information, new events may commonly intrude into the shaping of intention. For example, what if the teacher overhears your daughter discussing the events with another friend and offers a sharp repudiation that she and her friend should 'mind their own business.' If the repudiation then leads to a narrative more focused on the teacher's censorious presence, and of solidarity with Nina as part of a community of victims of the teacher's arbitrary and vindictive use of authority, the narrative intention has shifted dramatically (from the original 'intention,' a weighing of the events that led to her friend's punishment, with evaluation of the fairness of the teacher's response.)

Nina's story is an example of what Bamberg, Georgakopoulou, and others have termed a 'small story' (2004, 2005). It is iterative, evolving, and emergent in particular communicative contexts. For example, consider Nina's recounting of the tale to her friend group that evening over video chat—the idioms of their sensemaking will differ from what Nina shares with her parents, but will also be drawn from larger sociocultural contexts. Her story, and the ephemerality of intention within it, demonstrates how perspective, intention, and narrativity are experienced on multiple levels, including in perceptual cognition.

Whereas the 'small stories' framework traces the emergence and development of intention in dialogue, this example helps us see its necessary antecedent: pre-dialogic narrative processing. Intention is dynamic and integrated with the emergence of narrativity, rather than *a priori*. We process experiences by organizing them with narrative features, and this processing stimulates intentions to construct communicable narratives. Through this processing, the sociocultural contexts insinuated in dialogic communication affect pre-intentional narrative processing as well.

Incidentally, this squares with a commonsense view of how some novels are written—an author may intend to create a narrative, but the intention to create a novel that offers a specific implicature (say, a commentary on middle-class Americans' increasing addiction to screens) may emerge once a certain degree of narrativity has been established.

This leads to further qualification of the earlier contention that a 'threshold' notion of narrativity is problematic. All elements of narrativity, *including* 'intention,' are potentially dynamic rather than static in ordinary narratives.[1] However, there is a temporal feature of narratives that would seem unlikely in natural instances of narrativity. Intentional communication involves expectation management. Artifactual narratives typically cue expectations for subsequent dynamics (through, for instance, foreshadowing), and the perceived quality of a narrative involves how these internal expectations are managed in the context of explicit or implicit communicative strategies/structures as well as being communicable artifacts. That is, they involve discursive structuring of events, as is immediately apparent in narratives in which a climactic moment or a final condition is offered at the outset of the narrative, followed by an account of the events leading to it. Yet the shaping of experience by expectation is actually an ordinary subconscious feature of perception generally.

Overall, then, narrativity describes relations that can be represented artifactually or simply observed. Narrativity forms the basis of artifactual and non-artifactual narratives alike. And narrativity emerges in a feedback coupling with intention and perspective, rather than being derivative. That is, processing for narrativity constitutes intention and perspective even as it is constituted by it.

This dynamic characterizes immediate and ongoing *post hoc* sensemaking, while not necessarily indicating the perspective, adopted by some strains of narrative hermeneutics, that experience is always already interpretation and reflective thought involves a "double hermeneutic" (an interpretation of interpretation) (Meretoja 2022, p. 279). Understood as such, narrativity exists in the substrate of reflective thought engaged with ongoing experience, configuring experiences as it undergoes new experiences. If in narrativist accounts 'telling' is the location where particular intentions and perspectives are articulated, and if in the 'small stories' of ordinary interaction dialogue spurs dynamism in intentions and perspectives, the substrate of mutually constitutive reflection and experience is the site of early configurations of both.

Specifically, experience's emergent form reflects ongoing, dynamic parsing of temporality, sociality, events, and contexts. Psychologist Jerome Bruner, who was introduced in Chap. 2, Sect. 2.3, is probably the best-known early theorist to propose that narrative structures our thinking. In his influential early formulation (1986), he argues that: "We organize our experience and our memory of human happenings mainly in the form of narrative…Narratives, then, are a version of reality whose acceptability is governed by convention and 'narrative necessity' rather than by empirical verification and logical requiredness" (pp. 4–5). Bruner sees three ways narrative is integrated in our cognition. First, narratives are constructed in the service of 'folk psychology'—narrative is a means of understanding social events based upon beliefs about others' beliefs and predictable behavior. Narratives help explain when deviations from normative individual or group behaviors occur (see *Acts of Meaning*, Chap. 2). Second, narrative is the stuff of autobiography—a central feature of consciousness is the continual construction of a coherent life story (and this reflexive process 'codes' life events in relation to conventional narratives, and through these narratives inculcate normative values). Third, narratives (derived from cultural learning through our experiences) come to "achieve the power to structure perceptual experience, to organize memory, to segment and purpose-build the very 'events' of a life" (1987, p. 15).

This final point signals a radical tendency in Bruner's views: narratives not only are *post hoc* forms of processing experience but also are constitutive of some experiences. In a late essay on the legacy of narrative discourse pioneers Labov and Waletzky, Bruner develops his speculations about the structuring power of narrative: basic cognitive "schemas," such as Johnson's 1989 SOURCE-PATH-GOAL schema, "probably provide the beginning-middle-end armature on which stories are built" (Bruner 1997, p. 66). Bruner values linguistic actions (i.e., representing experience in language) and narrative wholes as the sources of narrativity. Bruner thus provides a two-sided approach to narrative—on the one hand, there is an 'armature' in ordinary cognitive processing upon which, on the other hand, culturally derived narrative prototypes fashion experience into meaning-laden narratives. Thus, Bruner is open to some proto-narrative processing in perception, but is ultimately allied with the top-down, *post hoc* approach.

Narrativist theories typically view narratives as emergent in language-based acts of configuration, even when they locate some proto-narrative processing in immediate experience. Paul Ricœur's groundbreaking work on time, for example, defines temporality as "that structure of existence that reaches language in narrativity" (1980: p. 165; qtd. in Ritivoi 2009, p. 29).

Within these theories, different approaches assume different 'givens' in experience subject to emplotment. Bruner's 'armature' and Ricœur's 'events' are necessary pre-conditions for *post hoc* acts of narrative configuration. Andreas Ritivoi notes that this is generally the case in narrativist views:

> a relatively widespread view deems narrative a series of events arranged into plausible and coherent connections through the operation of emplotment (Prince 1973; Abbott 2002). Because it organizes discrete entities—events—into a series, emplotment creates units of signification. Its function is to mediate between the 'manifold of events and the temporal unity of the story recounted; between the disparate components of the action—intentions, causes, and chance occurrences—and the sequence of the story' (Ricœur 1992: 141). Thus, emplotment functions as a form of explanation that tells us why an event happened, or why a character has behaved in a certain way. (2009, p. 33)

In this view, events are discrete and 'given.' This givenness, however, assumes natural patterns in experience or 'bottom-up' configuration of experience in basic cognition. For an event is structured by temporal and spatial boundaries, actants, and significant dynamisms. Events, in other words, are the preformed *'whats'* of experience. The emplotment process Ricœur describes involves attribution of the *'whys'* of experience by linking given events to other events (particularly via causal relations) as well as through abstractions, distal circumstances, and other elements.[2] If narrative (or narrativity) emerges in the configuration of events that are themselves not narrative, then narrativity is a second-order 'explanation' of experience.

Such a view of narrative's role in cognition points to a constitutive logic of narrative argued for in this book: heterogeneous concatenation. A simple view of narrative might involve homogeneous concatenation, in which the narrative consists of a sequence of events in a chronological, causal chain, like a Rube Goldberg machine. By contrast, the 'explanation' view of configuration suggests that event concatenation in narrative is heterogeneous, meaning that the linkages between events are not always chronological, causal, or physically manifested, but rather depend upon other cognitions (about intentions, general tendencies, and valuations, distal circumstances, contextual information, etc.). Heterogeneous concatenation describes a messy but rich network of top-down and bottom-up influences in shaping experiences. Heterogenous concatenation is part of the view that experiences generated at the 'low' level of perceptual cognition are shaped by the subject's sociocultural knowledge, values, and goals, and formed experiences are also subject to emplotment (which organizes and reformulates). These processes, moreover, exist simultaneously, and so-called formed experiences are subject to reformulation and recontextualization as they themselves shape what is perceived and parsed in low-level cognition.

How the emplotment process draws upon heterogenous elements, such as unconscious cognitive schema, ideas about selfhood, socially distributed narratives, and embodied, phenomenal experiences into particular narratives, is the subject of much debate. Richard Menary is skeptical of certain top-down views because of their lack of attention to social discourse and embodied experiences. Menary critiques two versions of the top-down thesis: first, that narratives unconsciously influence our cognition; second, that narrative construction is constitutive of selfhood.

For Menary, intersubjective experiences provide the basis for the narratives we create. Narrative configuration involves these embodied experiences being shaped via discourse.[3] While Menary's viewpoint is primarily focused upon narrative as *post hoc* configuration of social experiences, he also believes embodiment creates emergent narrativity in basic cognitive processing. For Menary, "a minimal embodied narrative" emerges in basic sequential relations between experiences,

> allowing for a subject of experiences (the minimal, embodied, feeling and perceiving self) and, therefore, anchors narratives in the unfolding sequence of embodied and embedded perceptions of an individual. This is quite different from the self as an abstract narrator. Narratives arise directly from the lived experience of the embodied subject and these narratives can be embellished and reflected upon if we need to find a meaningful form or structure in that sequence of experiences. (2008, p. 76)

In other words, Menary's model includes a baseline of narrativity in pre-linguistic experiences. Thus, although narrative configuration is linguistic, social, and generally 'higher order,' Menary's embodied view involves an emergent narrativity in the basic processing of experience.

Given the temporality and linguistic nature these models ascribed to configuration, Menary's and other views might seem to suggest a simple linear progression from experiences to narrativization despite the proto-narrative character or narrativity associated with these experiences. However, I believe it likely that, as Ricœur's framework suggests, complex feedback processes are at work involving both remembered and new experiences. That is, configuration is dynamic and ongoing, integrated with new event experiences, and potentially reconfiguring past experiences as new experiences unfold.

To illustrate this dynamic, consider a brief example: imagine you have a narrative 'stewing' in your brain about the unfairness of a former friend's behavior toward you in relation to a group of friends. You may be uncertain about the motivations of the bad actor, as well as the effects. You may also be uncertain about how blameworthy the bad actor is, and how to understand her psychology. Then, imagine a moment when you are preparing to go out with a subset of your friend group. The subject of the bad actor will come up. In preparation, you might crystallize the narrative by (temporarily) committing to certain evaluations of each point mentioned above. Even if you do not tell the story—which poses its own complications—in crystallizing the narrative you have communicated with yourself to prepare for a discursive context in which the other members of the group may have a variety of opinions, or differing opinions, of your former friend. A provisional commitment to a narrative, such as this, is quite ordinary (i.e., those you held before preparing for your night out). What's interesting is how this provisional commitment might impact your perceptions. For example, imagine that this same former friend reaches out to you in advance of a birthday party hosted for you by the group of friends. While a charitable view may interpret this communication as an attempt to rebuild the friendship, you may be primed to interpret it as an attempt by the former friend to wrangle an invitation to feel included in the group. The communication, in other words, is received in the context of (at least) potential interpretations that are folded within narratives regarding the friendship. In this case, your 'theory of mind' for the friend's motivations is shaped by an ongoing narrative you have about the friend's behavior toward you in relation to the group.

3.3   NARRATIVITY IN EXPERIENCE

Intention, configuration, and emplotment, then, can be enmeshed in ongoing cognitive processing of experiences. But how could this manifold of reflective and perceptual selection and biasing shape and be shaped by perception in the everchanging present instant? In *Towards a 'Natural' Narratology* (1996), Monika Fludernik defines narrativity, rather than narrative, in terms of "cognitive ('natural') parameters" (p. xi). Her theory is based on a combination of insights from the Labovian tradition of natural linguistics and Culler's concept of "naturalization" (xii). She focuses partly on oral narratives, in the spirit of sociologist Alfred Shutz's emphasis on "everyday experience" as prototypical of human relations, because they "cognitively correlate with perceptual parameters of human experience" (17). Moreover, these parameters, she believes, "remain in force even in more sophisticated written narratives" (12).

Her focus is on the way narrative evokes experience. That is, consuming narrative is subjective, dynamic, and embodied. It is both a form of experiencing and evocative of the experiences represented within a narrative. Part of Fludernik's emphasis on 'natural' narratives is her foregrounding of the ordinary, iterative nature of most narratives. She opposes older approaches to narrative that either insist on actantial parameters or treat narratives as relatively static (p. 12, p. 20). She also values models of narrative that emphasize dynamism (p. 21).

Fludernik describes narrativity as "a function of narrative texts [that] centers on experientiality of an anthropomorphic nature" (p. 26). Her experiential emphasis distinguishes her views from the traditions of narratology which locate narrativity "in the existence of a narrator" (p. 26), and which, as we've considered, persist in some contemporary ideas about narrative perspective. This is partly because Fludernik believes 'experientiality' is grounded in embodiment. So, narrative is distinctive partly because it represents embodied experience.

There are links here to Menary's foci on embodied experiences as prenarrative fodder and the emergence of minimal narratives in embodied experiences. Yet in both, the 'what' of embodiment that persists in linguistic narratives requires clarification.[4]

Herman notes a different objection, from Alber, to Fludernik's view. If experientiality is the defining feature of narrative, then understanding how narrative's experientiality is different from other forms of experientiality we'd be reluctant to call narrative, or conversely how non-narrative literary forms that also seem to evoke experientiality, is crucial to Fludernik's position, but not fully explained.[5]

For Fludernik, embodiment as a category subsumes specificity and individuality (which are cognitive) (p. 22). In turn, specificity and individuality are banal, ordinary features of cognition, as opposed to "pure sequentiality and ... causality," which "do not figure at all from a cognitive perspective" (p. 29). Since experientiality reflects embodied (and thus specific and individual) experiences, narratives only emerge from certain types of experiences. Fludernik concludes that "timeless or habitual situations do not trigger narrative dynamics, just as narratives cannot have everybody (or no one in particular) as their protagonist" (p. 29). Narrative features of consciousness emerge at a secondary level of cognitive processing, as a special case (here the theory recalls others that argue that narrative functions at the nexus of crises in the social order, though in this case it is related to individual experience). Fludernik offers a 'level II' that parallels Paul Ricoeur's Mimesis II, in which narrative configuration occurs.

One objection to this view, which we'll explore in detail in later chapters, is that 'presence' and 'reflection' are not discrete categories of experience—instead, the very 'schemata' or 'frames' that Fludernik draws upon are engaged in continual feedback loops that test inferences about 'reality' as inseparable parts of perceiving reality. This kind of 'reflection' is quite different from what Fludernik has in mind, I suspect, but since *Towards* was published a great deal of research has affirmed the need for models that draw perception and higher order cognitive processing together (see Chap. 6 and Sect. 7.6 for consideration of one of these models, the Predictive Processing framework).

A second objection is that Fludernik's description of the emergence of 'sequentiality' and 'causality' does not delve in detail into the markers that permit these properties to suddenly emerge. What are the mechanisms and markers that enable us to reliably discern sequential/causal chains? Overall, these objections are grounded in the fact that because Fludernik's focus is ultimately on providing a convincing account of how narrative operates, she emphasizes stages in cognition at which narrative properties are clearly discernable and is less interested in unpacking what led to them.

While reserving narrative to a special case, at a secondary level of consciousness, Fludernik theorizes a "three-part schema of—'situation-event (incidence)-reaction to event' which constitutes the core of all human action experience" (p. 29). This view is open to several questions: First, we should note that this schema, *operant in basic cognition*, seems to have implicitly narrative properties. As we'll see in reviewing more recent research on event recognition, cognized events involve cognition for boundary processing and agentive casting (or, to use Fludernik's term, 'actantial' selection). Second, Fludernik's model views 'event' and 'reaction to event' as constitutively separate, rather than potentially interleaved (i.e., the subject's ongoing response to event stimuli is part of defining the event itself). As she writes, initial reactions are subsequently processed through more complex evaluations:

> in narrating such experience, however, after the fact evaluations become important as a means of making narrative experience relevant to oneself and to others. All experience is therefore stored as emotionally charged remembrance, and it is reproduced in narrative form because it was memorable, funny, scary." (p. 29)

It seems commonsensical to argue that reaction precedes a process of evaluation that makes sense of experience narratively, specifically in relation to received narrative patterns with sociocultural import and in relation to larger narratives (e.g., and particularly, the 'narrative' of selfhood).

However, there is potentially something lost here—reaction (or, I'll argue, proto-evaluation) *in situ*, as inextricable from present time, as part of and contributing to the sensemaking that constitutes event recognition. Artifactual narratives, in Fludernik's model, ultimately reflect continuity with the emergence of experientiality in natural narratives. Fludernik writes: "Experiencing, just like telling, viewing or thinking, are holistic schemata known from real life and therefore can be used as building stones for the mimetic evocation of a fictional world" (p. 28). One of the related bundles of questions which bedevils thinking about schemata is *what is a schema and what, when, and how are experiences shaped through them?*

Conceiving of 'experiencing' as schemata seems rather counter-intuitive. However, in a response essay to a series of impressive articles in *Partial Thought* in 2018, Fludernik clarifies the difference between 'experience' and 'experientiality.' Where experience refers to our common understanding of the word, experientiality "links telling and experiencing in the dynamics of tellability…, hence sublating (in the sense of a Hegelian dialectics) the narration and the narrated in the concept of experientiality" (p. 341). So, experientiality is related to the evocation of experience in narrative production and reception.

Experience itself, however, is associated with forms of cognitive processing, rather than being simply given, and narrative forms are emergent in experiencing. In a chart Fludernik reproduces in her 2018 essay, narrativization occurs subsequent to 'human experience' but as 'mediation (narrativization) by means of consciousness (a complex natural category with several available frames to choose from).'

In an analysis of "four levels of cognitive narrative frames" Fludernik describes "experiencing" as a second-level natural mediating frame (p. 344). Below this mediation level, 'real-life parameters' including "events, motivation, goal, intention, cause, effect, [and] action" provide the basis for eventual narrativization (p. 344).

Subsequent chapters will consider research into the implicit structures of several 'real-life' elements as well as how action and reflection emerge through feedback with 'real-life parameters.' In other words, 'real-life parameters' and 'experiencing' are closely knit to the point of being mutually constitutive.

Fludernik's treatment of schemata as phenomena operant in the course of ordinary experiences, narrative construction, and narrative reception opens the way for a significant reconceptualization of experience. Her theories have advanced the notions we hold of how narratives characterize experience (as 'experientiality'). Taking ordinary narratives as her starting point, Fludernik adroitly remedies some of the problems with other views that view narrative as a mode. My interest in Fludernik's work is primarily in the possibilities it suggests for understanding the nature of 'experiencing' and 'real-life parameters' in relation to the ordinary, 'ready-to-hand' nature of narrative.

Engagement with schemata is central to the "narrative practice hypothesis." Children engage narrative schemata throughout childhood, and this helps them deploy culturally derived values and attitudes to immediate experience. This involves the patterns of narrative 'ascription' central to folk psychology, specifically evaluations that are inseparable from predictions about other individuals' behavior. Herman (2009) explains narrative as

> the fundamental resource used to construct explanations of others' behavior in terms of assumptions or hypotheses about their minds. Such explanations take the form of provisional, tentative ascriptions to others of motivations, beliefs, goals, and other mental states, including the what-it's-like dimension of experiencing the taste of a freshly sliced tomato, the sight of a dramatic sunset, or the pain of a twisted ankle. (p. 159)

Herman's description of 'provisional' and 'tentative' narratives points to the flexibility associated with cognitive narrative forms, which might be conceived as having features of networks as well as features of stepwise, fixed form artifacts.

In pointing to ascription in Theory of Mind, Herman highlights a role for narrative in social experience that is acceptable to a wide range of "discursive" views about how narrative and experience might be related. He contrasts this approach to a 'cognitive' approach that encompasses the questions considered in this book:

> a discursive approach to narrative and mind can be contrasted with a cognitivist approach. In the cognitivist approach, discourse (print texts, conversational interaction, graphic novels, films, etc.) can be viewed as a window onto underlying mental processes that form a kind of bedrock layer for psychological inquiry. By contrast, the discursive approach studies how the mind is oriented to and accounted for—that is, constructed—in systematic, norm-governed ways by participants in these and other modes of discourse production, e.g., through processes of positioning. (p. 152)

He notes that it is uncertain whether the hallmark of phenomenological experience—the subjective perceptual experience known as 'qualia'—can be accounted for within a discursive conception of mind. For the cognitivist approach, narrative discourse offers isomorphic relations to the processes and experiencing of qualia, rather than a direct rendering.

'Rendering,' rather than representation or enaction, because narrative discourse, even if it somehow manages to bridge the gap between referent and object, is accountable for creating a new discursive object with a referential relation to an original, rather than enacting it. So, in probing experience for narrative features, narrative discourse is paradoxically at the end of the investigation, rather than the start. To put this another way, and hopefully more simply, we can ask whether either the 'cognitivist' or the 'discursive' approaches, as Herman lays them out, are the same as or can shed direct light upon 'experiencing'? That is, are the features of evoking experience within narrative texts exactly in correspondence with narrative aspects of experience, if they exist?

I'm doubtful, though the approach Herman pursues is promising. Instead, we are left to decide, if narrativity is not just a tool for thinking, but is intrinsic to *how* we experience, and to what experience feels like, then we need to define what features of experience are best labeled 'narrative' before wondering how narrative texts evoke these features of experience in a 'doubling over' operation. In other words, the attempt to discern how cognitive operations work via how communicated narratives work can only be partial and approximate, even for theorists like Fludernik who consider 'natural' narratives that we generate automatically and to some degree unconsciously.

3.4   CRITIQUES OF 'MODE OF THINKING' PERSPECTIVES

Yet to consider narrative as a form of cognitive processing also understandably draws skepticism. Marie-Laure Ryan has considered the problems with attempts to view narrative "as a mode of thinking," noting that they are speculative (and thus of limited value for empirical science) and that they are inflationary (p. 481). In describing the 'inflationary' nature of the claim that narrative involves mental activity, Ryan writes:

> Many of these claims can be taken in two ways: one metaphorical and weak, the other literal and strong. It is in the literal sense that they are inflationary: for instance, the idea that narrative constructs reality is widely acceptable if

one interprets it as meaning that narrative gives form to that which it represents; but it is highly controversial if one interprets it as meaning that all
perceptions or experiences of reality have narrative form, or that reality is
inherently a construct of the (narrative) mind. (p. 482)

Ryan's criticism focuses upon a lack of granularity in 'mode of thinking'
accounts: "A trademark of inflationary theories is that they treat narrative
as an unanalyzed whole, rather than attributing the effects they claim for
storytelling to specific constituents of narrative" (p. 483). Ryan argues, for
example, against Mark Turner's description of 'narrative imagining' as
integral to human cognition:

> For Turner, noticing objects or events in our perceptual environment
> amounts to constructing embryonic stories about them…In this view, the
> mere action of focusing on a certain tree in the forest is a narrative act,
> because it makes the tree into the protagonist of a virtual story. But if
> "thinking about," i.e., distinguishing figure from ground, is always already
> storytelling, the task of defining narrative becomes both superfluous and
> impossible: superfluous, because it is no longer necessary to differentiate
> narrative from any other manifestation of human thought, and impossible,
> because it is inseparable from a complete theory of mind. (2007, p. 28)

Ryan's critique of Turner reflects an understandable worry about labeling any cognitive activity 'narrative,' and perhaps Turner's phrasing is, in
this instance, misleading. However, Turner's conception of 'foreground'
and 'background' seems to raise a question Ryan may misconstrue: it is
not that distinguishing 'foreground' from 'background' is 'narrative' *per
se*, but that such boundary definition is a continuous feature of cognition
that in some cases defies object-based logics. That is, foreground and
background definition reflect a selection process that entails an underlying
logic, and this logic can reflect narrative reasoning rather than logico-
deductive reasoning. One example I've been alluding to, but that I'll
explore in detail in a chapter on narrative and new models of cognition, is
temporal: What makes an event? What logic underlies event boundary
definition, and is it sometimes unconscious? I'll look at current research
and theorizing in this area in that later chapter (Chap. 5).

Here, however, I'd like to point to the range of candidate forms of narrative reasoning to give a sense of the range of features of experience that
current empirical models which rely upon artifactual notions of narrative

tend to overlook, and which a supplementary emphasis upon narrative processing would capture.

Ryan's primary objection to pro-narrative accounts involves their top-down nature. Ryan is not "denying ... the importance of narrative for social life, intelligence, memory, knowledge, and our sense of identity, but rather, the importance of conscious judgments of narrativity for the processing of verbal or visual information" (p. 32). Ryan's primary point is that labeling experience as narrative is not necessary for cognition such as object identification. Intriguingly, Ryan notes that this reservation points toward, rather than away from, investigation of the narrative features of basic cognition: "If defining narrative has any cognitive relevance, it is because the definition covers mental operations of a more fundamental nature than parsing global judgments of narrativity" (p. 33).

However, her dismissal of the holistic nature of narrative in mode of thinking accounts is characterized by an assumption that for narrative to be integral to cognition it must be pervasive. Ryan's construal of inflationary accounts overlooks potential subtleties in how constituents of narrative are treated—"all perceptions or experiences of reality have narrative form, or reality is inherently a construct of the (narrative) mind" (2010, p. 482). On the latter, the notion that we have a 'narrative mind' seems absurd. Most of the research into cognitive psychology suggests pervasive sharing of neural resources. Even well accepted ideas, such as the existence of the modular limbic system, have been strongly challenged. On her second claim, I don't think it is necessary to claim "all perceptions" have narrative properties to argue that constituents of narrative play a particular role in cognition.

Finally, Ryan's solution to the 'inflation' of narrative is to view stories as the endpoint of a variety of mental processes coming together: "We can avoid this impasse, without falling back on a segregationist conception of thinking that distinguishes narrative and non-narrative operations, by regarding narrative as the outcome of many different mental processes that operate both inside and outside stories." (2007, p. 28)

While the dangers of inflationary accounts Ryan describes are important, her analysis of what inflationary logics necessitate may obscure some useful inquiry into the very constituent mental processes she claims result in stories. For someone to argue that narrative constituents are characteristic of particular modes of cognition requires neither a belief that all experiences have narrative form, nor that reality is a narrative construct.

Instead, narrative features may be part of what we might call the 'boundary parameters' of some experiences—what receives consideration (selection), how it is conceptualized (definition), how this conceptualization embeds value—(valuation), for how long (extension), where (location), and in relation to what else (relationality). In these boundary parameters, experience may have features most logically described as 'narrative,' even if full-blown narratives are not viewed as immanent, or inchoate, or even direct shapers of experience.

Ryan seems to agree with this last point, as she argues that "a trademark of inflationary theories is that they treat narrative as an unanalyzed whole, rather than attributing the effects they claim for storytelling to specific constituents of narrative" (2010, p. 483). My focus will be on the emergence of these constituents of narrative into experience. Late in the book, I will 'inflate' this theory by speculating about how these constituents might figure into higher order reflection, particularly through memory and ideas about selfhood. However, the focus will be on how describing certain features of experience as 'narrative' not only provides a language for phenomena usually glossed over, but also provides a promising means of beginning to reconcile insights about cognition from a variety of disciplines and researchers.

Ryan, however, has a strong response to the kind of argument I am foreshadowing:

> The bottom-up interpretation denies that narrative requires specialized mental abilities—by this I mean abilities that we exercise only when we engage in narrative thinking. Imagine that A is causal reasoning, B is sequencing, C is mind reading: we use A when we boil water to cook an egg, B when we plan our time and schedule appointments, and C when we engage in conversation. But we would not call these activities storytelling, even though they involve operations that are crucial to narrative thinking. (2010, p. 484)

So, Ryan would likely respond to my list (selection, definition, valuation, extension, location, and relationality) by saying that none of these are inherently narrative.

While that is correct, all of these elements have manifestations that are peculiar to narrative, and in particular forms of cognition these elements mutually require manifestations of one another that reflect narrative logic. That is, selection of a dessert item at the grocery store probably has little

to do with narrative, but selection of individuals to focus on during a particular experience certainly might. The issue, in other words, is the basis of
selection. Where selection (or definition, valuation, etc.) at the grocery
store may be based in the anticipated satisfaction of appetites, other
instances of selection have a basis in narrative relations between elements
of experience.

For example, you are likely to focus upon the bereaved husband of your
departed friend during her funeral service. Moreover, you are likely to be
particularly attentive to how your friend's husband interacts with or avoids
your friend's long-term lover during the service. If these dynamics occupy
you, you will attentively evaluate each person's behaviors and emotional
condition, and this attentional focus's end point might involve an additional evaluation of when the interaction is no longer salient for either
party. While it would be overreaching to say a 'story' has occurred, or that
you have created a story, the cognitive processing you underwent—partly
automatically—has elements that arguably are best characterized as narrative. So while Ryan claims a special status for 'narrative thinking,' in which
constituents of ordinary cognition are combined, I believe the kinds of
experiences reflected in this social example can't be fully understood without some notion of 'narrativity' or narrative processing to explain their
interrelation. It is these kinds of features of some experiences that I wish
to understand further.

In this light, the argument I pursue in the chapters that follow depends
on different constituents, or different conceptions of the constituents,
than Ryan describes, as well as a theory about how value informs and
structures perception that draws upon recent research into the nature of
consciousness. We'll return to Ryan's way of developing a constituent-
based characterization of narrative in a subsequent chapter. In addition,
I'll take issue with the notion that all 'narrative thinking' must be 'storytelling,' and even the weaker claim (perhaps one Herman would be sympathetic to) that all narrative thinking is isomorphically related to
storytelling.

Despite the nuances, the primary point is that narratives probably don't
figure as wholes in most cognitive functions, and it doesn't make much
sense to call cognitive processes 'narrative' if they are simply constituents
of narrative (such as sequencing, causal reasoning, or mind reasoning)
whose products individually resemble narrative only if they engage in a
form of post hoc emplotment.

However, by considering the problems attendant on emphasizing narrative wholeness, retrospective configuration, language-basis, and other factors for reconciling the importance of narrative as a 'tool for thinking' with how experience happens, and how meaning accrues to it, I find it necessary to consider the possibility that ordinary cognitive functions involve features we most commonly associate with narrative, and these features get short shrift in studies of cognition because they do not fit into standard models of the outputs of basic processing, which include items like recognition of visual objects, sounds, smells, and the like. They do not fit what Hutto calls the 'object-based schema' that have traditionally guided the study of cognition. If they exist, they require process-oriented analyses that illuminate how experience emerges into meaningful temporal extensions.

In other words, artifactual narratives don't convincingly explain how in real time, as an event unfolds, some of its features have significance we would typically ascribe to narrative. Additionally, while there is widespread belief among pro-narrative thinkers that past experiences with narrative have an impact on at least some aspects of how we think, we are still at a quite early stage in understanding the means through which this occurs. If we want to make progress regarding how narrative figures into cognition, we'd do well to consider how narrative features emerge into experience.

This approach elaborates upon Jongepier's (2016) theorization of 'implicit narrativity':

> the coherence and intelligibility of our experiences is due to the fact that they are anchored in a larger, diachronic context, which ... takes an importantly embodied as well as a narrative dimension. Implicit narrativity ... is not marked by a certain sense of 'my life as a whole', not even of a shadowy kind, but rather by an absence of self-directed experiences. (p. 65)

Combining embodiment with narrativity, Jongepier's concept points to the importance of engaging 'low' as well as 'high' level cognitive processes.

In the next chapter, I'll identify features of narratives that may be emergent in ordinary experience. Subsequently, I'll consider how these features might be understood in conjunction with contemporary models of cognition and emotion. Specifically, in the next chapter I describe a number of features of narrative that occur naturally in the course of ordinary cognition. This involves a hybrid "top-down/bottom-up" perspective on narrativity. Such a model rests, foundationally, on an acceptance that there is something called 'narrativity,' and that it is distinctive from the condition of being a narrative. Second, it emphasizes processing rather than outcomes.[6]

I maintain that these narrative features of cognition exist, and that assumptions about narratives as artifacts in discussions of both text-based, published fictions and narrative in cognition contribute to obscuring their role in our ordinary work of making sense of experience as it happens and afterwards. This involves considering what seems 'given' in experiences, and how this givenness occurs. After articulating these narrative features, we'll consider how recent studies of cognition account for them, and how an 'object-based' epistemology leaves gaps that might be effectively explored via an emphasis upon processing, including narrative processing.

Notes

1. Intention may be emergent at the scene of communication as well—we may begin telling a story, anticipate how its trajectory might offend a particular constituency, and alter the details to match this audience.
2. A significant literature argues that contingency and counterfactuality are essential to definitions of narrative. Beatty reviews these ideas, including Gallie's and Prince's positing of unpredictability as crucial, Hawthorn's emphasis on plausible worlds and indeterminacy, Bremond's similar emphasis that narrative is not unilinear, Ryan's exploration of 'sideshadowing,' and Beatty's own emphasis on the importance of counterfactuals in the experience of narrative (2017).
3. "Narratives are important tools that provide us with a means for self-reflection and analysis. However, the inter-subjective nature of narratives indicates that the self should not be thought of as a private, inner entity. Narrative accounts of the self have the virtue of considering the self to be relational, structured in an intersubjective fashion, rather than thinking of the self as an independent substance with intrinsic properties" (2008, p. 74).
4. Daniel Hutto reflects on these issues in relation to radical enactivism:

   [We must] steer clear of the practice of imagining experiences in the abstract—experiences are not posits or theoretical constructs to be understood in vacuo. The only way to understand 'what-it-is-like' to have an experience is to actually undergo it or re-imagine undergoing it. Gaining insight into the phenomenal character of particular kinds of experience requires practical engagements, not theoretical insights. The kind of understanding we seek when we want to know 'what-it-is-like' to have such and such an experience requires responding in a way that is enactive, on-line and embodied or, alternatively, in a way that is re-enactive, off-line and imaginative—and still embodied. (Hutto 2006, p. 52) Hutto critiques approaches to understanding perception and cognition through "object-based schema," in which experiences are conceived as abstractions. Such abstractions are commonly described as narratives. So, Hutto's analysis applies to the chief proponents of the pro-narrative position as well. Yet it also applies to viewing narrative first as a category of [abstractions] rather than a descriptor of processes.

5. While this objection is interesting, it is primarily focused upon the nature of narrative, rather than the nature of cognition. In this, Alber, Herman, and Fludernik are quite reasonably pursuing narratological ambitions. To explore narrative as a 'tool for thinking' in basic cognition, and to understand how narrative figures into basic cognition we must explore whether experience always, sometimes, or never has narrative properties. We should call certain properties of experience 'narrative' if (a) there's no better name; (b) naming them exposes them to study; and (c) they reveal the integral nature of narrative as a processing logic operant in a variety of forms of cognition, and which therefore provides an important linkage between these forms.

6. Kukkonen (2014) views narrative as a 'process.' Some see narrative processing embedded in well-established functions of cognition, like perception (Carr 1986), while others see narrative processing occurring in tandem with living and experiencing. Some argue that narrative is how the mind operates, while others see it as a replication of experience. Some, like David Bone and Richard Menary, allude to narrativity in 'pre-narrative' or 'ante-narrative' processing, others see narrativity as language-based processing of certain features of cognition, while still others call for a fully natural narratology. All reflect a variation of 'bottom-up' narrativity, as opposed to other thinkers who view narrative only in terms of higher order features of cognition like abstraction, identity, and self-reflection.

References

Brockmeier, J. (2009). Stories to Remember: Narrative and the Time of Memory. *Storyworlds: A Journal of Narrative Studies, 1,* 115–132. https://doi.org/10.2307/25663011.

Brockmeier, J. (2015). *Beyond the archive: Memory, narrative, and the autobiographical process.* Oxford University Press.

Bruner, J. S. (1997). Labov and Waletzky Thirty Years On. *Journal of Narrative and Life History, 7*(1–4), 61–68. https://doi.org/10.1075/jnlh.7.06lab

Bruner, J. (1991). The Narrative Construction of Reality. *Critical Inquiry, 18*(1), 1–21. https://doi.org/10.2307/1343711.

Bruner, J. (2008). Culture and Mind: Their Fruitful Incommensurability. *Ethos*, 36(1), 29–45. https://doi.org/10.1111/j.1548-1352.2008.00002.x.

Currie, G. (2010). *Narratives and Narrators: A Philosophy of Stories*. OUP Oxford. http://site.ebrary.com/lib/morrismn/docDetail.action?docID=10360199.

Currie, G., Kieran, M., Meskin, A., & Robson, J. (Eds.). (2014). *Aesthetics and the sciences of mind* (First edition). Oxford University Press.

De Fina, A., & Georgakopoulou, A. (2011). *Analyzing Narrative: Discourse and Sociolinguistic Perspectives*. Cambridge University Press.

Herman, David (2003). "Stories as a Tool for Thinking." D. H. (ed). *Narrative Theory and the Cognitive Sciences*. Stanford: CSLI, 163–92.

Herman, D. (Ed.). (2007). *The Cambridge companion to narrative*. Cambridge University Press.

Herman, D. (2009). *Basic Elements of Narrative*. Wiley-Blackwell. https://doi.org/10.1002/9781444305920.

Herman, D. (2013). *Storytelling and the Sciences of Mind*. MIT Press.

Hutto, D. (2006). Impossible problems and careful expositions: reply to Myin and De Nul. John Benjamins Publishing Company.

Jongepier, F. Towards a constitutive account of implicit narrativity. *Phenom Cogn Sci* 15, 51–66 (2016). https://doi.org/10.1007/s11097-014-9368-9.

Kukkonen, K. (2014). Presence and Prediction: The Embodied Reader's Cascades of Cognition. *Style*, 48(3), 367–384. http://www.jstor.org/stable/10.5325/style.48.3.367.

Menary, R. (2014). *Cognitive integration: Mind and cognition unbounded*. Palgrave Macmillan.

Menary, R. (Ed.). (2006). *Radical enactivism: Intentionality, phenomenology and narrative. Focus on the philosophy of Daniel D. Hutto* (Vol. 2). John Benjamins Publishing.

Menary, R. (2008). Embodied Narratives. *Journal of Consciousness Studies*, 15(6), 63–84.

Menary, R. (2010). Introduction to the special issue on 4E cognition. *Phenomenology and the Cognitive Sciences*, 9(4), 459–463. https://doi.org/10.1007/s11097-010-9187-6.

Menary, R. (2013). Cognitive integration, encultured cognition and the socially extended mind. *Cognitive Systems Research*, 25–26, 26–34. https://doi.org/10.1016/j.cogsys.2013.05.002.

Meretoja, H. (2013). Philosophical underpinnings of the narrative turn in theory and fiction. *The travelling concepts of narrative*, 93–117.

Meretoja, H. (2022). Life and narrative. *The Routledge Companion to Narrative Theory*, 273–285. https://doi.org/10.4324/9781003100157-26.

Ricœur, P., and K. McLaughlin. (2009). *Time and Narrative. Vol. 1*. Rpt., Univ. of Chicago Press.

Ritivoi, A.D. (2009). Explaining People: Narrative and the Study of Identity. *StoryWorlds: A Journal of Narrative Studies*, *1*(1), 25–41. https://doi.org/10.1353/stw.0.0000.

Ryan, M. (2007). Toward a definition of narrative. In D. Herman (Ed.), *The Cambridge Companion to Narrative* (Cambridge Companions to Literature, pp. 22–36). Cambridge: Cambridge University Press. https://doi.org/10.1017/CCOL0521856965.002.

Ryan, M. (2010). Narratology and Cognitive Science: A Problematic Relation. *Style*, *44*(4), 469–495. http://www.jstor.org/stable/10.5325/style.44.4.469.

Turner, M. (1998). *The Literary Mind: The Origins of Thought and Language*. Paperback, Oxford Univ. Press.

Warner Bros. (2013). Picture presents an Annapurna Pictures production; produced by Megan Ellison, Spike Jonze, Vincent Landay; written and directed by Spike Jonze. Her. Burbank, CA :Distributed by Warner Home Video.

CHAPTER 4

Narrativity and Reading Narratives

The previous chapter argued that the formation of narrative intentions reveals inchoate narrativity in the manifold between perception and reflection, specifically in the reception and anticipation of experiences. This chapter characterizes low-level cognitive processes associated with narrativity by considering the cognitive processing that occurs during the reading of narratives. It surveys recent research on narrative as well as studies of the links between experiences of the real world and imagined fictional worlds. It builds on Fludernik's concept of 'experientiality' (see Chap. 3, Sect. 3.3) to describe the abstraction processes of both ordinary experiences and narrative reading in terms of the role the felt quality of experiences plays in information processing. This leads to a taxonomy of emergent structures in reading and ordinary experiences, including emergent qualities such as relational salience and dynamic valuation. The chapter concludes by describing the bottom-up aspects of reading narrative from these experiential, weakly narrative building blocks.

Humans have the remarkable capacity to have experiences while reading narratives. Even before accounting for how this works, understanding the information processing involved in reading narratives is challenging:

This chapter is also published under the same title in *Narrative and Cognition in Literature and Science* (De Gruyter 2024).

© The Author(s), under exclusive license to Springer Nature Switzerland AG 2023
B. Miller, *Narrativity in Cognition*,
https://doi.org/10.1007/978-3-031-40349-1_4

Meretoja (2022) describes reading narratives as a "triple hermeneutic," in which the basic interpretative processes of perception and ordinary sense-making are supplemented with a third interpretive level (p. 13).

Reading narratives is a complex informational task. To read a narrative text, a reader confronts written words and forms concepts that, through the reading process, are developed and related to other concepts into a complete story, about which the skilled reader can derive summary information. The extraction and synthesis of information draws upon the reader's repositories of social, natural, and aesthetic knowledge, and as such may be thought of as a process of translation.

Anyone who has seen a filmic adaptation of a beloved novel and has been disconcerted by the casting and acting of a key character has confronted this. When a protagonist seems not as you imagined her, the fact of your translation of words into concepts that are not precisely indicated in the text becomes clear. The making and synthesis of concepts from words involve significant cognitive processing. Given the nature of the concepts and the significance of time to their relations, the reader must coordinate discrete concepts with the whole of a narrative, as well as new concepts that emerge because of the relations of concepts that become apparent as the narrative is read. Both the working through of a reading of a text and subsequent reflection involve, then, complex cognitive work. To understand reading narratives, we must closely consider how readers translate texts into time-dependent informational/conceptual networks.

It would seem even more daunting to understand how these concepts generate experiences as they are formed and coordinated. As one prominent narrative theorist puts the matter, a fundamental feature of narratives is that they convey qualia.[1] On first consideration, this would seem to make narratives a kind of super capacity. We generate and interrelate concepts by translating words, and as we generate them we have a phenomenologically rich experience of them.

This chapter argues that, while aesthetic experiences engendered by reading narratives are indeed extraordinary, the processes they are grounded in are mostly not. As several scholars have pointed out (see below), the processing model just described puts the cart before the horse: so-called qualia are not subsequent to information processing, but integral to it. This chapter contributes to this conversation by offering a set of gap-filling ideas to further develop models that foreground the phenomenology of reading narrative. Specifically, it argues for isomorphic processes in reading and ordinary experiences. Subsequently, it offers a taxonomic description of conceptual processing in reading narrative that distinguishes between high-level processes distinctive to reading and low-level processes common to all experiences, and it describes their interrelations. This foregrounds processes necessary for understanding and experiencing narrative that are also present in some non-reading experiences. In sum, reading narrative draws upon basic capacities that generate the phenomenology of experience and builds upon them. Moreover, in light of recent research blurring traditional lines between perception and conceptualization, the phenomenology and informational features of translating language likely combine in generating the imaginary simulations produced in reading narratives.

4.1   CURRENT IDEAS ABOUT READING AND READING NARRATIVE

Reading is a late developing, complex activity, and reading narrative engages emotional, analytical, spatial, temporal, and other capacities. There are debates about whether reading is primarily a 'bottom-up' or 'top-down' activity, though standard models acknowledge the need to accommodate both perspectives (Rayner et al. 2012, 22).[2] Theories of literacy have articulated a variety of models of the engagement of readers, evolving from views of readers as passive recipients to makers of meaning to, in recent decades, contingently positioned within social networks of meaning (Hruby et al. 2016).[3]

Recent research in cognitive neuroscience finds that reading 'recycles' particular brain areas used for other activities, though there is persistent debate about the degree of localization of reading (Dehaene 2014). Nevertheless, these findings support the idea that reading narrative engages ordinary cognitive processes in ways that can make reading 'feel' like non-reading experiences.

Vittorio Gallese has claimed, for example, that "solid empirical evidence shows that the neurobiological mechanisms interfacing us with the 'real world' largely overlap with those activated when we imagine fictional worlds both through images and words [...] the world of literature is 'felt' not too differently from how we feel the more prosaic world of our daily life" (Gallese et al. 2018, p. 376).

Phenomenological critics have historically sought to understand how readers interact with texts to produce meaning, describing a 'virtuality' of the work and reader's creative participation in building meaning through processing that shares deep features with Husserl's phenomenological model of how we experience time (Iser 1972, pp. 280–282).

Paul Armstrong, citing Gabrielle Starr and others, argues that reading narratives is an embodied form of 'skilled coping' that recruits emotional, cognitive, and other capacities. Armstrong argues that reading engages the 'hermeneutic circle' by which readers' developing understandings of parts of and anticipation of the wholes of narratives mutually inform one another (the whole is hypothesized during ongoing reading) (Armstrong 2013, see Chap. 3 in particular).

Richard Gerrig, Nicole Speer, Rolf Zwaan, and others have authored pioneering explorations of the cognitive processing required for rendering narratives meaningful, the various kinds of readerly experiences stimulated by narratives, and the linkages between them. "Schemas" are called upon in ongoing sensemaking of narrative texts.[4] Zwaan and colleagues propose an "Event Indexing Model" of narrative comprehension in which "comprehenders construct situation models from text by extracting events from the text and integrating these events on five different situational dimensions: time, space, causation, motivation, and protagonist" (Zwaan et al. 2001, p. 72). Speer and colleagues more recently propose that readers spontaneously segment narratives into events as part of ongoing situation modeling (Speer et al. 2007).[5]

The literature on schema and situation modeling in narrative comprehension emphasizes the importance of 'participation,' or ongoing hypothesis and inference building, as well as emotional 'transport' (Gerrig 1993, 2001). Burke builds upon the hedonic elements of this theory to hypothesize the existence of 'disportation'[6] and 'oceanic cognition' in the experience of reading stories, which reflect "distributed blends and combinations of basic multidirectional neural processes" (Burke 2015, p. 5). This 'bushy' or distributed model of cognition applies to reading and non-reading activities alike.

In describing 'participation,' 'transport,' 'coping,' and model building, these researchers propose that reading is simultaneously experiential (that is, reading is a kind of experience) and representational. Fludernik (2010, 2018) has explored this relation by distinguishing between experience and 'experientiality.' Experience is constituted through ordinary cognitive processes. Experientiality, by contrast, is representation or evocation of experience within artifactual narrative. But what is the cognitive work that goes into reading narratives? That is, how do we experience experientiality?

Marco Caracciolo explains experientiality as "tension between the linguistic structures [readers] engage with and their own past experiences" (2014, p. 47). He argues that two central mechanisms are responsible for this engagement: "'consciousness-attribution,' [i.e.,] the simple 'recognition' that a particular event referred to by the story is experiential [...] [and] 'consciousness-enactment' [which] [...] consists in empathizing with or mentally simulating the experience that we attribute to a fictional character" (Caracciolo 2014, p. 41).

These character-oriented processes may have larger implications for the relations between narrative and ordinary cognition. Mar (2011) has found that 'consciousness-enactment,' as Caracciolo puts it, may indeed be integral to reading narratives: Theory of Mind activities in general and narrative processing share significant overlaps in neural networks (Mar 2011).[7]

Various accounts of the experiential dimension of reading narrative may seem difficult to reconcile. Some involve intensive, and perhaps intentional, participation (as 'top-down' activities), while others happen bottom-up and automatically. Some focus on emotion as integral to cognition, while others take an information processing view. Jacobs (2015a) and colleagues offer an "eclectic, comprehensive" Neurocognitive Poetics Model (NCPM), which describes different forms of processing for 'foreground' (FG) and 'background' (BG) aspects of narratives,[8] located in different brain hemispheres. The model also accounts for differential aspects of readers, texts, and contexts as determinants of the reading process.

The model is of particular interest because it describes reading language-based narratives simultaneously in terms that comport with ordinary cognitive processing and in terms that emphasize processing language for specific features. Background generally maps to 'immersive processes' and Foreground to 'aesthetic' experiences (and in both cases, to accompanying emotional systems). Yet these mappings are partial. Jacobs' model suggests that experiences of narratives draw upon ordinary forms of processing by employing the same systems that generate 'foreground/background' distinctions in non-reading situations.

Reading text may draw upon these systems via processes of simulation. Caracciolo argues that "engaging with stories can trigger imaginative responses that simulate more basic models of interaction with the environ-ment, thus digging below mental representations and higher order cogni-tion" (2014, p. 11). For Caracciolo, "our experiential responses to non-actual events and existents depend on a simulative mechanism whereby we use our cognitive resources in an 'off-line' mode..., reacting to them as if they were actual" (2014, p. 32).

There are different systems that contribute to phenomenological feel-ings in ordinary experience, and potentially also to the simulative aspect of reading narrative. Emotion, in Jacobs' model, is integral to language pro-cessing, rather than subsequent to it. Emotional systems mediate the felt sense of experiences being embedded in a background "field that is vari-ously and continuously shaped by the biological make-up, culture, social positioning, and personal experience of every individual" (Caracciolo 2014, p. 57). Other theorists, notably Lawrence Barsalou, have argued for the identity of perceptual and cognitive processes ("cognition is inherently perceptual"), and linked the 'feel' of experiencing to non-linguistic per-ception (Barsalou 1999, p. 577). In this model, perceptions are stored in a manner that facilitates re-simulation, rather than categorical, taxonomic archiving of their properties and contents.[9]

The temporal aspects of having an experience and simulating one while reading narrative may provide a key for understanding simulation. Reading a fictional text, similarly to some forms of ordinary experience, can be described as accumulative sensemaking:[10] that is, sensemaking emerges and accrues via the temporal 'working through' of experience. Generally, this occurs through two forms of emotionally laden work associated with reading narrative: event segmentation and anticipation. First, reading a narrative involves the experience of meanings that depend on changing relations through time, which often reflect emotional dynamism and are structured in some relation to a conventional pattern.[11] Second, reading a narrative involves anticipatory feelings that grow from the prior experi-ences of the reader. As a reader, one begins (usually) as an unknowing subject who encounters narrative features and makes predictions about them. The effort and selection involved in these predictions create a struc-ture of anticipation that is inseparable from developing a sense of care for features of the narrative, usually particular agents or groups of agents. Taken together, the readerly experience of temporal extension and of an anticipatory, empathic economy operate in processing the representations of temporal extension and agentive care (i.e., the cares of agents within the story). This processing creates an experience in reading roughly parallel to the experience represented, helping to simulate qualia.[12]

Consider the emotional economy activated when we read, for example, a climactic moment in the fairy tale "Little Red Riding Hood." When the girl approaches the Wolf in bed dressed in her grandmother's clothes, our foreknowledge of the wolf's plans generates an anticipatory terror that we may or may not associate with the girl herself as she considers the Wolf's features. This state in the reader is the result of (a) understanding that the Wolf is a wolf, and knowing the threat wolves pose; and (b) prior knowledge of the Wolf's machinations and consumption of the grandmother. The moment of the girl's observations—"What big eyes you have," etc.— is shaped by terror at her vulnerability and anticipation of the conclusion of this event in the wolf's attack. The heightening of our emotions runs parallel to the girl's increased wonder at the non-grandmotherly features of the figure in the bed. Our evaluation of the girl in this moment, which may have earlier involved censure at her careless behavior during her journey, now modulates into fear for her safety grounded in an evaluation of her credulity. This double dynamism—at once experiencing the textual present in terms of what is to come and simultaneously experiencing an agent in a manner embedded in the moment (terror for her safety, in contrast to our prior evaluation)—makes the reading experience a 'working through' with a dynamic phenomenology.

Time is a key element of the 'working through' of narrative.[13] As they read, readers make provisional recognitions and associations between elements of their texts, which remain available for further synthesis. As they accumulate these recognitions, associations and syntheses contribute to sensemaking—answering the who, what, why, when, and how of a particular moment in the narrative by linking it to the past moments of the narrative as well as by projecting future developments.

Thus, 'sensemaking' pervades the experiential aspects of simulation in narrative reading in a manner similar to ordinary experience. In ordinary experience, the subject-in-experience processes the contacts of world and subject, (re)marking the familiar and unfamiliar, about which there are already well-formed beliefs, and about which new forms of experience and new dynamisms within and between them emerge.

What elements would characterize accumulative sensemaking in reading narrative? Katherine Nelson describes 'narrative dynamics' as "the structural glue that ties together the who, what, where, when, and why." Nelson views processing narrative as an activity involving "three essential components of narrative": "temporal perspective, the mental as well as physical perspective of self and of different others, and essential cultural knowledge of the unexperienced world" (Nelson 2003, p. 28). These components are emergent within reading experiences.

The emergent nature of meaning via these three components reflects a number of underlying, and quite ordinary, cognitive processes. Before articulating these, it is worthwhile to consider the qualities of narrative that readers are attracted to, and around which they build meanings. Meir Sternberg (2003) has identified several universal emotions—'narrative appetites'—associated with narrative processing: curiosity, suspense, and surprise. Curiosity is stimulated by past events, which prompt care about what is currently happening. Suspense is anticipatory—we predict and care for what will happen. Surprise reflects a breakdown in our expectations and prompts the emergence of new predictions.

These appetites drive and are satiated by several kinds of sensemaking activities that mutually influence one another: sequencing, selection, and evaluation for salience. To be clear, while narrative texts reflect such activities on the part of an author during composition, this section focuses on how characteristics of narrative stimulate sensemaking work in readers, comparing this readerly work to sensemaking in non-reading activity.

4.2   Sequencing

First, reading narrative involves active, ongoing attribution of meaning to unfolding sequences.[14] The text offers events and exposition in a particular order, and the reader actively processes each as s/he reads, making sense of the new in light of what has already been presented as well as in light of what's expected. Sequencing may be linear, as in the following narrative:

> Bored with his circumstances and feeling unloved, George hoped something big would happen to him on his birthday. He threw a penny into a wishing well and made his wish. The next day was his birthday. He arrived home after a dull day at work. When he flipped on the light, a tremendous shout of 'Surprise!' rose from his living room. He found his friends and a large chocolate cake in his apartment. His lover had thrown him a birthday party. George wept with joy. He felt lucky for the first time in years.

In an artifactual narrative, the sequencing may also be more complex: say, for instance, the above might be retold by beginning with George's tears, and then jumping back in time to the previous day and continuing the narrative back to the present.[15] In this case the order of presentation and the chronology of events differ. However, in both versions sequencing is important. This narrative, let's call it "George's Story," reflects chronological sequences which may be preserved in George's memories and reflections after the sequence is complete. Other sequences also exist, particularly the 'ordering' of the narrative as it is presented. Non-chronological sequences cue cognitive processing for meaning, as the reader ponders why the events are presented as they are. We see extreme versions of this in novels like Martin Amis's *Time's Arrow* (1991) and the film *Memento* (2000), in which important sequences (in the novel's case, subsuming the entirety of the artifact) are presented in reverse chronological order.

While chronological succession is characteristic of some sequences, it is typically not the only operant logic. Meaning-attribution depends on a reader's prior experiences with different narrative genres. Readers use these past experiences to make sense of what Vladimir Propp called the 'morphemes' of narratives, and to anticipate how particular units likely presage others in a familiar narrative grammar. Meaning depends upon how individual elements fulfill expectations regarding particular narrative functions, as well as upon how these elements are related through time.

Some sequencing is (in Herman's phrasing) 'causal-sequential.' For example, when George weeps, it appears to be caused by the presence of friends and/or the realization that he is not alone. If George's weeping is 'caused' by the presence of friends (in a behaviorist manner), it is immediate causal sequencing; if the weeping is caused by a realization that he is not alone, then it is an unrepresented cognitive process that has been anticipated earlier in the story. What seems most likely is that the weeping involves an amalgam of the experiential quality of his friends' presence (i.e., feeling their loving gazes and smiles, etc.) and an unrepresented cognitive process (George realizes 'oh, I am not alone after all').[16]

However, readers attribute meaning to other forms of narrative sequencing as well. For example, what if the last three sentences of George's story were replaced with "George felt a sudden convulsion in his chest and fell to the floor. He shook and gasped for air. As the dark closed around him, George thought he was sorry to miss the party."

What does the effect of such a change show? As we explored above, reading a narrative is participatory, rather than passive. In this case, the earlier portion of the story creates anticipation: Will George's loneliness be cured? In the first version, the answer is an emphatic 'yes.' In the second, however, the answer is mixed—a 'yes, sort of, but the shock induces a heart attack, and so George's death mitigates the recognition of community.' In this case, the feeling is more complex, and may stimulate reflection. By grappling with the dissonance between emotional anticipation, partial fulfillment, and sudden catastrophe, the reader may reflect on competing values, which can lead to more complex meanings: some things, like life, are more important than recognition from friends. Or, we have a psychological portrait of George, however hazily sketched, as valuing the wrong things; or, we have an implied statement about the desperate need for human community, couched in irony. In terms of Sternberg's (2003) narrative universal 'surprise,' this juxtaposition of versions reveals that 'surprise' reflects re-evaluation of particular elements of a narrative, and also (potentially) revaluation of the values readers deploy in processing the narrative. To put this simply, while both versions involve dynamism regarding George's loneliness, in the second version loneliness itself turns out to have been overvalued.

The key to appreciating the narrative in this case is to grapple with how emotional anticipation and fulfillment or disappointment are forms of cognitive processing associated with reading. This processing potentially leads to meanings. The reading experience might (and frequently does) involve empathic responses: the reader's grasping of the story as meaningful involves feeling along with the focalized consciousness. This partly explains why narratives in which the focalized consciousness is an unlikely subject for empathy (say, an evildoer) can be disturbing—processing the story involves resolving tension between a judgment and an empathic reading strategy.

External contexts that supervene as a narrative unfolds can cause retroactive revaluations of earlier events and expository statements. For example, what if the last four sentences of the original story were replaced with the following: "He found his friends, bound and gagged, and a chocolate cake with detonator wires strung to the front door. The agent from the enemy's spy service, masked but for a pair of twinkling eyes, gave him a wave as he rappelled away from the open window. George should never have allowed anyone to get close to him; it was the first rule of spycraft. The blast wave felt strangely warm, then unbearable, and then everything stopped." In this version of George's story, the last four sentences provide a shock via juxtaposition: the context of George's occupation and the grisly ending function as internal indexes of the final meaning of the story, making the opening emotional references resonate far differently.[17]

(Admittedly, different readers will have different reactions to the story—most probably find it emotionally overwrought. However, regardless of the reader's reaction, these new four sentences force a kind of re-thinking: things were not what they appeared.)

The effect of this sequence is relatively complex. On the one hand, the frisson one might feel in confronting this ending involves a radical reframing. You read the first bit with the belief that you understood the context in which the story occurred sufficiently. However, the narrative turn reveals that you have been left in the dark—that a key context has been withheld. This sort of thrill—perhaps a singular pleasure of narrative—results from a disruption and re-establishment of a normative contextual framework through which the narrative is processed. Context-based reframing exposes the ongoing situational processing that governs sequencing relations during reading.

Underlying sequencing processing are ongoing processes of selection. These would seem to be distinctively part of pre-formed narrative artifacts. Novels, for example, contain a finite number of words, and arguably a finite amount of information. Details come pre-selected—they are simply part of the text. As such, selection appears to be entirely part of authorship. Take our example, 'George's Story.' In composing the story, our author sat at her writing desk, processing bits of her observational experience, her research, and her imaginative creations during an exhausting process of synthesizing, reimagining, researching (through introspection or through life experiences or texts), writing, and revising. It's all after the fact that she composes "George's Story," even if the genesis of imaginative details is mysterious.

Pre-formed narratives offer additional layers of selection as features of the text. Suppose George himself 'tells the story' that comprises the major plot of the piece, and "George's Story" is actually something he has ruminated upon in his mind as a memory of the year he turned 30. Novels with this kind of structure are quite common, including works featuring the character Marlow as a narrator in some of Joseph Conrad's fictions, and in more recent work like Julian Barnes' *The Sense of an Ending* (2011). Surely creative, post-experiential processing has occurred, as George has 'configured' the story for us. These structures are distinctive to narratives that are read or told, rather than being aligned with ordinary elements of experience.[18]

However, attention to the selective design of a text should not obscure the role of selection in the work of reading. For example, George's emotional response to the surprise party as it is experienced probably reflects how elements of the surprise party (the good will reflected in his friends' and loved ones' smiles, for example) are selected for the ongoing story of his loneliness. As readers, part of our cognitive work is to detect the selections that have been made, to select among them, and to draw inferences about them. For example, how do George's emphases in telling the story reflect his view of himself? How does his presentation of his younger self reflect an older George? What details does he focus upon, and what does this reveal?

As we read, in other words, we do not simply receive selected information and extract pre-given meanings from it. Instead, reading involves intensive cognitive processing of selections (or selections of selections, to be precise) for meaning (see Jacobs and commentary on 'foreground' and 'background' (2015a, pp. 337–8). The 'givens' of the artifact exist, but they are continually prioritized, associated, and revisited.[19] In this sense, reading an artifactual narrative involves complexity—we make sense of its representations by building an internal representation of them. Just as we noted in the discussion of sequencing, in selection there is something like an 'end point'—after reading is complete, or perhaps after delay occasioned by forgetfulness, discussion, or other factors, we more or less settle on an understanding of a work that we might communicate if asked what we thought of it. However, the selection processing we undertake during reading is continual, and it has heuristic value, contributing to anticipation and emotional response. So, we are continuously engaged in selection within a growing set of selections in order to anticipate the form of the final set.

4.3   SALIENCE AND RELATIONALITY

So, if selection underlies the work of sequencing, on what basis are selections made? This points to a previously mentioned feature of readerly cognition, salience. To select a particular detail is to value it above others. Salience can be related to primary organismal needs, like hunger, or to threats, like a snake emerging from the wall above your bed. These can suppress or overshadow other features of concern. Certainly if you woke to a snake slithering from a crack in the corner of your bedroom wall you probably wouldn't think as much about the ceiling needing repainting! Salience can also be related to beliefs, such as George's belief that he is isolated and his life is dull. As readers, we might take George's circumstances as evidence for or against this belief. Thus, something quite unremarkable becomes remarkable. There's an important distinction here—in the snake example, salience is more or less a characteristic of an individual element of experience (the snake). This is how salience is generally treated in the scientific literature, along with a focus on salience related to personal well-being. In the 'beliefs about George' example, by contrast, salience emerges through the relation of otherwise unremarkable details to a key concern of the reader about George.

Because salience in individual elements is linked to overarching meanings, a feedback mechanism emerges in the reading process: meaning emerges from the entailment by salient elements of otherwise unremarkable elements, but most forms of salience are fundamentally guided by meaning. When a particular detail is freighted with implications for survival or well-being (a snake coming from the wall), comports with immediate goals, or has significant cultural meaning (such as a religious symbol), salience is experienced as 'given.' But in other cases, how does this work? In reading, threats and goals are generally not immediately pertinent. First, consider a device that is employed in narrative, in music, and in virtually any art form: repetition. When repetition occurs, we attend to the element repeated. Indeed, if we recognize no other significance to it, we actively seek it. Thus, repeated references to George's habit of brushing his hair from his eyes might take on additional significance if we see it as revealing of his inner psychological character. If this represents a 'depth-finding,' or 'vertical' form of significance seeking, another form is 'horizontal,' in the sense that salience is relational. Salience emerges through relations between particular features of texts. In literary studies, terms such as 'antagonist' and 'foil' describe characters whose salience exists primarily in relation to other characters.

Relationality is thus a crucial building block of understanding in the reading process. Two forms of relationality, at minimum, are processed more or less continuously during reading: first, condition changes for salient elements; second, relations between these parsed elements. The first of these we might term 'dynamic persistence.' We follow a particular feature of a narrative while processing its changes, creating a new analysis of the feature that can supervene upon the salience assigned to it in its relational role within the narrative. Processing for 'dynamic persistence' occurs when the reader compares different instances of the feature, either creating a static composite or deriving meaning from both the identity and difference in the feature as it changes through time. This occurs most visibly when we track the changes that occur in a particular character or place. The second kind of relationality involves relation to other elements in the narrative. Some examples of this are straightforward, as in a character who functions as a foil to another, but others entail processing the salient feature in relation to condition changes within the narrative. For example, there are many condition changes in "George's Story," including: temporal (from one day to another); spatial (from work to home); character-field (from only George to George and friends and loved ones); also, condition changes that reveal dynamic persistence, such as the character-psychological change from George's despair to George's joy.

There are a few insights we might immediately derive from describing relationality as a key focus of cognitive work during reading narratives. First, of the many relations between parsed elements that have significance, some follow a semantic, rather than a causal, circuit. For example, George's wish, early in the narrative, is related to his surprise party at the end. The reader is unlikely to infer that George's surprise party is caused by his wish, but it is a fulfillment of the wish nevertheless. That is to say, individual elements are implicitly related via associative or causal-sequential bonds. Second, relationality is not limited to human agency. Objects, changes, and features can have inchoate relational and emotional features. An object, such as a bridge the devil is rumored to have appeared on in a story, may become imbued with a felt sense of empathic terror in the reader for the child wandering across it late at night.

More ordinary objects may derive their value from implicit relationality. For example, the same home (clean, unoccupied except by the perceiver, nice, in a safe location, and unattended by any unusual circumstances) as experienced in the switch from work to home differs from home as a place one seldom is able to leave. Some texts, including famously *The Yellow Wallpaper* (1892) and *Room* (2010) offer features related to a single domestic space that shift with the passage of time to dramatize psychological changes in a primary character. Time spans can have relational properties as well. For example, the same day (filled with the same activities and interactions) takes its value from its relation to others. This is dramatized in the film *Groundhog Day* (1993), in which the repetition of a single day creates changing significance for the central character, and for the viewer.

Relationality exists between elements in a narrative or experience, but also between elements and themselves, elements and concepts, and elements and readers. One of the common structures of cognitive processing in reading artifactual narratives, as several examples above demonstrate, is derived from the reader's care for a particular central agent (in literary studies, usually designated the protagonist). Processing for relationality often centers around this agent in a multitude of ways. Table 4.1 offers a taxonomy of typical forms of relationality centered around a protagonist:

Arguably, reading involves negotiating any number of elements and tracking multiple relationalities for each. In viewing reading narrative as such, I am supplementing Armstrong's argument that reading involves ongoing processing of a "polyphonic harmony of value qualities" (2013, p. 24). In the examples I've given of spaces and time spans, readerly cognitive processing involves a doubled analysis of meaning—in assessing relational differences in time and space, readers (or viewers) assess the dynamics of a particular character or characters. However, relational processing is ongoing whether or not a particular object, time, or place reveals the inner psychological makeup of a character. Rather, it is part of what narratologists call 'world-building.'

The point is that the meanings that emerge through narrative features are constructed in part through the sequencing, selection, salience, and forms of relationality attendant upon the sensemaking activity of reading. Simultaneously, inchoate meanings (we might term them 'meaning-theories') guide processing for relationality, salience, selection, and sequencing. But our valuations of individual textual elements may seem to us natural, even 'given' rather than constructed.

Music provides a useful analogue: a middle-C on the piano can sound quite different if it is the tonic (the main note in a scale) rather than the seventh. Our auditory cognition, in what might be understood as a regular attribution error, parses the note relationally but attributes its value to the note itself. Moreover, this slippage is conventionally associated with values associated with cultural codes. For example, the final 'C#' in a Western classical piano sonata in the key of C#-minor creates a sense of finality or closure. This sense involves hearing the note differently from earlier iterations of the C# (for example, during an interlude in which the key shifts), but the valuation is associated with the note. Other features of the piece as a whole—its tempo, for instance—will similarly shape the valuation of the note.[20]

4.4   VALUATION

The lowest level of our charting of cognitive processes engaged in reading artifacts involves 'dynamic valuation.' Valuing, as I'm using the term here, means assigning characteristics to particular features of a narrative artifact that may cue additional processing. Value is a 'folded' concept, synthesizing characteristics of the object (which may be social, as in the price of a car, or situational, as in the temperature of a skillet on the stovetop) with relevance to the subject (as a source of pleasure, as a source of danger).[21]

That is to say, the objective and subjective values of a particular object are relative to other values (both like and apparently unlike), and they are subject to change. A subjective experience of narrativity thus begins with coordinated value processing through time, and develops in relation to higher order values, primarily future prediction.

Valuing begins with basic features that relate to readers' intuitions about the need for this additional processing, which may manifest in at least three forms: first, valuing elements-in-themselves as stimulants of predictions. Famously, a loaded gun on a wall in the beginning of a story may generate the prediction of it being fired. Predictions extend widely through the reading process and can be understood as the basis of the characterization of individual elements as well as the sociocultural milieu of an artifact. This processing can even be directly cued by the text, as in Austen's famous opening to *Pride and Prejudice* (1813): "It is a truth universally acknowledged, that a single man in possession of a good fortune, must be in want of a wife" (p. 1). In this sentence, the reader is cued to make predictions about the marriages of single men and women in the novel as we encounter them.

Second, readerly affective responses (involving the first type of relationship described in Table 4.1) to particular characters trigger valuations that are available for future relational processing. These affective responses reflect sociocultural conditioning, but also the reader's processing of the rest of the text. For example, an angry, antisocial character in *Pride and Prejudice* might trigger valuations of him as a threat to the social order; however, an angrier, even more rebellious character in a film like *Rebel Without a Cause* (1955) or *Cool Hand Luke* (1967) would likely trigger quite different affective responses. As the reader (or viewer) works through the narrative, these affective valuations may themselves become dynamic—in *Pride and Prejudice*, the angry character may turn out to be angry for good reason, or misunderstood, or in need of sympathy.[22]

Table 4.1 A Taxonomy of Relationalities

1. to reader	How does the element relate to the reader's sense of self and to prior experiences?
2. to prior manifestation	How does a particular incarnation of the element relate to an earlier incarnation?
3. to another element	How does the presence of another valued element condition the valuation of the element in question?
4. to future manifestation	What change is anticipated in the element, and how does that shape present evaluation of the element?
5. to the element as a concept	How does this manifestation of the element relate to a broader concept of this element (e.g., 'home,' or 'car' vs. a dilapidated structure or luxury vehicle)

A taxonomy of relationalities: common relationships parsed in reading narrative

Note: A particular element can be engaged in multiple relationships

Third, valuation in cognitive processing involves a subtle dynamic element, undergirding the predictive and affective dimensions. Certain features of a narrative may by nature of their inherent value as concepts (events such as marriages, objects such as diamond rings) attract more attention and focus than others. Other features, in virtue of greater focus (manifested in long, detailed descriptions, for instance), may be established as high value. In addition, working through a narrative involves dynamism regarding the nature and amount of attention devoted to a particular feature. Tracking value dynamism is a key building block for the salience, selection, and sequencing functions described above. Consider Henry James' novel *The Golden Bowl* (1904), for example. As the novel progresses, the titular bowl is initially valued as an aesthetic artifact, the presence of which has implications for how we understand the people who interact with and through it. Later, it becomes something quite different (an indicator of undisclosed interpersonal relations), but in this dynamism demands much deeper attention than we might otherwise accord it. This focus itself is cued by focus from a particular character on fine details of the bowl's flawed structure. In any event, for our purposes the bowl receives increasing attention as its role in the text shifts. That is, referring to the previous section, its salience increases as the register in which it is valued shifts.

Through these dynamic valuations (of agents, objects, settings, and the like), readers derive structures of understanding the narrative artifact that take shape around the continual work of heuristic prediction and revision, a changing affective economy, and through changing attentional commitments. While narrative artifacts inevitably contain external indexicals (i.e., references that point to particular known features of the real world), valuation dynamics develop meanings contingent upon relationships through time. To give a simple example, a novel might begin with an evil billionaire firing his secretary to blame her for what he calls an 'accounting error' in his portfolio. The secretary, who supports a cancer-ridden mother with her paltry salary, is put into an untenable situation. By the end, the billionaire's corruption is exposed, and he is left in much reduced, though still wealthy, circumstances. Meanwhile, the secretary has recovered from grief at her mother's passing and is starting out as a small business owner. Conceivably, the reader's experience of such a narrative could involve feeling the secretary has triumphed and the billionaire has fallen, although in terms of the most straightforward marker of value identified here—money—the billionaire still has considerably more. One way this works is that both characters experience change through the novel, with the billionaire on a downward trend and the secretary rising upward. The comparison of such trends provides a sense of satisfying closure to the crisis initiated by the billionaire's selfish malevolence and the secretary's vulnerability.[23]

Dynamic valuation, then, provides the basis upon which the higher levels of cognitive processing of narrative artifacts occurs. Note that I am not arguing that narrative artifacts don't contain characters, or scenes, or other narrative features—instead, I am focused on the cognitive processing readers undertake in encountering and making sense of them. As discussed at the beginning of this chapter, understanding a definition of narrative, or narrativity, that depends upon the interaction of readers with artifacts to describe what's special about narrative requires that we look carefully at the cognitive processing that readers undertake when they read.

4.5   Emergent Structures in Reading and Other Ordinary Experiences

Consider the typology of processing activities employed in reading and ordinary cognition in Table 4.2.[24] As described in earlier sections, the cognitive work involved in reading narrative mostly has analogues in ordinary cognition. No reading experiences are the same, of course, but there is a universal: as they read, subjects have experiences. What Gallese and others

Table 4.2 Processing structures in narrative reading and ordinary experiences

	Who	*Emergent processing structures*	*Emergent temporal structures*
I	Readers	Configured wholes	Time remembered
II	Readers	Proto-configurations (theorized parts and arcs based upon parsed events)	Whole-directed, anticipatory temporal figuration
III	Readers + ordinary subjects	Events	Processing time into 'temporality' via boundary processing & selection
IV	Readers + ordinary subjects	Structuration via context, causality, and association	Time-based associative networks
V	Readers + ordinary subjects	Dynamic valuations	Time primitives (i.e., proto-events)

have noted is that this experiencing involves simulation, and this simulation draws upon the same neural and cognitive resources as processing ordinary experiences. Simulation is ongoing—that is, it is not exclusively a retrospective 'making sense' of collected elements of an experience.[25]

Let's begin with the top level. This is associated with reading narrative artifacts, and generally not with other experiences. 'Configured wholes' refers to Paul Ricœur's (1984) theory that 'configuration' is a crucial cognitive process in understanding narrative. At this level, connections between major plot arcs, themes, contexts, and the like might be processed into a synthesis of something like the 'overall message' of the artifact. It is here that we often locate the inferential work of understanding the 'intention' embedded into the artifact. While this kind of processing does not occur exclusively after a reader finishes an artifact, this is prototypically the moment when the reader makes sense of the ending by recalling earlier parts.

In artifacts, some temporal markers are obvious—for example, in Virginia Woolf's *To the Lighthouse* (1927), the book begins with a scene and ends with a parallel scene ten years later. However, some might be intuitive—in interpreting a scene, we might not have a definite idea of how long it took, but we categorize it as a scene and have some intuitive range within which it falls (e.g., less than a day, more than a second; perhaps even something as specific as more than 30 minutes, but less than an hour). These units, in more or less fuzzy/defined form, become the material for top-level configuration.

The top level of 'configured wholes' involves readerly work in which those explicit and implicit temporal units (formally, scenes, chapters, and other structural units, but also uncodified parts) are synthesized into a notion of overall structure. If you have a poor memory, this configuration may be quite fuzzy, and may favor recent and highly dramatic or emotional points in the narrative over others. High-level 'configuration' may also be associated with 'disportation' (cf. Sect. 4.1). Nevertheless, in the course of reading, we frequently feel we've grasped the book, including the meaningfulness of its temporal structures.

Partly this has to do with the second level, again associated primarily with reading. This level involves 'proto-configurations.' As the reader progresses through the artifact, meta-concepts related to theme, tone, and plot and character arcs, informed by known conventions, emerge both consciously and intuitively. This configuring process is ongoing and dynamic, rather than summative (as in the first level). In addition to the reader not having yet reached the end of the artifact, a key difference is that configuration occurs as part of making sense of particular passages in the artifact. Linking earlier passages to the present can serve two functions simultaneously—it is sensemaking of the new, providing a localized form of context; in addition, it may be an anticipatory configuring activity, like a hypothesis.

Armstrong argues that reading creates an ongoing, spiraling 'hermeneutic circle,' a concept initially popularized by reader response critics. For Armstrong, this circle is strongly related to the multi-dimensional temporality of Edmund Husserl, Martin Heidegger, and others (2013, p. 56). Since this notion of temporality is not exclusive to reading, it is important to point to a particularity—the 'spiraling' involved in literary reading operates via an expectation of narrative closure. In ordinary experiences, schemas and scripts may condition such an expectation, albeit loosely. What's distinctive about the working-through experience of reading a work of literature (as opposed to ordinary experience), however, seems to be anticipation of a retrospective evaluative position regarding the structure of the work as a whole.[26] This anticipation manifests most obviously when a reader (or a viewer, in a film) feels an emergent sense of following the intention of the author or director.[27]

In artifactual narratives featuring a configuring narrator, the reader experiences temporal units that have been prefigured, as in the sentence:

"three hours later, the couple were married in a brief service." Here the time marker from the previous scene is clear. However, at this level there is implicit cognitive work happening—the reader has to imagine the 'brief service,' which in an Anglo-American context would probably mean less than 30 minutes, but more than two. In addition, the reader engages in some conscious and some intuitive cognitive work to make sense of implied temporal units, as in: "Later, she would feel the marriage had been a mistake."[28]

While the text may offer clear definitions of the temporal parameters and structures of the narrative, often these are left to the reader. For example, consider the following sentence: "After the tragedy, Amaya came to understand Nicholson better." The exact timeframe of Amaya's developing understanding is unclear, though the sequence (understanding occurring after the tragedy) is clear. In rendering this sequence meaningful, the reader is likely to do some additional cognitive work to form a fuzzy idea of the time parameters of Amaya's understanding, and perhaps indeed of the understanding as a process that unfolds in time.

In addition to grappling with the presence of a more or less explicit narrator, reading narratives often involves the configuration of multiple perspectives. Point-of-view shifts, in particular, are a striking feature of artifactual narratives. While ordinary experiences might include 'perspective taking' through theory of mind activities, the dramatic juxtaposition of different fully articulated perspectives requires unique cognitive work for the reader.[29] David Miall and Don Kuiken describe the work of perspective management and synthesis into a "felt perspective, often a personal one, which inheres in a literary text's expressively rich aesthetic components" (2001, p. 292).

There is an additional kind of temporal experience that conditions the reader. As the reading experience progresses, the reader, additionally, 'goes through' the temporality—the literal time it takes to read has a relationship to the temporal units represented within the work. To make sense of this, consider a famous technique from the French New Wave movement in film. In Jean-Luc Godard's *Weekend* (1967), a traffic jam is depicted as the camera slowly pans along a line of stationary automobiles. The film forces the viewer to endure a boringly long duration that may induce an experience, or at least emotions, sympathetic to that of actually being stuck in a traffic jam. Earlier, I argued that readerly qualia are stimulated through the substance and form of a particular representation of experience (the 'experiential' component of narrative), and that this combination of representations of experiences and stimulated experiences for the reader together embody what I think Herman means about how qualia are 'conveyed' in narrative artifacts. The time and work of reading, in other words, conditions the reader's appraisal of the artifact's representations, including appraisal of the temporality of narrative events.

These top two levels, then, seem largely confined to the experiences of readers engaging artifacts. The next two levels, however, clearly are parts of the ordinary cognitive processing of subjects in experience. Reading engages these processes too, but in ways that reflect the particular conditions of this activity. Just as proto-configurations, in level two, can be considered an important anticipatory architecture for configured wholes, in level one, so levels three and four represent underlying frameworks through which the top levels might be developed. However, whereas proto-configurations mostly precede the retrospective configuration of the whole, the bottom three levels are simultaneous and interleaved. Moreover, the bottom three levels are each constituent of the level just above them.

Before we consider the lower three levels, let's consider the role of language in simulation. Simulation is complex: it is representation typically focused on perceptual faculties, with language playing a lesser or facilitating role. Earlier, we considered the idea, introduced above through Vittorio Gallese and Marco Caracciolo, that reading literature involves simulation that draws upon the same neural areas that help us navigate ordinary experiences. One route to understanding how this works is to consider how ordinary perception is translated into information that is designed to be employed in simulations, and how memory processes facilitate simulation.

Some scholars have described non-linguistic 'perceptual symbol systems' that support, and indeed require, re-enactment of an earlier state for the retrieval of memory. In the model from Lawrence Barsalou (adapted by Speed et al. 2015), amodal and perceptual symbol systems are contrasted. Whereas in amodal systems perceptual information is translated into non-representational, taxonomic information, in perceptual symbol systems perceptual information is preserved in an association area, causing neural simulation of the original information upon re-activation. Speed et al. (2015) propose a semantic architecture that combines linguistic and non-linguistic components, and that would thus help account for how narrative reading involves a combination of simulation and difference from ordinary experience.

Without the grammar afforded by language, then, what is the grammar of the simulations afforded by perceptual symbol systems? In part, ongoing simulations predict and respond to the coordination of 'dynamic relational salience' (level 3). This means, as explored earlier, identification of what matters based on its relation to or association with other features of experience that matter. A common example of this involves attention to agents in experience. If a particular agent has strong attentional focus, and that agent is herself strongly focused on another agent, then that other agent may grow in 'salience'—in relative importance for the future provision of attentional resources.

Relational salience does not need to be about agents, however. A context might make one feature of experience particularly important, and a causal chain might make an ordinarily unimportant feature crucial. As such, relational salience plays an important role in the ongoing work of sensemaking, by familiarizing the unfamiliar through its relations with the familiar.[30]

Relational salience draws upon the reader's affective and analytic responses as well. As Gerrig's pioneering work on participation demonstrates, responses to texts are not passive—instead, readers bring particular biases to the text, and the text's internal cues about affective identification (such as the use of first-person perspective and different perspectives) bias how events, agents, and other elements are evaluated (2001, esp. pp. 310–323).

As the reader builds networks of dynamic relational salience, textual time begins to take on meaningful shape. Via the influence of context or shifts in relational networks away from and back to states of relative equilibrium, the subject's experience is marked with temporally anchored changes in relational salience that provide memorable future reference points, and provide a framework about which proto-configurations occur.

The third processing level, focused on defining events, occurs for both the reader and the non-reading subject in experience. Event segmentation and processing creates units out of the continuous flow of a read text or an experience. However, reading for events leverages textual cues not available in ordinary life. Whereas for the subject in experience relational salience and temporal processing are emergent, growing out of processing in relation to prior experience, for the reader the artifact is more or less strewn with expository, formatting, and other cues embedded in features as subtle as parataxis and other grammatical forms that suggest particular relational and temporal dynamics, and thus give shape to events.

These textual features frequently create a distinctive experience of temporality by creating surprising juxtapositions of events. Zwaan and colleagues describe this property as 'displacement':[31] "In real life, we experience events as a continuous flow. Because of its design feature of displacement, language allows speakers and writers to jump forward or backward in time. This creates discrepancies between how we experience events in real life and how we experience them vicariously through language" (Zwaan et al. 2001, pp. 71–2). Nevertheless, the experience engendered in reading often contributes to a form of active processing that depends on the displacement we experience in mediating present activities via memory and anticipation. Consider, to illustrate this idea, the well-known scene at the end of the film *The Usual Suspects* (1995) in which the heretofore unwitting police detective realizes that the story he's been told is in fact an assemblage of details taken from articles and paraphernalia the suspect had observed in the detective's office. The realization offers an example of radical reconfiguration of the detective's understanding, and we witness his remembrance of moments that revealed the sources of the suspect's narrative. The scene is recounted as a form of active, real-time processing (the detective drops a cup of coffee, which falls in slow motion as he recalls details from the witness' testimony and connects them to items on his office walls). While most examples of displacement do not have this immediate revaluative role, typically displacement is deployed for the continued construction of the narrative's dynamic relational salience network, which in turn helps revalue the diegetic present. The point is that texts have particularly complex tools for depicting the emergence and evolution of our understanding of narrative salience networks.

This form of processing is crucial to understanding how the simulations engendered by reading relate to the ongoing sensemaking we ordinarily associate with experience. This level suggests an immediately fruitful type of processing to explore if we'd like to understand what the work of reading narratives might tell us about cognition more generally.

The second level, or 'structuration,' involves the primitive forms of the sequencing, selection, and relational valuation dynamics described in the previous section. Note that sequencing, selection, and relational valuation occur throughout the upper levels of the processing chart as well, but that these dynamics are emergent in primitive forms at this level.

Finally, the most basic level involves 'dynamic valuations' (also dealt with in the previous section). This means, simply, that portions of experience are assigned values, and that those values change (i.e., the elements of experience are tracked through time and assigned new values as they change). Consider a simple example of this: you see your child looking at a pencil you've been writing the grocery list with. You might notice features of the pencil—its age and condition, its sharpness—and value the pencil accordingly in the same moment that you recognize it. If your child picks up the pencil, its value might change—perhaps you see the pencil as an instrument of your child's curiosity, or as a container of dangerous lead he might ingest. If your child brings the pencil to show you and the sharp tip gets close to your eye, you might revalue the pencil as a threat. These valuation changes, both within a particular set of predictions about the future and in terms of a break from one set of predictions in favor of another, as when the pencil becomes a threat to your well-being, are quite ordinary.

Further, these values and changes in them are crucial networks from which meanings emerge. This kaleidoscopic level of dynamic valuation not only precedes time-sense, but is the stuff out of which primitive time units are constructed. While dynamic valuations are constructed via cognitive processing, they are experienced as 'givens' by the subject-in-experience, as they happen automatically, and can only be constructed consciously through dedicated attention. For readers, these dynamic valuations can be taken as signs of intention, as a subtle form of perspective even when a narrative's narrator is relatively transparent. They are built into the language of the text, and the reader receives them in the course of simply processing the language into meaningful concepts. Jacobs and colleagues have noted the importance of stylistic devices in literature for 'foregrounding' particular ideas. Certainly, alliteration, metaphor, and other devices highlight particular textual details, bringing them into the 'slow' evaluative reading streams Jacobs' hypothesizes.[32] Additionally, textual perspective is revealed through valuative claims embedded in texts.

For a hyperbolic example of these phenomena, consider the opening lines of *101 Dalmatians*:

A large car was coming towards the Dearlys. It drew up at a big house just ahead of them, and a tall woman came out onto the front-door steps. She was wearing a tight-fitting emerald satin dress, several ropes of rubies, and an absolutely simple white mink cloak. Her hair was parted severely down the middle and one half of it was black and the other white—rather unusual.

> "Why, that's Cruella de Vil," said Mrs. Dearly. "We were at school together. She was expelled for drinking ink."
>
> "Come in and meet my husband," said Cruella. The absolutely simple white mink cloak slipped from her shoulders to the floor. Mr. Dearly picked it up.
>
> "What a beautiful cloak," he said. "But you'll find it too warm for this evening."
>
> "I never find anything too warm," said Cruella. "I wear furs all the year round. I sleep between ermine sheets. I worship furs, I live for furs! That's why I married a furrier."
>
> Then Mr. De Vil came in. Cruella introduced him and then said, "Where are those two delightful dogs?"
>
> Pongo and Missis came forward politely.
>
> "Wouldn't they make enchanting fur coats?" Said Cruella to her husband.
>
> Pongo gave a sharp, menacing bark. (Smith, p. 1)

The passage is suffused with aptronyms, including the 'Dearlys' goodness and naivete, and Cruella's cruelty. There are narratorial evaluations, indicated in phrases such as 'absolutely simple' and 'rather unusual.' There are social codes built in, such as the connotation of wealth associated with the de Vils through 'big house,' 'ropes of rubies,' and the like. The characters offer valuative observations of one another, such as Mrs. Dearly's report of the reason for Cruella's expulsion from school. Finally, the passage offers value dynamism in Pongo's change from civility to assertion. There is little 'dynamism' in this passage, as it is introductory.

This feature of textuality—the insertion of dynamic valuation claims at a basic semantic level—is a fundamental differentiator between reading narrative and other experiences. Values associated with particular word associations evoke particular value systems intuitively, thus making the experience of experientiality overdetermined in a manner that seems unique to narrative. However, the central idea here is that valuation is a multimodal, ongoing form of basic processing that enriches ongoing experience, and by so doing creates the conditions for the higher levels. While such valuations seem 'built in,' processing a text is a continuous form of cognitive work in which the reader coordinates them, reacts to them, and employs them to develop networks of dynamic relationality, as well as meaningful units of time.

In sum, these levels all describe forms of cognitive processing, some of which seem more particular to acts of extended reading, and others which occur in both reading and in other forms of ordinary cognition, with differences regarding the activity and passivity of parts of the processing.

One of the key elements that, for many theorists, distinguishes narrative reading experiences from ordinary experiences is the inclusion of narrative 'perspectives' within the artifacts themselves. The model I've offered here suggests additional complexity to an already complex notion— 'perspectives' may manifest at lower and higher levels of cognitive processing of the artifact. This is because levels two, three, and four are simultaneous and interleaved. Proto-configurations are provisionally based on relational salience, which is provisionally based on provisional dynamic valuations in a daunting complexity.

These bottom three levels thus describe reading, but they also describe the processing that occurs in ordinary cognition. While the subject-in-experience may seldom, or never, achieve the summative activity suggested in level one, negotiating the world involves continuous valuation, assessments of multiple forms of salience and relationality, and redoubts of proto-configurations that contribute to the sensemaking of ongoing experience. This all occurs in the course of parsing time into an increasingly semantic temporality.

This section has presented a taxonomy of processes engaged in reading and in other ordinary forms of cognition, and drawn linkages between reading and experience at the level of structuring elements of experience, whether perceptual or representational, into networks of dynamic valuation that help define the meaningful temporal units of narratives.

4.6   Conclusion

Reading narratives is experiential, and so it combines cognitive processes associated with reading and dynamics associated with narrative. Prior scholarship addressing the experiences created by narrative reading through concepts like 'experientiality' can be developed by considering how narrative reading is ordinary and how it is particular. The experiential aspects of narrative reading are integral to, rather than the effect of, sensemaking processes at lower levels of comprehension.

These views have a number of implications for studies of reading, cognition, and narrative around the relationships between representation and feeling. Briefly, an orthodox view is that narratives are felicitous information structures, offering a flexibility for recording and extracting information from heterogenous experience. In this view, narrative is a representational structure. An alternative view is that narrative is comprised of associative and temporal relationships that bridge representations and feelings through complex, dynamic forms of valuation. As a (third) supplement to this view, these relationships are often inextricable from, and constitutive, of meaning, including the meaning attributed to particular temporal extensions and dynamics.

If the first view is orthodox, the second is progressive. It can accommodate the first view because information structures are relational—what's new is the inclusion of multimodal, non-representational valuation mechanisms, such as emotion. The third, supplementary view is potentially radical. If valuation is primary, relationality and informational structuring exist downstream of the most basic form of sensemaking.

Taken together, these various levels of cognitive processing can be summed up in the following description of narrative that foregrounds processing: Narrative processing is ongoing meaning-directed generation and processing of emergent temporal structures consisting of related value-dynamic sequences involving value-dynamic selected agents, mediated by socio-cultural contexts. Crucially, this description applies both within and between events. Events are not given. Rather, they are constructed in perception and subsequent processing in relation to one another. If classical descriptions of narrativity are analogous to the sequencing and relationships between each stone in a string of pearls (in which the pearls—events—are pre-given), in this model the pearls themselves form in a reciprocal, generative process simultaneous with their arrangement along the string. That is, events are fashioned even as they are related to one another.

In the next few chapters, we'll consider some prominent recent theories of how ordinary cognition works, with an eye toward how these theories might relate to the processing dynamics we've just considered.

NOTES

1. As referenced earlier (Chapter 2), narratologist David Herman defines narrative as "a basic human strategy for coming to terms with time, process, and change" (Herman 2009, 2). Narrative representations include several elements, including "a specific discourse context or occasion for telling […] [a process that] cues interpreters to draw inferences about a structured time-course of particularized events […] [that] […] introduce some sort of disruption or disequilibrium into a storyworld involving human or human-like agents [while] also convey[ing] the *experience* of living through

this storyworld-in-flux, highlighting the pressure of events on real or imagined consciousnesses affected by the occurrences at issue" (Herman 2009, 14).

Herman concludes from this description that the phenomenology of narrative is crucial and connects it to the nature of cognition: "narrative is centrally concerned with *qualia*, a term used by philosophers of mind to refer to the sense of 'what it is like' for someone or something to have a particular experience [...] recent research on narrative bears importantly on debates concerning the nature of consciousness itself" (Herman 2009, 14).

Herman thus identifies four parameters for narrative representation. The inclusion of qualia raises questions about how a post hoc representation can include 'going through' the experience represented. That is, can processing ink on a page, for example, have the phenomenology of an event depicted in a narrative—say, the traumatic experience of a shipwreck?

In Herman's view, it is 'conveyed,' meaning it is representation that elicits a subjective feeling that resonates with what the subject imagines being-a-bat, or some other qualia, might be like. What's attractive, though, about narrative, is that it seems to give us the experience of 'living-through' a storyworld via the 'pressure' of events on consciousness. In other words, qualia are stimulated in the reading process (within the reader) that simulate the qualia represented.

2. Rayner et al. reflect that "our model of the reading process can best be described as a bottom-up model in which the reader gets some help from top-down processes" (2012, 22). Rayner et al. (2012, Ch. 1) provide a strong overview of the history of reading theories.

3. Hruby et al. (2016) provide a history of theories of literacy that variously model readers.

4. Paul Armstrong notes a change in Gerrig's model from schemas to "fluid[,] [...] idiosyncratic" processing of narrative texts through reference to "general knowledge" (Armstrong 2013, p. 196). See also Gerrig and Egidi (2003) and Gerrig (2010).

5. Zwaan hypothesizes that event processing precedes language acquisition: "Our general hypothesis is that the mechanisms involved in situation-model construction from language are derived from the mechanisms of situation-model construction in the real world. Children first learn to understand basic events, such as the movement of a person or an object in the environment, before they learn to understand the phrases that describe these events" (Zwaan et al. 2001, p. 73).

6. Refers to a heightened affective state that creates a felt sense of being in motion. Burke argues literary reading stimulates disportation, and that the

existence of disportation points to the interrelatedness of affect and cognition (see Burke 2015, pp. 4–5).

7. Mar notes several important caveats and grounds for future investigation, including a lack of deep understanding of how TOM and narrative comprehension are linked; the implication of the same neural network(s) in other activities, like future thinking and autobiographical memory; and a need to understand our tendency to anthropomorphize as part of understanding (Mar 2011, p. 125). For an introduction to how literary studies has approached Theory of Mind, see Zunshine (2006).

8. Jacobs adopts a pragmatic approach to identifying foreground (FG) and background (BG) features, emphasizing different effects. Whereas FG elements are textual sites of significant focus and attention, BG elements facilitate a sense of immersion (Jacobs 2015a, p. 7).

9. Some scholars have articulated models that fold together the linguistic and non-linguistic. For a perspective on how linguistic and embodied information contribute to word meanings, see Speed et al. (2015). Other scholars have theorized that emotion is crucial to perception. See, for example, Pessoa (2013).

10. Sensemaking is a term used in a variety of contexts, but here I am referring to the version associated with Ezequial Di Paolo. This version places the individual at the center of dynamic couplings that engender meaning. However, the dominant strand of theorizations of sensemaking, associated with Weick (1995), focuses on sensemaking's deep and inherent sociality.

11. The time spent reading is also experienced by readers. In reading, readers respond affectively to the duration of reading, and to this duration's relation to the representations drawn from the text.

12. I believe the processing described here and Caracciolo's 'consciousness attribution' and 'consciousness enactment' are mutually constitutive.

13. The felt sense of 'working through' or working toward understanding is common to non-narrative reading as well. However, the nature of narratives contributes to a conceptual integration of the 'working through' into the meaning of the whole, whereas in most other reading 'working through' is quickly forgotten as the reader integrates concepts into a summative memory of the reading.

14. By meaningful sequencing, I mean that reading a narrative requires coordinating parts by linking them in meaningful ways. Meanings, in this context, can relate to changes in entities about which the reader cares; and they can be part of larger social schema.

15. See Zwaan and Radvansky (1998) for an analysis of the particulars of linear ('iconic') sequencing and the achronological temporal structures often found in literary texts.

16. Apprehending causal history is crucial, not only to following the plot but also for extracting the kinds of meanings Currie emphasizes. That is, in

processing (hearing, viewing, reading) narrative, this causal history is crucial for higher order evaluation (who is morally culpable, for example?). However, experience is inseparable from understanding causal history. And the way causal history is understood arguably involves three components: (1) selection of components (delimiting the when, the where, the what (occurs), and the who (the agents and receivers of action, not necessarily human). (Importantly, because experience is rich, this is selective—much (most?) is excluded); (2) baseline evaluations of each component; (3) evaluations of dynamics. We process for causal history through interleaved processes of selection and evaluation. This interleaving occurs within interleaved acts of perception and higher order cognition.

17. Paul Ricœur (1984) describes the ongoing importance of 'configuration' in grasping narrative. Such juxtapositions point to how ongoing configuration can involve dramatic swings in a reader's understanding of a text.

18. Some literary theorists might argue that these structures are homologous to Theory of Mind (TOM), which is common to both narrative texts and ordinary cognitive experience. However, I believe the structure described is distinctive, and since this argument is reconcilable with the general position of TOM theorists, it does not seem worth pursuing at length.

19. To illustrate this, consider the experience of reading a mystery novel. As you proceed through the work, you are weighing particular information and constructing theories that render the crime meaningful in terms of the social agents who exist within the framework of the plot.

20. Armstrong notes deep similarities between music and literary reading in the sense that both involve working through experience to produce emergent meanings: "melody is not an objective entity but a developing temporal construct" (2013, p. 96).

21. This folding is useful—it entails enfolded subjective and objective processes. Simply, 'valuing' is both objective and subjective.

22. The point isn't that the character is good or bad—the point is that the reader assigns a value (this manipulability is a signature of the role of processing).

23. One opportunity of process-oriented rather than object-oriented models of cognition is that it may lead to re-examination of valuation and salience. Rather than the abstractions 'good,' 'bad,' 'beautiful,' 'ugly,' 'advantageous,' 'threatening,' and the like, they highlight values based on imagined (sometimes fantasized) actions related to identity concerns.

24. By exploring these dynamics, we complement the 'top-down' approach (where the seminal example of a narrative is a finished, communicable verbal or written text) with a bottom-up approach (where acts of narrative comprehension take center stage as the reader synthesizes and evaluates features of the narrative, ultimately developing an emergent sense of the meanings of parts or the whole). This bottom-up perspective may shed a

different light upon what is at the 'top' (that is, the nature of 'finished, communicable verbal or written texts').

25. To characterize the simulation in reading as 'closed-form' would be to repeat the errors associated with artifactual views of narrative in earlier cognition.

26. This might not be consistently the case. Consider a rather ordinary example: say you've gotten tickets with a friend to a concert for a band you love, but you are not a 'night person.' The experience of the concert might be one of mixed positive and negative feelings (enjoying the music vs. fighting off sleepiness and grouchiness). In addition, though, you might experience feelings of processing the experience with an eye toward how you will recount it later, including your evaluation. This may subtly alter your experience of the concert.

27. One certainly might argue that this kind of anticipation occurs in other circumstances. However, what's distinctive about consuming artifacts is how the 'working through' experience is permeated by a sense of anticipating this retrospective evaluative moment, which (again) can manifest as a feeling of tracking authorial intention.

28. Armstrong describes 'gap-filling' as a key form of cognitive processing that distinguishes reading. See Armstrong (2013, p. 84).

29. There is a potential critique of this position. Say that you believe that juxtaposed perspectives in narratives have correlatives in ordinary experiences in the retrospective gathering of perspectives on a particular situation or event (the juxtaposition of perspectives in artifactual narratives sometimes works like this). Then, *in situ* ordinary experiences might include a mentalized juxtaposition of imagined perspectives in the mind of the subject. However, this example seems overblown: the complexity of processing a particular experience would seem to preclude this kind of mental gymnastics.

30. Armstrong describes familiar/unfamiliar 'grafting,' while many scholars, notably Gerrig, emphasize the dynamic, ongoing deployment of schemas (Armstrong 2013, p. 72).

31. The displacement creates cognitive work that results in a proto-configuration, although one might want to call the displacement itself the proto-configuration. Here the point is to assess the materials from which proto-configurations are drawn.

32. Foregrounding may have important effects with regard to the reader's self-perspective as well: Miall and Kuiken (2001) offer a "defamiliarization-reconceptualization cycle" theory, which states that when a reader encounters stylistically foregrounded language in a text, his/her schemata may be inadequate for comprehension. As a result, the feelings evoked by the text facilitate alternative perspectives which can direct and motivate readers to search for new understandings.

References

Armstrong, Paul. *How Literature Plays with the Brain: The Neuroscience of Reading and Art*. Baltimore: Johns Hopkins University Press, (2013).

Austen, J. (2002). *Pride and prejudice*. Penguin Books.

Barsalou, Lawrence W. "Perceptual Symbol Systems." *Behavioral and Brain Sciences* 22.4 (1999): 577–660. https://doi.org/10.1017/S0140525X99002149.

Barsalou, Lawrence W., W. Kyle Simmons, Aron K. Barbey, and Christine D. Wilson. "Grounding Conceptual Knowledge in Modality-Specific Systems." *Trends in Cognitive Sciences* 7.2 (2003): 84–91.

Burke, Michael. "The Neuroaesthetics of Prose Fiction: Pitfalls, Parameters and Prospects." *Frontiers in Human Neuroscience* 9 (2015): art. 442. https://doi.org/10.3389/fnhum.2015.00442.

Caracciolo, Marco. *The Experientiality of Narrative: An Enactivist Approach*. Berlin and Boston: De Gruyter, (2014). https://doi.org/10.1515/9783110365658.

Dehaene, Stanislas. "*Reading in the Brain* Revised and Extended: Response to Comments." *Mind & Language* 29.3 (2014): 320–335. https://doi.org/10.1111/mila.12053.

Di Paolo, Ezequial. "Extended Life." *Topoi* 28 (2009): 9–21. https://doi.org/10.1007/s11245-008-9042-3.

Fludernik, Monika. "Narratology in the Twenty-First Century: The Cognitive Approach to Narrative." *PMLA* 125.4 (2010): 924–930. http://www.jstor.org/stable/41058291 (22 August 2021).

Fludernik, Monika. "Towards a 'Natural' Narratology Twenty Years After." *Partial Answers: Journal of Literature and the History of Ideas* 16.2 (2018): 329–347. https://doi.org/10.1353/pan.2018.0023.

Gallese, Vittorio, and Hannah Chapelle Wojciehowski, with Patrick Colm Hogan. Interview. "Embodiment and Universals." *Literary Universals Project*. University of Connecticut, 25 September 2018. https://literary-universals.uconn.edu/2018/09/25/embodiment-and-universals/# (22 August 2021).

Gerrig, Richard J. *Experiencing Narrative Worlds: On the Psychological Activities of Reading*. New Haven and London: Yale University Press, 1993.

Gerrig, Richard J. "Perspective as Participation." *New Perspectives on Narrative Perspective*. Eds. Willie van Peer and Seymour Chatman. Albany: State University of New York Press, 2001. 303–323.

Gerrig, Richard J. "Readers' Experiences of Narrative Gaps." *Storyworlds: A Journal of Narrative Studies* 2.1 (2010): 19–37.

Gerrig, Richard J., and Giovanna Egidi. "Cognitive Physiological Foundations of Narrative Experiences." *Narrative Theory and the Cognitive Sciences*. Ed. David Herman. Stanford, CA: CSLI, 2003. 33–55.

Herman, David. *Basic Elements of Narrative*. Malden, MA et al.: Wiley-Blackwell, 2009.

Hruby, George G. et al. "The metatheoretical assumptions of literacy engagement: A preliminary centennial history." *Review of Research in Education* 40.1 (2016): 588–643.

Iser, Wolfgang. "The Reading Process: A Phenomenological Approach." *New Literary History* 3.2 (1972): 279–299. https://doi.org/10.2307/468316.

Jacobs, Arthur M. "Neurokognitive Poetik: Elemente eines Modells des literarischen Lesens." *Gehirn und Gedicht: Wie wir unsere Wirklichkeiten konstruieren*. By Raoul Schrott with Arthur M. Jacobs. Munich: Carl Hanser Verlag, 2011. 492–520.

Jacobs, Arthur M. "Affektive und ästhetische Prozesse beim Lesen: Anfänge einer neurokognitiven Poetik." *Sprachen der Emotion: Kultur, Kunst, Gesellschaft*. Eds. Gunter Gebauer and Markus Edler. Frankfurt a. M. and New York: Campus, 2014. 134–154.

Jacobs, Arthur M. "Neurocognitive Poetics: Methods and Models for Investigating the Neuronal and Cognitive-Affective Bases of Literature Reception." *Frontiers in Human Neuroscience* 9 (2015a): art. 186. https://doi.org/10.3389/fnhum.2015.00186.

Jacobs, Arthur M. "Towards a Neurocognitive Poetics Model of Literary Reading." *Towards a Cognitive Neuroscience of Natural Language Use*. Ed. Roel M. Willems. Cambridge: Cambridge University Press, 2015b. 135–159.

James, Henry. (2009). *The Golden Bowl*. Oxford: Oxford University Press.

Mar, Raymond A. "The Neural Bases of Social Cognition and Story Comprehension." *Annual Review of Psychology* 62.1 (2011): 103–134. https://doi.org/10.1146/annurev-psych-120709-145406.

Meretoja, H. (2022). Life and narrative. *The Routledge Companion to Narrative Theory*, 273-285. https://doi.org/10.4324/9781003100157-26

Miall, David S., and Don Kuiken. "Shifting Perspectives: Readers' Feelings and Literary Response." *New Perspectives on Narrative Perspective*. Eds. Willie van Peer and Seymour Chatman. Albany: State University of New York Press, 2001. 289–301.

Nelson, Katherine. "Narrative and the Emergence of a Consciousness of Self." *Narrative and Consciousness: Literature, Psychology and the Brain*. Eds. Gary D. Fireman, Ted E. McVay, and Owen J. Flanagan. Oxford: Oxford University Press, 2003. 17–36. https://doi.org/10.1093/acprof:oso/9780195140057.003.0002.

Pessoa, Luiz. *The Cognitive-Emotional Brain: From Interactions to Integration*. Cambridge, MA: MIT Press, 2013.

Rayner, Keith, Alexander Pollatsek, Jane Ashby, and Charles Clifton. *Psychology of Reading*. 2nd edition. New York and London: Psychology Press, 2012.

Ricœur, Paul. *Time and Narrative.* Vol. 1. Trans. Kathleen McLaughlin and David Pellauer. Chicago and London: The University of Chicago Press, 1984.

Sinding, M., Heydenreich, A. & Mecke, K. (2024). *Narrative and Cognition in Literature and Science.* De Gruyter.

Smith, D. (1984). *The 101 dalmatians.* Puffin Books.

Speed, Laura J., David P. Vinson, and Gabriella Vigliocco. "Representing Meaning." *Handbook of Cognitive Linguistics.* Eds. Ewa Dąbrowska and Dagmar Divjak. Berlin and Boston: Mouton de Gruyter, 2015. 190–211.

Speer, Nicole K., Jeffrey M. Zacks, and Jeremy R. Reynolds. "Human Brain Activity Time-Locked to Narrative Event Boundaries." *Psychological Science* 18.5 (2007): 449–455. https://doi.org/10.1111/j.1467-9280.2007.01920.x.

Sternberg, Meir. "Universals of Narrative and Their Cognitivist Fortunes (I)." *Poetics Today* 24.2 (2003): 297–395.

Weick, Karl E. *Sensemaking in Organizations.* Thousand Oaks et al.: Sage Publications, 1995.

Zwaan, Rolf A., and Gabriel A. Radvansky. "Situation Models in Language Comprehension and Memory." *Psychological Bulletin* 123.2 (1998): 162–185. https://doi.org/10.1037/0033-2909.123.2.162.

Zwaan, Rolf A., Carol J. Madden, and Robert A. Stanfield. "Time in Narrative Comprehension: A Cognitive Perspective." *The Psychology and Sociology of Literature: In Honor of Elrud Ibsch.* Eds. Dick H. Schram and Gerard Steen. Amsterdam and Philidelphia: John Benjamins, 2001. 71–86.

Zunshine, Lisa. *Why We Read Fiction: Theory of Mind and the Novel.* Columbus: Ohio State University Press, 2006.

CHAPTER 5

Cognition: Contemporary Views and Debates

This chapter briefly surveys contemporary models of cognition as a primer for readers unfamiliar with these ideas. In later chapters, particular aspects of these theories will be specified in relation to ideas about experience being structured by narrative processing. The survey is not comprehensive; rather, it introduces concepts necessary for following later arguments.

To begin, it's worth noting that the term *cognition*, like *narrative*, has a long history[1] and currently is subject to robust debate and criticism. Recent years have witnessed robust debates over the definition of cognition, the existence of a 'mark of the cognitive,'[2] the necessity and/or exclusivity of representation in cognition,[3] and whether non- and anti-representational processes should be considered cognitive.

The approaches to cognition highlighted in this chapter share the premise that cognition is complex, and that established models are inadequate for fully explaining it. The variety of processing tasks associated with cognition, from basic visual perception to higher order abstract reflection and conceptualization, is bewildering. In addition, a theory of cognition must reconcile apparently discrete processes with one another and explain the emergence of 'late' processes (e.g., when does something become conscious?). Within these tasks, sub-processes pose similar challenges (e.g., within perception).

Many older theories of cognition are subject to critiques of 'computationalism,' in which the human mind operates on the same processing

© The Author(s), under exclusive license to Springer Nature Switzerland AG 2023
B. Miller, *Narrativity in Cognition*,
https://doi.org/10.1007/978-3-031-40349-1_5

principles as a computer. Also, older theories are subject to Hurley's critique of so-called sandwich models of cognition, in which perceptions lead to cognitions, which subsequently lead to actions in stepwise, unidirectional processes. As Burr notes,

> Hurley saw a number of problems or limitations with this account. For example, this serial process would be insufficiently dynamic to cope with the time pressures of a constantly changing environment. In the time taken to construct a representation and plan an action by integrating the necessary information, the environment may have changed, which would render the current model (and any actions based on it) inaccurate. (p. 3)`

In addition, older models reflect unresolved debates about the modularity, functional anatomy, and knowability of features of mind. New models have emerged, influenced by network theories of parallel distributed processing, plasticity, and integrative views of classically discrete functions (e.g., emotion and cognition). In contrast to 'brain-as-computing-device' and 'brain-in-a-vat' theorizations of cognition, some of these models favor integrating bodily interactions with the environment with cognitive processing.

If, as Chaps. 2 and 3 suggest, the case for narrative as central to cognition faltered because it depended upon ambiguous and usually artifactual conceptualizations of narrative, the new theories of cognition, with their emphases upon networked, highly iterative, and trans-modular forms of complex processing, are more hostile still to the integration of artifacts.

If we are to speculate that weak narrativity (as a form or feature of processing, rather than as the deployment of an established, static narrative object) is implicit in cognition, newer models of cognition, which reject the stepwise nature of the 'sandwich model,' may provide fertile terrain.

In this case, weak narrativity would emerge either via global structural dynamics or through individuated forms of processing. If the former, we must examine points of emergence and function within these global systems. If the latter, we must consider how global structural dynamics might support these individuated processes, and how weak narrativity contributes to other cognitive processes (i.e., what is produced in narrative processing, and how does that become a cognitive resource).

5.1   CURRENT GLOBAL THEORIES OF COGNITION

Current discussions of the global structure of cognition center on two broad theoretical frameworks, Global Workspace Theory and Local Recurrence Theory, which exist in tension with one another.[4]

According to Global Workspace Theory (Baars 2005), cognition operates through information processing in encapsulated modules such as vision, language, and memory. These modules broadcast to one another, and certain broadcasts comprise conscious awareness. For proponents of Global Workspace Theory, "it's all in the dynamics" (Dehaene 2016). That is, specific 'workspace' neurons are activated when other modular systems reach thresholds, broadcasting a signal across the global workspace. Thus, neural function operates on two 'tracks,' one of which gathers information, performs error detection, and stimulates consciousness; the other, characterized by awareness and conscious intention, is consciousness itself. The two tracks allow us to perform more computations than we'd otherwise be capable of (Dehaene 2016). Thus, we are conscious of the active signals propagated across the workspace, while we are not conscious of signals confined to other modular systems that have not reached thresholds for 'workspace' activation.

Evidence for this model includes the relative lateness of conscious perception, the (theorized) imperative that task switching occurs consciously, and the emergence of apparently spontaneous thoughts. According to Baars et al., Global Workspace Theory posits "the limited capacity of conscious contents at any given moment, compared to the vastness and complexity of unconscious neuronal circuits. Thus, consciousness is associated with limited capacity, seriality, and integration, whereas comparable unconscious processes are of much greater capacity, parallelism, and distributed autonomy" (Baars 2005).

Local recurrence theory, by contrast, locates the emergence of conscious awareness in the feedforward and feedback activity that occurs in individual neural systems. For example, feedforward and feedback activity between a region of visual cortex and higher activity centers in the brain comprise conscious awareness.

There is a third form of theorizing important to debates about the location of and processing which produces conscious awareness: Higher Order Theory (HOT) (see Chap. 7, Sect. 7.10, and Chap. 8).

The three theories differ regarding the role of higher cognitive functions, the importance of attention and its relation to consciousness, the richness or sparseness of the phenomenology of experience, the role of working memory, and the neural location(s) of the emergence of consciousness.

In relation to the hypothesis that experience exhibits weak narrativity (i.e., that we experience our perceptions as structured by selection, boundary definition, and agentive relationality in the service of temporal parsing into weakly narrative event sequences), these theories provide distinctions between conscious and subconscious neural activity and offer models for how the subconscious becomes conscious. They do not seem particularly hospitable to meaning-making at the level of basic cognitive processes, but the possibility is not foreclosed. For example, the 'thresholds' emphasized in Global Workspace Theory may involve weakly narrative features, including deviations from expectations, and the like. Similarly, what rises to 'higher order' consciousness may involve narrative-based adjustments to certain forms of higher-order thought (such as autobiographical details), but they also might involve more basic narrative patterns or deviations from patterns that require additional processing.

5.2   Recent Established and Emerging Theories of Particular Systems

5.2.1   Memory Systems

While these remain the dominant theories of how global cognition works, and how consciousness and/or awareness manifests, there have been several influential models of features of cognition that might provide fertile ground for theories about narrative processing as component to cognition.

Perhaps the most robust, and most relevant to our purposes, of these is the progress made in recent decades regarding our understanding of memory. The findings of recent research are leading theorists to reconsider established models of memory. From approximately 1960 until quite recently, memory research evolved around three categorizations of memory: short versus long term, declarative versus non-declarative (sometimes designated 'procedural'), and, within the category of declarative memory, episodic versus semantic memory.

Currently, the nature of short-term perceptual memory and working memory is disputed. Block (2011) argues for the 'overflow hypothesis,' which suggests that sub-personal recall of experiences exceeds conscious recall of short-term memory. That is, we unconsciously remember more than we are able to consciously access.

Similarly, theories about the nature and function of forms of declarative memory have shifted considerably. Declarative memory can be consciously articulated, while non-declarative memory reflects learning of a skill or unreflective process (some researchers also refer to 'explicit' (declarative) and 'implicit' (non-declarative) memory). Within declarative memory, Endel Tulving famously distinguishes between 'episodic' and 'semantic' memory. For Tulving (2002), the human capacity for "mental time travel" points to "a neurocognitive (mind/brain) system ... called episodic memory" (pp. 2–3).

Semantic memory involves facts—"Cleveland is a city," "My car is a Dodge," "my church holds a regular service on Saturday evenings"— where episodic memory involves events from one's experience—"My first kiss with my future partner." Episodic memories are distinguished by phenomenological detail—how an event unfolded, and what it felt like, for example.

Because of the isomorphism between episodic memories and narratives, we'll consider Tulving's and other's findings about episodic memory in some detail. In his classic definition, Tulving observes that episodic memory-retrieval is an event-like neural activity; that is, it is experiential. The episodic memory system is comprised of a number of components, including a "sense of subjective time, autonoetic awareness, and self" (p. 2). "Autonoetic" is distinctive from the "noetic" awareness typically associated with semantic memory insofar as it is recalled with (often robust) markers of the where and/or when of a memory. The difference is commonplace. For example, while semantic memory includes knowing that 5 is the square root of 25, episodic memory involves *remembering* (in some sense, re-experiencing) your 5th-grade math teacher's square root lessons, which were accompanied by cartoon drawings of trees with equilateral subterranean structures ('square roots'!).

Researchers frequently employ the distinction between knowing (noesis) and remembering (autonoesis). Piolino et al. (2009) define autonoesis as "a sense of self in time and the mental reliving of subjective experiences arising from the encoding context" in experimental designs (p. 2). Tulving emphasizes how special this function is: "Episodic memory is oriented to the past in a way in which no other kind of memory, or memory system, is. It is the only memory system that allows people to consciously re-experience past experiences" (np).

So while the phenomenology of experience is retained via autonoesis in episodic memories, the two categories of declarative memory aren't mutually exclusive. For example, an episodic memory draws upon semantic memory, as in: "I was in my Dodge Dart overlooking the Cleveland skyline when I first kissed my future partner. I was driving us to an evening church service and decided to take a chance and pull the car off at a wayside rest to declare my feelings. My heart pounded, but I made my confession. We kissed. It was a beautiful Saturday evening, with the setting sun lighting up a long, thin line of clouds." As Tulving notes, "all memory tasks are multiply determined" (1995).

This speculation reflects a shift in conceptualizations of memory. Tulving (2002) describes episodic memory as "a hypothetical memory system...Episodic memory is not just a particular type of retained and retrieved information, and it is not just a particular kind of mental experience, although it is systematically related to both of these." He views the episodic memory system as a structure of underlying neural, behavioral, and cognitive components potentially shared with other memory systems. Tulving offers a flexible conceptualization of episodic memory: when considering whether "long-term memory is "best regarded as comprising multiple independent systems..., as a processing framework..., or as a complex function which can be used in a flexible and task-appropriate manner?," he answers that the correct answer may be "at the very least all of the above" (p. 1). He describes memory systems (including episodic and semantic) as "related to one another in terms of processes of encoding, storage, and retrieval":

> The central assumption of this SPI model—serial, parallel, independent—is that the relations among systems are process specific. Information is encoded into systems serially, and encoding in one system is contingent on the successful processing of the information in another system; information is stored in different systems in parallel; and information from each system can be retrieved independently of information in other systems. (1995, p. 839 (abstract))

So, for Tulving episodic and semantic systems have different relations during different forms of processing.

Tulving (2002) argues that episodic memory is likely unique to humans, and he speculates that episodic memory evolved in humans from semantic memory processes common in other species: "Many nonhuman animals, especially mammals and birds, possess well-developed knowledge-of-the-world (declarative, or semantic, memory) systems and are capable of acquiring vast amounts of flexibly expressible information" (p. 7).

At some point in human evolution, possibly rather recently, episodic memory emerged as an "embellishment" of the semantic memory system (2002, p. 7). The details of this emergence are unknown, and one can only speculate about them (Tulving 2002). It is not even certain that the evolution of episodic memory was a part of (neo)Darwinian evolution. Episodic memory may represent an instance of the Baldwin effect (Baldwin 1902; Richards 1989).[5]

The speculation that episodic memory evolved from semantic memory is supported by research that suggests that, within the lifespan of the individual, episodic memory is a "late-developing" and "early-deteriorating" memory system (2005, p. 5). Over time, memories shift from episodic to semantic:

> with the passage of time and the repetition of similar events in the phenomenal experience of remembering real-world events, there is a shift away from autonoetic consciousness and towards noetic consciousness, i.e. from episodic to semantic memory. (Conway 1997; Robinson and Swanson 1993)

> This shift is in line with the idea that most features of very long-term memories become semanticized over time (Cermak 1984), becoming a mixture of semantic knowledge and specific experiences. (see also Piolino et al. 2007; Westmacott and Moscovitch 2003). (Piolino et al. 2009, p. 2315)

While contemporary researchers note this shift toward semanticization, they do not claim that *all* episodic memory is semanticized. That is, our memories do not shift in a linear manner from "Remembrances" to "Knowledge" (i.e., we don't necessarily move from episodic memories of events, like vivid remembering of giving a public speech in 5th grade, to knowledge that we gave a public speech in 5th grade, and that it caused much anxiety but turned out well). Piolino et al. see a "reminiscence bump" during adolescence:

> There is a strong body of evidence that, rather than being only determined by the length of the retention interval, the distribution of episodic AMs across a long lifespan reflects the survival of vivid memories from late adolescence and early adulthood compared with other remote periods—the

so-called reminiscence bump (Rubin Wetzler, & Nebes, 1986; Rubin &Schulkind, 1997; Rubin, Rahhal, & Poon, 1998)—which represents a potent landmark for the current self (Conway & Pleydell-Pearce, 2000), serving to maintain a sense of identity and continuity in the present. (p. 2315)

So, long-term memory exhibits change over time toward semanticization. Given episodic memory's late evolutionary development, the autonoetic properties of episodic memories may be viewed as means of refining the subject's capture of semantic features of his experiences.

5.2.2   *The Default Mode Network*

The dynamic role memory systems play in organizing our experiences and orienting us toward the future is revealed in relatively recent research exploring the "Default Mode Network." The DMN, described in 2001 by Marc Raichle and colleagues, is "a series of interconnected subsystems that converge on key 'hubs,' in particular the posterior cingulate cortex, that are connected with the medial temporal lobe memory system" (Buckner et al. 2008, p. 11). The network

> is the most active brain system when individuals are left to think to themselves undisturbed. The default network also increases activity during mental explorations referenced to oneself including remembering, considering hypothetical social interactions, and thinking about one's own future. These properties suggest that the default mode network facilitates flexible mental explorations—simulations—that provide a means to prepare for upcoming, self-relevant events before they happen. (p. 30)

It is active when "individuals are engaged in internally focused tasks including autobiographical memory retrieval, envisioning the future, and conceiving the perspectives of others" and may function to "plan for the future, navigate social interactions, and maximize the utility of moments when we are not otherwise engaged by the external world" (p. 11).

Because the DMN is most active when environmental demands on attention are low, several functional processes have been proposed for it. One theory, which Buckner et al. call the 'Sentinel' view, sees the DMN as a monitoring network that registers changes in the environs during intervals in which attention is focused on internal mentation. Alternatively, the

DMN may support internal mentation itself, contributing to "constructing dynamic mental simulations based on personal past experiences such as used during remembering" (p. 18). This may facilitate thinking about the future and imagining alternative scenarios and perspectives (p. 19).

The DMN may draw upon "sensory, motor, and emotional systems to represent the content of...imagined events" (p. 31). Buckner et al. cite the theory of Hassabis and Maguire (2007), who describe this process as "scene construction, a term emphasizing that mental simulation often unfolds in one's mind as an imagined scene with rich visual and spatial content" (see also Hassabis and Maguire 2007) (p. 31).[6]

Scene construction may be a central feature of internal mentation. However, if the Default Mode Network's function is primarily, or even partly, to play the 'sentinel' role, one may speculate about how the 'sentinel' operates. The sentinel is a change monitor, gathering data about valuation dynamisms, with particular emphasis upon valuation dynamisms that signal emergent threats to the subject. However, the normative parameters of the field being observed may be heavily mediated by expectations, not only about particular objective features of the environs, but also about anticipated changes within the environs and their meanings.[7]

This recent work on memory and the DMN contributes to new formulations of the primacy of anticipatory cognition. As Suddendorf and Corballlis memorably put it, "we predominantly stand in the present facing the future rather than looking back to the past" (p. 147). The next chapter considers in greater detail what recent research suggests about how memory processes capture the present in narrative episodes, and what role episodic memories and other components of cognition play in the simulation activities theorized in the DMN.

Some anticipatory theories of cognition suggest that present perception is constructed, rather than received, through dynamics in the brain's motor and other systems, as well as in the interactions of body and world.

5.3   Constructivist Theories of Cognition

This section briefly features two emerging theories of cognition that are radically 'constructive.' In contrast to classical models of cognition (see the critique of the 'sandwich model' above), in constructivist theories brain activity actively shapes the nature and parameters of perception and cognition. That is, what we experience is in part shaped by intensive cognitive activity, including processes of sub-personal selection and simulation.

Constructivist theories offer a continuum of ideas about the relative encapsulation of cognition within neural systems (internalism) versus the role of extra-neural processing mechanisms.

A number of recent scholars suggest that prediction plays a key role in perception. Predictive Processing models invoke the principle of neural frugality and hierarchical Bayesian models to suggest overlapping processes that produce complex results. Neural frugality implies the likelihood of temporary neural assemblages that might comprise concatenated, provisional structures. Bayesian models might account for higher order feelings integral to perception, such as perspective and selfhood.

Pioneered by Karl Friston and colleagues,[8] predictive processing is a computational framework used to describe "perception, action, cognition, and their relationships in a single, conceptually unified manner" (Wiese and Metzinger 2017, p. 1).[9] In Wiese and Metzinger (2017), Predictive Processing is defined as "*hierarchical* predictive coding, involving *precison-mediated* prediction error minimization, enabling predictive *control*" (3).[10] It is a "unified theory of brain function [that] seeks to explain all aspects of mind and cognition" (Hohwy 2017, p. 1). In lay terms, this means that cognitive activity involves making predictions about what is experienced (based on prior knowledge) and refining those predictions by comparing predictions to sensory inputs to minimize errors. High-error predictions can be accorded greater attention, which may involve action to refine predictions.

The framework utilizes Bayesian statistical analysis to model the process of prediction error minimization.[11] Underlying this process is the 'free energy principle,' which postulates that organisms will seek relative stability and equilibrium, including relief from uncertainty. As a result, 'perception' is the result of active inference, which constructs models of the world, rather than of passive reception: "the deliverances of the sense organs [are] the basis for *inferences* about the ultimate causes of those stimulations. Beliefs about the world (explicit as well as tacit) both result from and constrain these inferences" (Anderson 2010, p. 3).

The predictive framework depends on the minimization of 'suprisal' or 'free energy,' which are effectively measures of indeterminacy. These factors are minimized through a process of 'active inference,' which typically involves a combination of error minimization (through feedforward and feedback loops in which the discrepancy between predictions and sensory inputs is reduced) and through action, which may orient the subject in a way that alters the sensory inputs to bring them in line with predictions.[12]

In this model, the organism understands the world in part by its impacts upon its own interoceptive, proprioceptive, homeostatic, and other states and its inferences about the near-term future of those states. Predictive processing thus implies that perception is actively linked to homeostatic control and the continued flourishing of the organism, rather than con-sisting wholly of the passive reception of inputs. For some PP theorists, the goal of perception and action is to "disambiguate the hidden causal structure of the environment" in the service of flourishing (Bruineberg, p. 7). For others, it is directed toward an "optimal state for the animal-environment system" (p. 8). This manifests in the ways the organism and environment mutually constrain one another so that the various states of each is compatible with organismal flourishing.

Bruineberg considers the implications of this *enactive* model:

> What the agent needs to be modeling then is not the relation between sen-sory stimulation and the causal structure of the environment *per se*, but rather the relation between sensory stimulation and its ways of living/flour-ishing in an ecological niche with a particular action-related structure. The generative model of the agent is thus shaped by previous experience result-ing in more and more subtle refinements to the context-sensitive relevance of available affordances. (p. 11)

The upshot is that "there is no clear demarcation between … epistemic and purposive actions": the "agent's history of interactions with the envi-ronment [is] based on a concern to improve grip" (p. 11). This leads to a fundamental, basic sense of selfhood and agency built into the organism's modeling of its interface with the environs: "the self in active inference is not accessible as an explicit belief or encountered as a thing but shows up in the way the agent is drawn to improve its grip on the situation" (pp. 14–15).[13]

Within this framework, traditionally vexing philosophical and scientific questions about the nature of mental representations of the world, the links between attention and conscious awareness, and the nature and func-tion of agency assume new (though perhaps no less difficult) forms.

Selection and attention,[14] for example, are theorized as mechanisms for "achieving greater precision in predictions … as well as reflecting … relative salience," perhaps resulting from transient neural networks[15] (Wiese and Metzinger, p. 9; Clark 2017, p. 17). Representational content, particularly the contents that constitute phenomenal awareness, could not be qualia as traditionally understood (i.e., translations of external stimuli onto interior percepts).

Instead, representations must emerge in prediction-making and prediction error detection processes, which might mean representations that combine descriptive and action-oriented content, or which are not attributable to either external signals or internal processing. Agency, finally, might be grounded in internal prediction-making neural mechanisms, or in feedback loops between these mechanisms and external stimuli.[16]

The ecological account of experience as skilled perceiving offered by Gibson (2014) and developed by a variety of dynamic thinkers into what we call the 4E perspective has given rise to many theories about the relations between primary perception, cognition, embodiment, and self. The 4E (embodied, enactive, embedded, extended) approach to cognition is an umbrella term for a range of theories with some quite different implications.

Embodied cognition views consciousness as a coping mechanism for the organism within its environment, and it offers an alternative to the dominant theories of cognitive science, which view the mind as a symbol manipulating faculty that calculates the organism's situation and prospective actions. Michelle Maiese terms a strong version of this perspective *Essentially Embodied Consciousness*: "consciousness is not just instrumentally dependent on the body, but constitutively dependent" (i.e., its content is derived from embodied experience) (p. 1).

According to Michael O'Donovan-Andersen,

> The knowing self is not just the sensing mind, but the living, moving, intruding, fully embodied interactive self, a self which can access the world by means other than the epistemic text of interpreted sensation. This opens the possibility of an epistemology which allows the world to provide epistemic friction, revealing that skepticism, in those very areas of scientific knowledge where it seems most plausible, can be subverted by insisting that the knowing, thinking, interpreting self is more fully and thoroughly embodied than Cartesianism admits. (p. 4)

Lawrence Shapiro (2011) delineates two approaches to embodied cognition. One depends upon the controversial notion that the mind is "offloaded" into the environment. In this view, cognition occurs in objects we interact with in a way that makes them *part* of what we refer to as mind. Using a smartphone, for example, involves offloading needed information onto silicon. Thinking and interacting with the world occur through complex couplings between the organism, prostheses like the smartphone, and features of the environment that afford particular types of interaction useful to the organism.

Shapiro's second strand of embodied cognition emphasizes the insufficiency of the SENSE-THINK-ACT circuit, which is foundational for cognitive studies. For researchers pursuing an embodied approach, thinking should not be described as an autonomous "step" in a linear, sequential process. Instead, reflexivity is integrated into a nearly instantaneous feedback loop. Thus in the embodied cognition view, the activity described as "SENSE-THINK" is really a complex dynamic system in which thinking and sensing are tightly related and mutually condition one another. Recursive patterns also occur in the "THINK-ACT" portion of the circuit. What we conventionally describe separately as thinking and acting are in fact mutually imbricated not only with one another but also with sensing. Perhaps dancing with a partner to known music with lyrics provides a useful example here—the sounds and bodily response are orchestrated in rhythmic and semantic ways, and complex social messages are conveyed to and received from the partner, others, and oneself. This example also points out the role affect can play in cognition.

Other models of cognition account for complex feedback loops as well. Daniel Dennett's *multiple drafts model* dispenses with a controlling agency of thought and envisions mind as a self-organizing symbolic system simulating potential actions in the world. Perceptual inputs shape the articulation of potential responses, and the sense of an organism's self—as the "observer" of thoughts and as a controlling agency—turns out to be an illusion. Dennett concludes, famously, that this modeling produces an illusion of continuity in consciousness processes that are in fact intermittent (Dennett 1991).

The multiple drafts model can help us see how the self is a configured, functional illusion. It usefully provides a bridge between organism-environment processes and social processes, insofar as the configured illusion of self is explicitly functional. More basically, Dennett's model provides a grounding for an understanding of experience, although from a computational perspective on cognition.

Embodied cognition, by contrast, argues for complex and semantically rich interactions between environment and self at a presymbolic, or "pre-reflective," level. Evan Thompson (2007) argues for two sources of a sense of continuity: our complex time sense and a pre-reflective form of self-consciousness. Pre-reflective self-awareness can be simply described as the continuous feeling of experiencing. Thompson refers to Dan Zahavi's description of this feature of consciousness as simultaneously static and dynamic: "pre-reflective self-awareness is streaming because it is constitutive of the streaming or flowing experiences themselves, not a pure and empty awareness that appears on its own. By the same token, it is standing because it is an ever-present and unchanging feature of consciousness" (p. 328). The persistence of the flow of experience, in other words, marks our presence to ourselves. This awareness provides a fundamental sense of continuity through time, even though it is not a repository of the characteristics of self. Rather, it is the perspective around which experience is organized. Thompson notes Naomi Eilan's similar model of "perspectival awareness" in terms of this implication: "such awareness is not yet 'the capacity for detached reflection on oneself' that develops along with language and conceptual thinking, but it is enough to suggest a kind of ladder or continuum between bodily interaction with the world and developed reflectivity" (p. 20). As we consider how this ladder is traversed, we will consider the limiting conditions this perspectival awareness, manifest in the organism's interface with the environment, places upon higher order self-consciousness.

The other crucial factor in the organism's sense of continuity is the growth of the sense of time. Thompson draws upon the notions of duration associated with E.R. Clay, William James, J. Ellis McTaggart, and Henri Bergson, but emphasizes Edmund Husserl's model. For Husserl, experience consists not of a succession of moments, but of durations in which the present is infused with a sense of becoming ("primal impression"), of passing into the past and into memory ("retention"), and of anticipation ("protention"). The "thickness" of immediate experience links it inevitably to secondary processes of memory, comparison, and anticipation which group these experiential durations further. The inseparability of these durations from memory and anticipatory processes builds pre-reflective self-awareness into primal experience (Thompson 320–3).

The individual's Husserlian way of experiencing temporal presence is functional—it permits the pattern creation upon which learning is based while organizing experience around a common perspective through which needs can be satisfied and upon which more abstract conceptualizations can occur.

Taken together, this thick notion of time and the persistence of pre-reflective self-awareness constitute a disposition toward continuity basic to the organism's interface with the world, and productive of a primal self-image. In configuring duration blocks, the organism simultaneously generates a world oriented around a perspectival center while creating a learning mechanism for establishing relative dispositional advantages toward particular experience blocks that bear a similarity to others. A nascent sense of self grows out of pre-reflective self-awareness and the configuring being-in-time. The ongoing consequences of this model are first that the emergent self is caught between pre-reflective self-awareness and self-objectification; second, the sense of self is subject to multiple temporalities, including Husserl's thick notion of the present, our episodic or situational sense (fostered by the structures of memory), and the life span. Each of these temporalities is subject to configuration and the reciprocal influence of other temporal "levels."

The enactivist approach is perhaps the most radical of the 4E approaches in its focus on the constitutive nature of meaning-making. Theories of enactive cognition describe cognition as dependent upon dynamic interactions between subjects and their environments. Enaction describes continuous, iterative engagement in activity (broadly defined) to make sense of the relation between self and world and generating opportunities for such activity. Ezequiel di Paolo (2014) writes:

> In enaction, sense-making is first of all an ongoing activity which is rooted in bodies as precarious self-sustaining identities constituted by material, organic, cognitive, and sociocultural processes. To make sense is for a body to encounter value and significance in the world, and these relate ultimately to the body's precarious, multi-layered identity. Sense-making is not something that happens in the body, or in the brain, but it always implies a relational and value laden coherence between body and world—the world does not present itself as sense-data to be interpreted, but is itself a participant in the sense-making process and often the stage where my sense-making is enacted through my actions and those of others. Sense-making is not primarily a high-level voluntary interpretation of the world...but bodily and worldly activities of all sorts, from biological and pre-reflective to conscious and linguistic. In all these cases, sense-making is always affective. (p. xii)

The affective dimension of the enactive approach links it to new theories of emotion as a form of cognition, which we'll consider in Chap. 7. Before considering this account, however, let's briefly consider the relationship between the predictive processing and 4E accounts. There are debates within the scholarship about the degree to which Predictive Processing commits one to 'neurocentric seclusion' (Clark 2017, p. 2). Conversely, a central critique of 4E approaches, from the PP scholarship and elsewhere, is that 4E approaches are dismissive of boundaries that delimit the necessary and sufficient conditions of cognitive activity.[17] So, some PP approaches are critiqued for being too 'internalist,' fabricating experience in a manner reminiscent of the allegory of Plato's cave, while 4E approaches can seem to deny distinctions about what constitutes 'cognitive' activity in the service of conflating all inputs into cognitive processing with the processing itself.

Supporters of both theories have addressed these critiques and, in so doing, gestured toward reconciling the 4E and PP approaches. Andy Clark, one of the pioneers of 4E theories, embraced a PP approach that squares with the 4E account in *Surfing Uncertainty* (2015). Clark (2017) argues that 4E theorists "do not seek to deny the existence or importance of systemic boundaries blanketing the organism from the wider world. Instead, such theorists (see Clark 2004) stress the multiplicity, flexibility, and transformability of those boundaries, and the way the choice of what boundaries to stress reflects the explanatory interests and projects of the theorist" (np). Anderson claims that predictive processing should be understood in terms conducive with the 4E approach, describing "the perceptual system [as] an exploratory and not an inferential system" (2017, p. 7)).[18]

The next chapter considers recent theories of the relationship between event processing and episodic memory, with a focus upon how recent constructivist accounts might provide a framework conducive to theories of narrative processing.

NOTES

1. For overviews of this history, see Green (1996). See also Miller (2003) and Cromwell and Panksepp (2011).
2. The debate about the existence of a 'mark of the cognitive' seems to have been ignited by Rowlands (2009) and Adams and Garrison (2013), though many other scholars have taken the question up.

3. See Ramsey (2017) for a review of this debate.
4. The following discussion borrows from Hakwon Lau's talk "Hot Topics" at the 2016 Science of Consciousness Conference in Tucson, AZ.
5. The Baldwin effect, a controversial but generally accepted part of evolutionary theory, posits that flexible learning capacities can figure into natural selection. Specifically, culturally developed traits can become genetic.
6. These dynamics might be described as narrative processing—'scene construction' is characterized by selecting, coordinating, valuing, and establishing dynamism with meaningful parts through durations. There are many theories about the roles the DMN may play in 'constructivist' forms of cognition, introduced later in this chapter. Note Andrews-Hanna et al.'s (2010) summary:

> A challenge to the field has been to disentangle such high-level tasks into component processes. Some have suggested a role for components of the default network in scene construction (Hassabis and Maguire 2007), contextual associations (Bar 2007), and conceptual processing (Binder et al. 2009). Others have suggested a role for the default network in social (Mitchell 2006; Schilbach et al. 2008), self-referential, or affective cognition (Gusnard et al. 2001; Wicker et al. 2003; D'Argembeau et al. 2005, 2009) with minimal emphasis on mnemonic or prospective processes (but see D'Argembeau et al. 2009). Schacter and Addis (2007) highlighted that future-oriented thoughts, which strongly drive activity in the default network, are inherently constructive, building on multiple episodic memories. They further argued that mental simulation based on memory is a core process of future-oriented cognition (Schacter et al. 2007). The divergence across these perspectives, perhaps exemplified best by the different emphases in Hassabis and Maguire's scene construction model (Hassabis and Maguire 2007) and D'Argembeau et al.'s emphasis on self-referential cognition (D'Argembeau et al. 2005, 2009), suggests that the default network likely comprises multiple interacting subsystems (e.g., Hassabis et al. 2007a; Buckner et al. 2008). (550)

7. This idea contributes to the idea of weak narrativity. Recall the value dynamic definition of narrativity as a means of temporalizing experience presented in the last chapter. In light of such a definition, the DMN may contribute to weak narrativity in experience. It may have some explanatory value for understanding how the boundaries of event processing and episodic memories are established through the recruitment of the 'sentinel's attention to changes/dynamisms that are unexpected. If in ordinary life the 'sensemaking' of ordinary vs. extraordinary changes depends on narrative expectations, then the gathering of them would themselves involve relations to anticipated narrative structures.

8. Friston's predictive processing framework is based on the "AIM" model. According to Bucci and Grasso, "Hobson and Friston base their view on the combination of the famous AIM model (Hobson et al. 2000) and the free energy principle (Friston 2010)3. The AIM model makes use of a multidimensional state-space for keeping track of the brain's changes in activation (A), input-output gating (I) and neurochemical modulation (M)." (p. 4).

9. Bruineberg traces a long lineage for the Predictive Processing framework, back to von Helmholz, while noting its recent formulations:

> After computationalism, connectionism, and (embodied) dynamicism, cognitive science has over the last few years seen the resurgence of a paradigm that might be dubbed "predictivism": the idea that brains are fundamentally in the business of predicting sensory input…This paradigm is based on older ideas in psychology and physiology (Von Helmholtz 1860/1962), and has been revived by parallels that have been discovered between machine learning algorithms and the anatomy of the brain (Dayan and Hinton 1996; Friston et al. 2006). The emergence of the paradigm of "predictivism" has sparked great interest in philosophy of mind and philosophy of cognitive science, mainly through the work of Clark (2013, 2016) and that of Hohwy (2013, 2016). This interest has led to a vast number of papers attempting to ground concepts from phenomenology, philosophy of mind and psychopathology in predictive architectures (see for example Hohwy 2007; Limanowski and Blankenburg 2013; Apps and Tsakiris 2014; Hohwy et al. 2016). (2017, p. 1)

10. According to Dewhurst,

> the predictive processing systems described by Hohwy and Clark are hierarchical; they consist of a nested hierarchy of precision/error units, with each level of the hierarchy predicting the current state of the unit below, which is then compared to the actual state of that unit and updated (in the next iteration) in response to any error signals that it receives. This hierarchy bottoms out in units that predict inputs received via sensory transduction, and tops out with a very abstract model, perhaps just predicting general causal laws or regularities. (np)

11. Some versions of this theory are referred to as also referred to as 'the Bayesian brain hypothesis' (Seth and Critchley 2013).

12. When perceptual inputs don't match predictions closely, more processing, including more and more varied predictions, may occur. This is labor intensive because of this 'mentalist' activity, but also because of how it integrates in preparing the organism for action in response. When inputs

are a relative match for predictions, less processing of details of experience may be entailed, reducing the energy devoted to attention to that particular task. Take the example of performing a routine task, such as tying one's shoes, that is so familiar as to require only tactile feedback responses. Ordinarily, the hands easily find both laces and the tying occurs without the need for visual input. However, in a unusual case one might not feel one of the lace-ends, and require a visual glance to locate it (tucked, for example, in one's shoe).

13. It may be helpful to consider the granularity of predictions in so-called low-level cognition (we'll consdier 'high-level' cognition in a later chapter). When we think of what a 'prediction' is, we might tend to imagine it is a holistic representation about a distal event ("When Mary arrives, I bet she'll say the travel was easy, even though she's been delayed for hours"). However, the predictions that form the basis of this theory are more granular and immediate. Consider, for example, the anticipation of impact you might have as a fastball approaches your catcher's mitt. The prediction is valenced, inseparable from both micro-muscular adjustments of the hand in the glove and from nerve suppression of pain reflexes to 'absorb the blow.' Low-level, basic predictions in the PP framework might be understood in this light—what's radical is that the perception of the event (in this case the fastball's impact) is inseparable from micro-muscular adjustments, nerve suppression, and the neural processes that cue them.

14. Attention is partly a way of achieving greater precision in predictions, as well as reflecting the relative salience of particular features of the environment. (Wiese and Metzinger, p. 9). For some, attention plays a more critical role in constructing experience:

> Attentional mechanisms, that story suggests, alter patterns of inner (neural) effective connectivity so as to enforce information flows that are highly specialized for the task at hand (Clark 2016; Clark in press). Attention, if this is correct, itself imposes a kind of transient organizational form, with its own distinctive Markov blanket organization (marked by temporary conditional statistical independencies), upon the brain. Attentional mechanisms may thus be seen as driving the formation and dissolution of a short-lived Markov partitioning within the neural economy itself, temporarily insulating some aspects of on-board processing from others according to the changing demands of task and context. These transient neuronal ensembles then recruit (and may also be recruited by) shifting coalitions of bodily and worldly elements, resulting in the repeated construction of temporary task-specific devices that span brain, body, and world. In this way, the ebb and flow of neural influence is matched by an ebb and flow of bodily and worldly influence. It is the progressive generation and maintenance of these nested

transient partitionings, swept up in the circular causal dynamics that bind perception and action, that enables living beings to persist and minimize free energy across their lifespan. (Clark 2017, p. 17)

15. According to Burr, precision-weighting is considered to be a "process by which the brain increases the gain on the prediction errors that are estimated to provide the most reliable sensory information, conditional on the higher-level prediction" (Burr, 2017, p. 12).

16. Hohwy (2017) associates the free energy principle with agency, describing the agent as "simply a model...engaged in prediction error minimization through action and through optimization of model parameters" (Hohwy 2017, p. 3). This depends upon a form of internalism—the predictive processes are based upon the interaction of models with sensory inputs which might be understood in the spirit of 'qualia' or 'percepts'—they reflect the impacts of the environs on the organism, rather than directly representing the environs themselves. Thus, the PP framework entails 'scepticism' in the sense that there is no direct encounter with the real. In addition, the model provides agency in the sense that it continuously changes to anticipate changes in sensory states (as opposed to viewing 'agency' in terms of a separate entity controlling the predictive process).

17. Ned Block (2005) has mounted a forceful critique of 4E approaches.

18. Anderson invokes the ecological model of perception that has inspired 4E theory: "It is the overall job of perceptual systems to keep organisms in contact with the values of relevant organism-environment relationships (the closeness of the obstacle; the penetrability of the surface). Put differently, the world properties it is important to pick out for the purpose of reconstruction are not the same as those that best support interaction, and psychology has tended to (mistakenly) focus on the former class of properties to the exclusion of the latter. This, of course, is the thought behind the Gibsonian affordance-based theories of perception that have been widely influential in embodied cognition (Gibson 1979; Orlandi 2014). Affordances are relationships between things in the world and an organism's abilities (Chemero 2009)" (Anderson 2010, p. 8).

References

Adams, F., & Garrison, R. (2013). The Mark of the Cognitive. *Minds and Machines*, *23*(3), 339–352.

Anderson, M. L. (2010). Neural reuse: A fundamental organizational principle of the brain. *Behavioral and Brain Sciences*, *33*(04), 245–266. https://doi.org/10.1017/S0140525X10000853

Andrews-Hanna, J. R., Reidler, J. S., Sepulcre, J., Poulin, R., & Buckner, R. L. (2010). Functional-anatomic fractionation of the brain's default network. *Neuron, 65*(4), 550–562.

Baars, B. J. (2005). Global workspace theory of consciousness: toward a cognitive neuroscience of human experience. *Progress in Brain Research, 150*, 45–53.

Block, N. (2005). Review Reviewed Work(s): Action in Perception by Alva Noë. *The Journal of Philosophy, 102*(5), 259–272. http://www.jstor.org/stable/3655560.

Block, N. (2011). Perceptual consciousness overflows cognitive access. *Trends in Cognitive Sciences, 15*(12), 567–575. https://doi.org/10.1016/j.tics.2011.11.001.

Bruineberg, J., Kiverstein, J., & Rietveld, E. (2018). The anticipating brain is not a scientist: the free-energy principle from an ecological-enactive perspective. *Synthese, 195*(6), 2417–2444.

Bucci, A., & Grasso, M. (2017). Sleep and dreaming in the predictive processing framework. In T. Metzinger & W. Wiese (Eds.). *Philosophy and Predictive Processing*: 6. Frankfurt am Main: MIND Group.

Buckner, R. L., Andrews-Hanna, J. R., & Schacter, D. L. (2008). The Brain's Default Network: Anatomy, Function, and Relevance to Disease. *Annals of the New York Academy of Sciences, 1124*(1), 1–38. https://doi.org/10.1196/annals.1440.011.

Burr, C. (2017). Embodied decisions and the predictive brain. https://predictive-mind.net/epubs/embodied-decisions-and-the-predictive-brain/OEBPS/07_Burr.xhtml.

Clark, Andy. (2015). *Surfing Uncertainty: Prediction, Action, and the Embodied Mind*. Oxford University Press.

Clark, A. (2004). Feature-placing and proto-objects. *Philosophical Psychology, 17*(4), 443–469. https://doi.org/10.1080/0951508042000304171

Clark, A. (2017). How to knit your own Markov blanket. https://predictive-mind.net/epubs/how-to-knit-your-own-markov-blanket/OEBPS/03_Clark.xhtml.

Conway, M. A. (1997). *Cognitive Models of Memory*. MIT Press.

Cromwell, H. C., & Panksepp, J. (2011). Rethinking the cognitive revolution from a neural perspective: How overuse/misuse of the term 'cognition' and the neglect of affective controls in behavioral neuroscience could be delaying progress in understanding the BrainMind. *Neuroscience & Biobehavioral Reviews, 35*(9), 2026–2035. https://doi.org/10.1016/j.neubiorev.2011.02.008

De Jaegher, H., & Di Paolo, E. (2007). Participatory sense-making: An enactive approach to social cognition. *Phenomenology and the Cognitive Sciences, 6*, 485–507.

Dehaene, S. (2016). *Plenary Address*. 2016 Science of Consciousness Conference in Tucson, AZ.

Dennett, D. C. (1993). *Consciousness Explained*. Penguin UK.

Dennett, D. C. (1992) The Self as a Center of Narrative Gravity. In: F. Kessel, P. Cole and D. Johnson (eds.) *Self and Consciousness: Multiple Perspectives*. Hillsdale, NJ: Erlbaum.

Di Paolo, E. A. (2014). Foreword. in M. Cappuccio and T. Froese (eds.). *Enactive Cognition at the Edge of Sense-Making Making Sense of Non-Sense*, NYC: Palgrave, Macmillan, pp. xi–xv.

Eilan, N. "Consciousness, self-consciousness and communication." *Reading Merleau-Ponty*. Routledge, 2007. 130–150.

Fair, D. A., Cohen, A. L., Dosenbach, N. U. F., Church, J. A., Miezin, F. M., Barch, D. M., Raichle, M. E., Petersen, S. E., & Schlaggar, B. L. (2008). The Maturing Architecture of the Brain's Default Network. *Proceedings of the National Academy of Sciences of the United States of America*, *105*(10), 4028–4032. https://doi.org/10.2307/25461360.

Friston, K. (2010). The free-energy principle: A unified brain theory? *Nature Reviews Neuroscience*, *11*(2), 127–138. https://doi.org/10.1038/nrn2787.

Gibson, J. J. (2014). *The ecological approach to visual perception: Classic edition*. Psychology Press. https://books.google.com/books?hl=en&lr=&id=8BSLB QAAQBAJ&oi=fnd&pg=PP1&dq=james+gibson&ots=zNC37M

Green, C. D. (1996). Where did the word "cognitive" come from anyway? *Canadian Psychology/Psychologie canadienne*, *37*(1), 31–39. https://doi.org/10.1037/0708-5591.37.1.31

Hassabis, D., & Maguire, E. A. (2007). Deconstructing episodic memory with construction. *Trends in Cognitive Sciences*, *11*(7), 299–306. https://doi.org/10.1016/j.tics.2007.05.001.

Hohwy, J. (2013). *The predictive mind* (First edition). Oxford University Press.

Hohwy, J. (2017). How to entrain your evil demon. https://predictive-mind.net/papers/how-to-entrain-your-evil-demon.

Hurley, S. Perception And Action: Alternative Views. *Synthese* **129**, 3–40 (2001). https://doi.org/10.1023/A:1012643006930.

Miller, G. A. (2003). The cognitive revolution: A historical perspective. *Trends in Cognitive Sciences*, *7*(3), 141–144. https://doi.org/10.1016/S1364-6613(03)00029-9

Piolino, P., Desgranges, B., & Eustache, F. (2009). Episodic autobiographical memories over the course of time: Cognitive, neuropsychological and neuroimaging findings. *Neuropsychologia*, *47*(11), 2314–2329.

Raichle, M. E. (2015). The brain's default mode network. *Annual Review of Neuroscience*, *38*, 433–447.

Ramsey, W. (2017). Must cognition be representational? *Synthese*, *194*(11), 4197–4214. https://doi.org/10.1007/s11229-014-0644-6

Richards, R. J. (1989). *American Journal of Sociology*, *95*(1), 258–260. JSTOR. www.jstor.org/stable/2780451

Robinson, J., & Swanson, K. (1993) Field and observer modes of remembering. *Memory*, *1*(3), 169–184, https://doi.org/10.1080/09658219308258230

Seth, A. K., & Critchley, H. D. (2013). Extending predictive processing to the body: Emotion as interoceptive inference. *Behavioral and Brain Sciences*, *36*(03), 227–228. https://doi.org/10.1017/S0140525X12002270

Shapiro, L. (2011). *Embodied cognition*. Routledge/Taylor & Francis Group.

Suddendorf, T., Addis, D. R., & Corballis, M. C. (2011). Mental time travel and shaping of the human mind. *M. Bar*, 344–354.

Suddendorf, T., & Corballis, M. C. (2007). The evolution of foresight: What is mental time travel, and is it unique to humans?. *Behavioral and Brain Sciences*, *30*(3), 299–313.

Thompson, E. (2007). *Mind in life: Biology, phenomenology, and the sciences of mind*. Belknap Press/Harvard University Press.

Tulving, E. (1995). Organization of memory: Quo vadis? In *The cognitive neurosciences*. (pp. 839–853). The MIT Press.

Tulving, E. (2002). Episodic Memory: From Mind to Brain. *Annual Review of Psychology*, *53*(1), 1–25 (online unpaginated version). https://doi.org/10.1146/annurev.psych.53.100901.135114.

Wiese, W., & Metzinger, T. (2017). Vanilla PP for philosophers: A primer on predictive processing.

Zahavi, D. (2007). Self and Other: The Limits of Narrative Understanding. *Royal Institute of Philosophy Supplement*, *60*, 179–202. Cambridge Core. https://doi.org/10.1017/S1358246107000094.

Zahavi, D. (2018). Consciousness, Self-Consciousness, Selfhood: A Reply to some Critics. *Review of Philosophy and Psychology*, *9*(3), 703–718. https://doi.org/10.1007/s13164-018-0403-6.

Zahavi, D., & Kriegel, U. (2015). For-me-ness: What it is and what it is not. In *Philosophy of mind and phenomenology* (pp. 48–66). Routledge.

CHAPTER 6

Events and Weak Narrativity

Chapters 3 and 4 argue for the dependence of a viable narrative practice hypothesis on weak narrativity as component to basic cognitive processing, and Chap. 5 introduced prominent models of cognition based upon prediction, a 'default' mode of cognition, and embodiment. This chapter argues that weak narrativity exists in low-level cognition. Weak narrativity is characteristic of how we process our experiences as events.

6.1   TIME PROCESSING: PRESENCE AND SEGMENTATION

Cognitive systems are complex, and hard distinctions between low-level and higher order systems are problematic. Research that demonstrates how integral they are to one another provides evidence of the irreducibility of cognition to a set of discrete functional systems. Theories such as the Default Mode Network, Global Workspace, and others, introduced in Chap. 5, provide further evidence that cognitive processes are heterogenous but deeply intertwined. As empirical research continues to reveal how cognition works, our understanding becomes more complex and diverse, rather than simplified into a unified theory.

Our experiences of time reveal complexity in subjective experience. Time is not experienced as unitary, but as chunked into sometimes clearly defined and sometimes ambiguous parts and intensities. The passage of experience involves duration as well as a succession of instantaneous

© The Author(s), under exclusive license to Springer Nature
Switzerland AG 2023
B. Miller, *Narrativity in Cognition*,
https://doi.org/10.1007/978-3-031-40349-1_6

moments. With the alternation between attending closely to the perceptual experiences of the present environs and 'default mode' cognition (in which attention to the immediate environment is reduced to a sentinel role while internal cognitive processes are more intensive), experience is segmented.

William James's famous description of consciousness offers an early account of this 'chunkiness.' The stream metaphor was, for James, a way to contest the orthodoxy of late nineteenth-century science. Radical in his time, James rejects the idea that experience consists of a chain of individual units:

> The traditional psychology talks like one who should say a river consists of nothing but pailsful, spoonsful, quartpotsful, barrelsful, and other moulded forms of water. Even were the pails and the pots all actually standing in the stream, still between them the free water would continue to flow. It is just this free water of consciousness that psychologists resolutely overlook. Every definite image in the mind is steeped and dyed in the free water that flows round it. With it goes the sense of its relations, near and remote, the dying echo of whence it came to us, the dawning sense of whither it is to lead. The significance, the value, of the image is all in this halo or penumbra that surrounds and escorts it,—or rather that is fused into one with it and has become bone of its bone and flesh of its flesh; leaving it, it is true, an image of the same thing it was before, but making it an image of that thing newly taken and freshly understood. (p. 255)

James' description verges on several paradoxes: the 'free water' of consciousness is simultaneously a 'halo' or 'penumbra' of particular images; it 'surrounds and escorts,' but also (or 'rather') is 'fused' with the image. The image is thus self-identical and particular to its momentary manifestation. James' metaphor of 'steeping' and 'dyeing' resolves these semi-paradoxes. Any image of consciousness is suffused with its 'near and remote' relations, and thus with its past and future (anticipated) changes. James thus suggests that our experiences are in part determined by complex *relational dynamism*. The subjective nature of our experiences, and the particularity of their phenomenology, results from near and distant self-relations as well as relations with 'free' features of consciousness.

James' description illuminates how temporality figures into cognition.[1] Time is not experienced in itself, but as a feature of ongoing consciousness and of particular experiences. Also, time is not experienced as unitary. It is 'chunked' into sometimes clearly defined and sometimes ambiguous parts and intensities. The parts result from the nature of experience, which involves durations as well as a succession of instantaneous moments. The intensities reflect the nature of those experiences. When attention is highly focused on a succession of percepts, time is experienced differently from when attention to percepts is less focused and the subject is engaged in rumination. Through these parts and varying intensities, experience is segmented.

For example, imagine doing a boring, repetitive task like sweeping a large empty room (say, an empty rectangular dance ballroom). The sweeper might at times forget his bodily motion and feel relatively detached from his surroundings. Imagine that he enters a state of reverie as he recalls a particular evening from his youth. The way he experiences present time would be modulated by the memory, including a possible experience of a gap in present time experience. Then, imagine the sweeper's reveries are interrupted when he stubs his toe on a nail sticking out of the flooring. The initial moments of pain return the sweeper's attention to the present, and that return may include an intensified focus that makes a few seconds seem longer than they would in a period in which no intense perceptions are experienced.

In this simple example there are several factors governing the experience of time. First, the sweeper's own moods and thoughts have durations. These reflect the sweeper's particular attributes as well as larger contexts, such as stressors in the sweeper's life. Also, the sweeper's circadian rhythms and metabolic processes create temporally extended feelings of fatigue and wakefulness, hunger or satiety, and the like. Also, external cues, such as the sweeper's progress through his task, the light coming in through the windows, and unanticipated sounds and interruptions shape temporal experience, as would communicative cues such as the time displayed on his mobile phone.

Taken together, these various processes comprise temporal experience or experiences. Are they fully synthesized into a singular 'temporal experience'? It seems more likely that the sweeper has competing 'temporal experiences,' and that shifts between these comprise the phenomenology of temporal experience. So, the changes described above between states of attention are segmented during a baseline of messy, shifting factors that comprise the sweeper's sense of time. This complexity can occur without the sweeper intentionally training his attention upon time, or upon a particular goal-directed task.

The addition of goal-directed intentionality brings further complexity to this situation. Imagine, for example, that the sweeper's supervisor has recently criticized his work in a particular area of the room, and threatened him with consequences if he doesn't improve. So, when the sweeper comes upon this area, he may train particular focus on this area, which may have additional consequences for how he experiences the time spent in this area versus other parts of the room, and his memory of the work might include an outsized weighting of this part of the work in relation to the amount of time the work took to complete.

As our example suggests, experiences of time are multiply determined by a variety of cognitive processes. These processes exist in competitive 'push-pull' relations among one another and are also shaped by our baseline capacities. Carlos Montemayor explains that our time sense is determined in part by 'cognitive clocks' with capacity limitations of about three seconds (see also Wittmann, pp. 45–50). These clocks mark sensory experiences, which facilitate the coordination of representations of time with "other representations, such as spatial representations and even episodic-like memories" (*Minding Time*, p. xiii, p. xii).

Yet we also experience, via anticipation and working memory, a sense of ongoing continuity that lasts beyond these three second intervals. Our experience involves, as Henri Bergson noted, a feeling of duration. That is, instead of taking each moment independently, they are experienced as a continuity. As Marc Wittmann describes the matter,

> What do we mean when we speak of the "present moment," the "instant," or the "now"? Experience has presence. When we see, hear, and feel something, we do so at this very moment: right now. What was only just present belongs to the past in the next moment. In this way, a flow of felt time emerges: we anticipate an event, then we experience it, and shortly thereafter it lies in the past. We experience duration. Conversely, one can also say that we are constantly living in the moment always exactly now. To be sure, events and our experience of them change in status: first they are expected in the future, then they are experienced fleetingly, and finally they remain only in our memory. All the same, our experiences are tied to the moment. A familiar saying holds that we live from one moment to the next—that we move from one instant to the following one, as it were. However, it might be more appropriate to say that our conscious experience is determined by a constant being-present through which events pass: from futurity, which is not yet fixed, to what is experienced in the moment, and then onward, into the past. (p. 44)

Wittmann's model of 'felt time' describes a steady-state phenomenological character for the present, or as he puts it, a 'constant being-present' (p. xiii). Simultaneously, experience is segmented into events which have some existence for us in the future, in the present, and in the past.

This duality is paradoxical in the sense that dynamism, represented in a stream of different events, seems to be coupled with a static state ('constant being-present'). If this stasis is generated by a particular orientation toward present events, and present events are natural phenomena that our orientation disposes us to anticipate and remember, the paradox is apparently resolved.

However, in this description the cognitive work of anticipating and remembering must be considered. There is a continual simulation of future events, which requires residual grappling with events in the past. The seemingly constant state of presence, in other words, is an active processing state. So, the paradox is resolved not by an orientation/event dyad, but by understanding how feelings of continuity emerge in an active processing state.

The example of the sweeper tracks shifts in attention between present sensory inputs (including the feelings associated with the work, such as changes wrought by the onset of fatigue; stubbing his toe; internal physical feelings (such as the onset of hunger), and the condition of the area subject to his boss's criticism) and internal reflections (including planning thoughts associated with completing the work, a memory of an evening from youth, replaying the confrontation with his boss, and thoughts about a potential partner he's recently met). How can these quite different foci of attention be felt as part of continuous processing? The answer is partly embedded in the question: feelings of presence are highly associated with a phenomenology of modulating attention.

In addition, the 'passage' of events from future to present to past describes a sequential, serial chain that requires elaboration in four areas. First, does the event experience have a phenomenology that differs from the phenomenology of the feeling of presence? As a corollary, if the phenomenology of event experience subsumes the feeling of presence, how does the sense of continuity-in-presence manifest? Second, what defines events? Are the boundaries natural or constructed? As they unfold, are event boundaries containers of their constituents or defined by them? Third, can events contain events? As a corollary, what are the typical time signatures of events—that is, how long at minimum and maximum can they be, and how much 'content' can they contain, to be a singular event?

Fourth, if events are anticipated, experienced, and remembered, how do events from these different time stages influence one another? To specify, do other events prime us to anticipate, experience, and remember events in particular ways? As a corollary, how do schema develop from experiences with events, and how are schema deployed in making sense of events?

In what follows, I'll explore these questions regarding attention and events by considering recent research that illuminates their function. Along the way, I'll highlight the emergence in event segmentation and episodic memory processes of dynamics fundamental to the definition of weak narrativity described in chapters 3 and 4. Narrative processing is ongoing meaning-directed generation and processing of emergent temporal structures consisting of related value-dynamic sequences involving value-dynamic selected agents, mediated by socio-cultural contexts. Subsequently, I'll argue that weak narrativity provides a coherent means of characterizing these processes within an overdetermined 'messy ecology' of emergent temporal and semantic experiences. In this way, weak narrativity is helpful for making sense of the phenomenology of event experiences.

6.2   ATTENTION AND EVENTS

Attention is fundamental to time experiences. It is simultaneously responsive to environmental conditions and subject to intentional control. Webb and Graziano (2015) promote a model of attention—Attention Schema Theory—that acknowledges this complexity: "top–down versus bottom–up distinction[s] in attention research … [are] flawed … because some effects do not fall neatly into either category" (p. 4).

Attention Schema Theory offers a partial answer to the questions raised above: How does modulating attention relate to an ongoing feeling of presence? For Webb and Graziano, the key is that attention is greater than, and subsumes, awareness. Awareness is dynamic and selective but continuous: "awareness is an internal model of attention useful for the control of attention" (p. 5). This internal model creates a sense of "subjective awareness. *A creature with an attention schema should be a creature that concludes it is aware*" (p. 6).

The feeling Wittmann describes of 'constant being-present' is the phenomenology of awareness. As Webb and Graziano put it, the observing perspective produced by our attention schema is experienced as "an amorphous, nonphysical, internal power, an ability to know, to experience, and to respond, a roving mental focus—the essence of covert attention without the underpinning details" (p. 43).

The awareness model, then, comprises a selection from the attentional field that reflects particular priorities. The model provides subjective continuity to our experiences. How these selections are made and coordinated in dynamic, unfolding time, and how they are formulated into units that we can recall and ultimately use to guide our future attention shapes event construction.

Events, as Thomas Shipley (2008) suggests, "appear to be a fundamental unit of experience" (p. 5). Events are experienced in the temporal present, and they are refined and repurposed in episodic memory. Events can be imagined, during which the outcomes and meanings of events may seem manifest in the unfolding of the event. Even during present, actual events, subjects often predict outcomes and meanings and apply them to ongoing dynamics.[2]

The degree to which events are autonomous from and precede human attention is subject to debate. For theorists subscribing to naturalism, event boundaries occur naturally rather than only as part of meaning-laden human intercourse. In this view events typically manifest in patterns of dynamic changes occurring in a single object or agent. Take the following example of a natural event: a tree falls in the forest. The observer observes the event by perceiving the increased volume of the creaking of the wood and the motion of the tree relative to its surroundings. She tracks the fall until it is complete and the tree is settled into a new position on the forest floor (i.e., indicating the end of the event: the dynamism has stopped). Once the settling has ceased, the subject either attends to the consequences of this event (animals are scattering, more sunlight enters the grove from the direction formerly occupied by the tree, etc.), or simply switches attention to some other event or feature of reality.[3] In this case, the event is perceived via multimodal dynamic patterns of onset, development, and cessation. For example, the sounds that contribute to event definition include the onset and increased volume of the cracking wood, and the cessation of sound related to the tree.

In an event such as this, cognition may involve ongoing construction of predictions that guide and even correspond to perception. However, perception is initially reactive—the event occurs in the world, and the subject's cognition tries to make sense of it.

Constructivists offer a different portrait of events. In their perspective, the mind actively selects and organizes perceptions into meaningful, and ultimately memorable, event units that in turn help guide future cognitive activity. That is, cognition involves constructing events as units of experiential meaning. For the constructivist, the mind organizes experience based on predictions, conceptual knowledge, and prior experiences. Perception is not merely receptive—instead, it is cognitively structured from the outset. Events are not purely naturalistic phenomena but rather are a key part of how we define and structure experience. An event is never 'natural'; instead, it is always constructed into meaningful scenes, units, etc. via cognition. As Schwartz argues, "events are what we make of them" (p. 54).

To illustrate this difference, consider our experience of events depicted in film. Generally, new events are experienced by the film viewer as inextricable from meanings established regarding agents and other events in the film. For example, a film director might create the following scene for a spy thriller: a secret agent (spy #1) obtains a forbidden document and seeks to leave a city to deliver it to his handlers. An opposing secret agent (spy #2) seeks to stop spy #1 from escaping. Spy #1 enters a large urban crowd and attempts to blend in. Spy #2 tracks him through costume changes and rapid switches in modes of transport and direction. Spy #1 creates obstacles behind him; spy #2 eludes these obstacles. Eventually the options for locating spy #1 dwindle and spy #2 either captures him or is eluded. Cut scene.

In this analogy, we see several key differences from the naturalistic event of a tree falling in the forest. First, the actors in the scene come laden with semantic meanings—identities—as 'spy 1' and 'spy 2' (established in some manner prior to the scene, for the sake of simplicity). Second, their dynamic changes are meaning-laden, rather than natural. Spy 1 is more or less in danger of capture, and spy 2 is more or less close to success in capturing her target. In this instance, dynamic changes do not have self-contained meanings (such as the cracking noises that signal the tree falling and the cessation of noises that indicate the end of the event). Instead, dynamic changes create states that indicate a higher likelihood of other dynamic changes (simply, when spy 1 hides behind the door when spy 2 enters the room, spy 1's capture and both of their deaths seem likely imminent possibilities).

Third, rather than singular dynamism, we have coordination of two dynamisms (changes in spy 1 and spy 2's conditions, both independently and relative to one another). These dynamisms depend heavily on understanding the goals of each agent, and from a higher order synthesis of the situation that makes the event's meanings (e.g., danger to the republic or populace on some level). Taken together, each agent's condition is evaluated in terms of the relative proximity of the other (for spy 1, close proximity of spy 2 changes his value to more endangered; for spy 2, close

proximity changes her value to more likely to achieve her goal by apprehending spy 1).

Boundary delimitation and selection are foundational to these dynamics. In this example, the two agents might be selected out of a crowd that
includes hundreds of other people. The film director cues this selection
through camera syntax, such as centering each agent in the frame, close
ups, repetition, tracking each agent's eyes, and the like. Through these
cinematic codes, they become figures highlighted against the 'ground' of
the urban crowd.

Finally, selection is inseparable from context-based affective valuations
(and perhaps other forms of emotional valuation as well). In this case, our
understanding of each agent's relation to social and political hegemonies
has primed an affective relation for the audience. For example, perhaps spy
1 is a foreign mole threatening a beloved homeland; or perhaps spy 1 is
exposing deep corruption among the powers that be. Spy 2 is selected in
relation to spy 1. If we value spy 1 as 'bad' or 'good' (or, in all likelihood,
something a bit more complex), spy 2's motives are similarly shaded. In
turn, our valuation of spy 2 depends upon her relation to her quest in relation to our valuation of it (and so on...). This all depends on our evaluation of the more general conditions that prevail in the filmic universe. So,
if 'selection' involves a distinguishing of 'figure' from 'ground,' this selection is strongly relational and intertwined with more abstract contextual
valuations (derived both from the director's choices and from our own
value systems).

As may seem obvious, both scenarios—the tree falling and the spy
thriller—are quite distant from how we understand events during daily
experience. The tree falling scenario may not be an 'event' in any meaningful sense at all—it is merely a 'happening' in the world to which the
subject may or may not attend, which may or may not have meaning,
dependent on factors such as its proximity to the subject, its uniqueness,
and its relevance relative to other factors within the subject's perceptual
frame or internal ruminations. The second is a generic, highly designed
narrative example that has little to do with how we typically experience the
world. Obviously, no filmmaker cues and guides our perceptions of the
world through camera work, mise en scène, editing, and other techniques.

Actually experienced events typically seem more dependent upon
human valuations than the tree falling, and less designed than the film—
we have in these examples relative extremes that might support naturalistic
and constructivist accounts. One significant difference is that the example
of the tree falling exists without obvious reference to a context outside of

its own dynamism (and in naturalistic views, any attempt to find meaning in the event—say, signs of rot in the forest, an omen of evil, or an instance of the ordinary course of nature—is applied retroactively, rather than part of the event itself). By contrast, the film scene is decipherable as an event, or chain of events, because of prior representations of the agents and their relations to the social order, as well as, potentially, iconic representational cues in the agents' features, comportment, or style that signifies particular meanings. In addition, the two 'events' are quite different in temporal extension and complexity, and the film scene may be best understood as a narrativized chain of individual events that form a chain of meaning.

Yet if we consider these hypothetical scenarios on a continuum within which events fall, their similarities may be as instructive as their differences. Each, obviously, is bounded by time markers: a beginning and an end. Each has a meaningful sequence of internal changes, with meaning determined by progress toward the ground (for the tree), and by relative and related increases in proximities to danger (for spy 1) and success (for spy 2). For each the sequence is predicated on changes in stability: from a relatively stable state, into increased instability and dynamism, and back to a relatively stable, though different, state. Moreover, the second stable state can be reassessed to form a *propositional*, and thus abstractable, account of the event as a whole: the tree has fallen, spy 1 has been captured or has escaped (or better, the chase has failed or succeeded). This propositional accounting is open to additional meanings. From a cognitive perspective, the events' passages entail both an initial attention change (to the tree or spies) and a closing attentional change (either to other stimuli or to rumination on the implication of the events).

Given these differences and similarities, how do we define and characterize events? One definition has some of the structures we associate with closed-form narratives: "a segment of time at a given location that is perceived by an observer to have a beginning and an end" (Zacks and Tversky 2001, cited in Zacks et al. 2007, pp. 1–2). Other definitions of events are narrower, and involve the notion of goals. For example, in "Event Memory in Infancy and Early Childhood," Patricia Bauer notes that she uses "a definition of 'event' borrowed from Katherine Nelson (2003)": events "involve people in purposeful activities, and acting on objects and interacting with each other to achieve some result" (p. 11). Because purposeful activity unfolds over time, it has a beginning, a middle, and an end. Because the actions in events (if defined in terms of goals) are oriented toward a goal or result, there are often constraints on the order in which they unfold: actions preparatory to an outcome must occur before it in time. This definition excludes simple physical transformations such as fluttering because they do not involve actors engaged in purposeful activity. In contrast, the definition includes chains of activities as complex as world wars. Importantly for present purposes, it also includes the activities in which individuals engage as they move through a typical day.

Event definitions tend to be centered around the experiencing subject as a goal-driven actor. However, subjects can experience events as observers, and they can imagine events. These events require a modulation of what we ordinarily mean by 'goal-directedness,' but all three subject-event relation paradigms involve experience parsing in terms of value as well as identity. Value provides the bridge between identification and goals, and it provides a common mechanism for the three paradigms. Value is a synthetic concept (bringing together affect, action-orientation, object-identification, association, and identification) that is nevertheless not secondary to experience, or post-experiential. Instead, it is integral to online, real-time sensemaking (for a description of valuation as it relates to affect, see Chap. 7, esp. Sect. 7.4 to the end). It is attractive as a concept in part because it includes modal representation while also being translatable to amodal representation (see Barsalou 1999b, 2008).

What components characterize events? Despite differences, including their natural or cognitive origins, the examples we've considered of events (the tree falling and the spy scene) have a repetitive structure—a sequence of disruption of a prior order and resolution (that is, a return to a relatively static state, though not identical to the initial state[4]). One way to parse this in terms of processes, as seen earlier, is that an event's borders involve a transition from an explicit or implicit equilibriar state to a disequilibriar state, and then to a (different) equilibriar state. To enact these transitions, there is a state shift from a state of steady or increasing disruption, followed by a state of steady or increasing order.

Given this pattern characteristic of events, what comprises 'equilibrium' and 'disequilibrium?' That is, what indicates an 'orderly' versus a 'disrupted' state, and how does 'orderly' state 1 relate to 'orderly' state 2? Further, how do both orderly states relate to the disrupted state?

Alternations between equilibria and disequilibria may differ based upon whether they are unexpected or expected. Unexpected perceptions, such as the pain one feels as one stubs one's toe, create an immediate disequilibrium that resolves into a new equilibrium condition as the pain subsides. Expected perceptions, such as the firing of a rocket engine as one pushes the ignition button on a model rocket, are accompanied by a mediating sense of anticipation. Witness, in this case, the phenomenology of a rocket engine not firing after one has pushed the appropriate button. The non-happening may be experienced as an event precisely because it contravened expectations.

Shifts from disequilibrium to equilibrium conditions may typically trigger shifts from perceptual to reflective processing. For example, after unexpected events, like the stubbed toe, intrude into perception, they are followed by reflective processing during which the individual seeks identification of the source of pain and reflects upon the causes (which may have to do with immediate environmental or internal circumstances, or with long-term evaluations of self and context). Expected events have a more complex integration of reflective processing, as perceptual inputs are highly selected and viewed in terms of anticipated values. Reflective processing also occurs, as with unexpected events, immediately following the perception.

The question of whether events are natural or constructed is further complicated by their revision over time. Via thought, subjects frequently define, refine, or revise the boundaries of an event. However, in large part events come 'ready made'—that is, their temporal character and boundaries are not the product of conscious construction, but rather seem to exist as part of the character of experience.[5] Also, event processing requires 'binding' multimodal perceptual inputs, as well as bottom-up, sensorimotor and top-down, schematic or anticipatory inputs. As Shipley notes, "To the extent that separate aspects of an event are processed and combined, we must consider how event-feature binding is achieved. In an event, the space-time behavior of objects must be combined" (p. 21). Empirical evidence suggests that the binding of the natural occurs via mediation by models, which are learned, constructed forms. But it is hard to reconcile what Shipley describes—combined space-time behavior of object (and agents)—with the taxonomic, associative form we typically associate with schema. The next section considers two models of event processing which address questions of event boundary definition. Then, I argue for a way to make sense of the deployment of schema in experience based on emergent weakly narrative forms: sequenced, dynamic clusters of valuations parsed into temporal strands coincident with action to fact shifts.

6.3   IN-EVENT PROCESSING

One theory of event processing with considerable empirical support rests on the idea that the natural/constructed dichotomy is mediated through the nature of perception. In ecological and ideomotor approaches, perception is not passive reception of stimuli, as the classical model would have it, but involves active picking up of information from the environment. This active perceiving is inseparable from action and action-planning.

In Hommel's Theory of Event Coding (TEC), events are encoded in event files that bind action plans to perceptual inputs, which in turn mediate the perception of future events.

Action plans are instantiations of goals that, in turn, develop through time via the subject's experience of her ability to affect the world. TEC "assumes that humans are able to register features of (self- or other-produced) events and to integrate the codes of these features into event files" (Hommel, 2004).[6] These event files are representations in the sense that "they stand for events that do not need to be present" (Hommel 2019, p. 87). According to Memelink and Hommel,

> TEC claims that perception and action features are coded in a common format and assumes that perception, attention, intention, and action share and operate on a common representational domain (Prinz 1990). This notion implies that *perceiving an object and acting upon that object is essentially the same process and involves the same network of represented features.* Accordingly, perception may influence action, and vice versa. (2017, p. 250, emphasis added)

TEC provides a model for the mechanisms of event encoding, but as Hommel notes, the boundary definition and internal mechanisms of events are more elusive: "How is an event defined? This question is notoriously difficult with regard to perceptual objects and it is even more difficult regarding events. When and under which (exogenous and endogenous) circumstances will a percept and an action plan be integrated into the same event file, and when into separate files?" (Hommel 2004, p. 499).

A partial answer lies in what Memelink and Hommel term 'intentional weighting'—that is, our intentions to act prime perception of particular features of the environment integral to intended actions (Memelink and Hommel 2013). Their theorized intentional weighting mechanism "operates on all feature dimensions that are involved in discriminating between task relevant and task irrelevant stimuli and/or responses," and it weights particular categories of stimulus rather than particular stimulus values (so, color as a category, rather than red) (2013, p. 252).

The intention-weighting principle has a similar explanatory benefit to the notion of 'affordances' in earlier ecological views, but leaves room for greater flexibility in perception, as particular stimuli are selected for attention, but not necessarily processed in terms of their task-relevance. This is a valuation mechanism, integral to internal event definition. Nevertheless, it does not seem to offer a nuanced theory of *value dynamism* within events (by value dynamism, I mean changes in the values of agents, objects, and other features within the event—see the definition of weak narrativity above).[7]

Event definition may be partly explained by combining Hommel's 'intentional weighting' with value dynamism. In this model, events are internally defined by coordinated tracking of the dynamism attending to actors that are intentionally weighted. Importantly, this reverses the traditional relationship between an event's 'container' boundaries (the beginning and ending) and changes in the value of actors and other features *within* the event. Instead, changes in value are boundary defining. That is, the 'container' is made by its 'internal' elements.[8] Recent findings about event duration support an inside-out model of event emergence. Faber and Gennari (2015) argue that the experience of event duration depends upon the similarities and differences among subevents.

To envision the difference, consider this alteration of a traditional view of boundaries as containers of events (i.e., defining events by first delimiting their outer boundaries (their beginnings and ends)). To stay close to the container metaphor, imagine the formation of a droplet on a countertop. When liquid hits the countertop, the liquid spreads until the combination of its inertia, surface tension, and the shape and slope of the countertop arrest it into a static form (along with other factors). The internal elements, combined with the environment and a dynamic action create the shape and size of the droplet. In event terms, the beginning and end emerge from these dynamics.[9]

So, we seek an explanation of how event boundaries (like beginnings and endings) are related to changes in the values of the elements within the event. Moreover, we require explanation of the more complex phenomenon of relational valuation dynamism. That is, how do the relationships between agents, objects, and other features change, and how does this affect the perceived value of each (see the spy thriller example for an illustration of this). That is, how do 'weightings' of particular stimuli depend upon proximity and relation to other stimuli?

Overall, the 'task-orientation' of TEC, as of ideomotor theories in general, may seem limiting. As the next chapter explores, affective valuation may play a significant role in perceptual weighting, as may accidental factors such as prior familiarity, strangeness, beauty, 'pop-out' qualities (e.g., a strong odor in relation to other environmental stimuli). In addition, analogical similarity to highly valued remembered stimuli may shape selection and weighting. Moshe Bar theorizes that the brain continually generates analogies or "associations as the building blocks of predictions...that prime our subsequent perception, cognition and action" (2007, p. 280).[10]

Simply put, not everything we experience as events is derived from top-down, subjective goals. Even if it is possible to reduce each of these 'weighting' qualities, and other forms of valuation, to 'action-orientation,' such an explanation would entail a wide range of valuations that reflect prior action-oriented encodings rather than the simpler mechanism of task-oriented selection Hommel and colleagues envision. To reduce all to action orientation, while perhaps explanatory of a subject's experiential history, does not seem promising as a means of explaining the totality of top-down weighting occurring in perceptual presence. If the model requires that we see in perceptual presence a deep history of weightings that can be abundant, potentially contradictory, and still ultimately grounded in (initial/learned) action-orientation, then we begin to approach a view of perceptual selection with a rich phenomenology.[11] However, even in such a model we are (a) only experiencing action-orientation in a distal manner; and (b) not explaining how the boundaries of and internal dynamics of events are processed. Therefore, it seems likely that the task-orientation dynamics described in TEC play a significant and foundational role in selection but are not fully explanatory of how we understand events.

While goals have been well-documented to shape selection, our varied experiences suggest the need for an expanded view of the causes of selection. Consider the famous 'Gorilla and Basketball' experiment, in which subjects were instructed to count the number of passes successfully completed by basketball players in a brief video. In the course of the video, a figure in a gorilla suit crosses in front of the camera, yet many of the participants did not report seeing this figure. This experiment has been used to illustrate how task-orientation creates selective attention (see Simons and Chabris 1999 for a popular treatment of the 'inattentional blindness' phenomenon).

We may not see the gorilla while we are counting the number of times the ball is passed between players when we are instructed to focus solely on a singular task, but we should remember that this was a lab experiment, and the subjects were instructed to focus upon counting passes of the basketball. Our ordinary mode of experiencing is not cued in this narrowly goal-directed manner. Instead, we derive the task at hand from a muddier experience, and we manage task-orientation alongside other less structured 'sentinel' and exploratory attentional tasks (see Buckner et al. 2008, p. 19 for 'The Sentinel Hypothesis' regarding the Default Mode Network (also Chap. 5, Sect. 5.2.2)). Our event processing involves parsing what we are doing, but also what is happening outside of our doing, and this more passive information gathering seems evolutionarily vital.

In addition, once we've theorized the mechanisms of event boundary setting, we will look at their potential effects. Event borders, as they emerge, may contribute to in-event processing, event segmentation, episodic memory encoding and retrieval of events, and likely in the feedback through which these processes affect one another, as well as the ways other aspects of sensemaking and higher order cognition affect and are affected by them. Theories of how events are defined vary in their view of representations of the present, of the past, and of similar events; of their views of time perception and its relation to event definition; and of how high- and low-level processing are related (Buckner 2010, pp. 4–7).

6.4   PREDICTION FAILURE AND EVENT BOUNDARIES

So, what determines when an event starts and stops, where it occurs and where (proximally) it is understood to not occur, who and what are involved, and what dynamics reside within an event (versus what dynamics are extra-event)? TEC theorizes that our experiences of events beginning and ending correspond to the opening and closing of event files. Yet, as noted above, this correspondence does not solve the problem of how event parameters are defined. Zacks and colleagues have pioneered some of the most insightful research into this question. Events and their boundaries are, like narratives,[12] 'fuzzy' (2007, p. 2). They focus on an 'everyday' notion of events typically characterized by certain types ('meals,' e.g.), goal-directedness, animate agents, and short duration (seconds to tens of minutes) (2007, p. 2). Their Event Segmentation Theory (EST) seeks to explain "how human observers segment continuous activity into discrete events" (p. 2). The basic mechanism derives from the Predictive Processing framework:

One central proposal of the EST model is that event segmentation is a spontaneous outcome of ongoing perception and arises at points where perceptual predictions begin to fail or change. This change in perceptual predictions is considered to occur at many different levels simultaneously and is a consequence of the failure of a currently active set of predictions, which are rapidly dysfacilitated and superseded by a more accurate set of predictions. The period of epoch between two such consecutive changes current mental models is an *event* (see Zacks et al. 2007, for a review of the extensive body of data demonstrating high sensitivity to event boundaries). (*Understanding Events*, p. 591)

EST hypothesizes that event boundaries are defined by changes in ongoing predictive processing.[13] In the course of a subject experiencing an event, an event model guides predictions that shape perception (Zacks et al. 2007, p. 3). The event model is an evolving, temporary framework that synthesizes information from event schemata stored in long-term memory with information from prediction errors. Event schemata store "prior knowledge about goals and plans and prior statistical learning" (p. 11).

As an event proceeds, predictions are relatively accurate. However, as it ends, prediction error increases, causing a reset of the event model. When such a reset occurs, an event boundary is set. This model does not, however, view event processing as a serial chain of single, discrete events—EST hypothesizes that event segmentation occurs "simultaneously on a multitude of timescales, spanning a few seconds to tens of minutes" (p. 5). As such it differs from TEC, which seems focused on the short end of this time range.

Events are typically segmented in relation to high-level information like goals and plans, contexts, similarities to previously experienced events, and low-level physical stimuli, especially physical changes. Event perception and segmentation, as noted in the summary of TEC, integrate multimodal information. Richmond and Zacks (2017) note that event models "nonlinearly" transform sensory and motor information into "re-representation[s] of the world" that facilitate "efficient learning and robust extrapolation" (p. 3).

So, EST offers an alternating pattern of relative stability followed by disruption and, subsequently a return to relative stability (marking the instantiation of a new, currently accurate set of predictions). This pattern of "stability punctuated by phasic transitions … segment[s] ongoing experience into a succession of events" (p. 18). In so doing, it manifests the patterns of equilibrium-disequilibrium-equilibrium described at the beginning of this chapter, but in a quite different manner. Events, as described earlier, are structured in equilibrium-disequilibrium-equilibrium cycles *internal* to the (narrative) event. So, where for EST the cycle characterizes the sometimes tumultuous transitions *between* events (and thus seems reminiscent of Thomas Kuhn's well-known model of paradigm shifts in scientific discovery), understanding events also requires understanding the governing internal logic of events and the processes that produce them and make them available for further cognition.

Speer, Zacks, and Reynolds offer this account of how readers parse narratives into events:

> As incoming information about the current event becomes less consistent with the current mental model, readers are more likely to update the current model to more accurately represent the state of the world (Gernsbacher, 1990; Reynolds, Zacks, & Braver, in press; van Dijk & Kintsch, 1983; Zacks, Speer, Swallow, Braver, & Reynolds, 2007; Zwaan & Radvansky, 1998). Therefore, readers may explicitly perceive the points where characters, goals, and other elements change as event boundaries because these changes drive the updating of readers' mental models at those points. (p. 454)

The proximity of narrative reading to event segmentation provides some support for the notion that we are particularly attuned to narrative and apply the same cognitive processes to making sense of experience that we employ when reading a novel. Indeed, Speer et al. argue that "this process of segmentation [used in detecting the structure of narrated activities] is part of a larger, modality-independent system involved in the comprehension of everyday activities" (p. 454).

In contrast to my characterization, though, Speer et al. describe internal segmentation on the basis of change. However, such a view creates a new issue to explain: the ongoing grasping together of the change-points into a meaningful unity. That is to say, to account for our experience of events as meaningful context-related sequences, we need to account for how the markers laid down by failures in predictive modeling are processed together into ongoing syntheses.

EST hypothesizes, as an implication of its view that event segmentation occurs at multiple timescales simultaneously, that there are principles for hierarchically arranging timescales into coarse and fine-grained predictions nested at multiple levels (p. 19). For example, Zacks considers "getting ready for work" a candidate coarse-grained event, with "brushing teeth" a nested, but still coarse event consisting of fine-grained events like "putting toothpaste on a toothbrush" (p. 19). In addition, Richmond, Zacks et al. describe *discontinuous* events, such as "building a sculpture," and connects EST to Kubovy's "concurrent strands" framework, in which "one might have different representational strands for the many facets of one's life, including home, work/school, etc.) (p. 19).[14] In EST, people "selectively attend to one timescale" (p. 8).[15]

This view of events extends EST well beyond the temporal limits hypothesized in TEC, as well as beyond the direct action plan-percept coupling fundamental to TEC. It therefore may be commensurate with theories of accreting autobiographical narratives considered in some humanistic accounts of narrative and human experience. Before linking into these higher order theories, however, let's consider the linkages between narrativity and event definition and segmentation inchoate in the psychological research.

To do so, we'll examine research regarding episodic memories, which Zacks and colleagues see as linked to event processing. How episodic memories are formed out of experience, in what state they exist, and how and to what ends they are deployed comprise a crucial part of cognitive processing that combines affective valuations with sensemaking operations such as recognition of changes and selection and boundary delimitation of place, time, objects, and agents. As such, they seem valuable candidate phenomena for weak narrativity, and their function in relation both to higher order processes and to mediating predictive processing may thereby reveal whether there is anything characteristically narrative about low-level cognition, especially event processing.

6.5   MEMORY AND EVENT PROCESSING

While in classical views of cognition memory areas of the brain function as a storehouse for remembered events, more recent research emphasizes the role memory plays in processing present experiences. This newer emphasis reflects the predictive processing framework. EST sees deep affinities between event segmentation and episodic memories, and between controlling actions and understanding others' actions (Richmond and Zacks 2017).

Much of this change in views has been prompted by research on the hippocampus, which is typically understood in the popular imagination as the seat of memory. In the last 20 years, researchers have found the hippocampus to be highly active in tasks not associated with reflecting on one's past.[16] Specifically, hippocampal processing of stored perceptual data and associations is essential to simulation. As Suddendorf and Corballis dramatically put the case (quoted in the previous chapter), "we predominantly stand in the present facing the future rather than looking back to the past" (2007).[17] Schacter and Addis, who pioneered this research, propose the "*constructive episodic simulation hypothesis*" (Schacter and Addis 2007, 2009):

> episodic memory provides a source of details for future event simulations, such that past and future events draw on similar information stored in episodic memory and rely on similar cognitive processes during event construction, such as self-referential processing and imagery. Furthermore, we have suggested that the constructive nature of episodic memory supports the flexible recombination of stored details into a coherent simulation of a new event that has not been experienced previously in the same form. This process of flexible recombination is thought to rely on relational processing abilities that are heavily dependent on the hippocampal formation (e.g., Eichenbaum 2001), with recent evidence implicating the anterior hippocampus specifically in recombining episodic details into novel events. (Addis and Schacter 2008)

One implication of this view with regard to event processing is that grasping together details such as imagery and value-for-self into a meaningful time extended sequence (an event) is implicit in processing events as well as reflecting upon and imagining them. Schacter and Addis have hypothesized 'IMAGINING' as a cognitive system that groups together memory, predictive processing, and creative thinking into a common set of interrelated processes.

Several other recent findings about episodic memory processing bear upon event processing. The predictive processing model of episodic memories fits with a view of simultaneous top-down and bottom-up processing.[18] Episodic memories likely shape holistic aspects of present temporal experiences as well as providing sources of details.

Kim (2010) suggests that "many episodic-retrieval-related activations may actually reflect more general attention/executive operations," rather than salience functions (p. 1648). Further, episodic memories provide schematic information that affects how we experience present events. In a research review on sequencing, Davachi and DuBrow (2015) suggest that the episodic or repeated nature of an experienced sequence may bias the source of temporal information for that sequence: "Temporal information based on a single experience may be biased toward relying on contextual features (e.g., 60 and 61), whereas repetition may bias the source of such information away from a specific spatiotemporal context and toward cued prediction of subsequent items in a sequence" (p. 99).Taken together, these findings suggest that a constructivist view of low-level cognition involves thinking of prior experiences as encoded for flexible reuse in segmenting present experiences into meaningful events.

Findings from Martin Conway offer additional insights into the mutual relation of event processing and episodic memories. Episodic memories "contain summary records of sensory-perceptual-conceptual-affective processing, ... always have a perspective (field or observer), ...represent short time slices of experience, ... are represented on a temporal dimension roughly in order of occurrence, ... make autobiographical remembering specific,... [and] are recollectively experienced when accessed" (p. 2306).

The temporal structure Conway attributes to episodic memories is similar to events. Both have their parameters and meanings in part determined by other events and organizing schema. Episodic memories are multimodal and have a phenomenology when activated. As 'summary' forms of 'sensory-perceptual-conceptual-affective processing,' they select and bind experiential details, and these summaries potentially include amodal (linguistic) conceptual information used to make sense of event experiences (p. 2306). The experience of recollection is closely associated with the relation of the event to the subject.

The similarity between events and episodic memories in terms of experiencing may provide a key insight for understanding internal event segmentation. The idea that remembering is experiential may seem surprising. Yet Conway (2005) proposes, contra the generally held view that emotions arise out of interruptions in goal processing, that 'cognitive feelings' (such as a sense of closure, accomplishment, and the need to shift attention) may play a role in event segmentation. He further proposes that

> many different forms of processing are accompanied by or associated with what we have termed cognitive feelings ... Cognitive feelings allow the individual to experience knowledge. By this view a person not only knows that he or she has just closed the door when leaving the house but also has a feeling, an experience, of a transition from one event to another. (p. 615)

In addition, Conway (2009) proposes that episodic memories have an action to fact semantic structure:

> We have proposed that the boundaries of episodic memories are marked at the opening boundary by information about actions and at the closing boundary by facts that are often details about the outcomes of actions (Williams et al., 2008). This is consistent with our more general view that episodic memory and autobiographical knowledge are about goals. That is to say they preserve information that is highly relevant to goal processing including goal generation, plan execution, outcomes and evaluations (for related views see Brewer & Dupree, 1983; Lichtenstein & Brewer, 1980). (p. 2306)

Action to fact patterns suggest that either during or after experiences we attend to relational valuation dynamisms internal to event structures. The experience of an 'observing perspective' and cognitive feelings of episodic memories, taken together, further suggest that these dynamic valuations have reference to the self. Research that emphasizes the integration of event selection and episodic memory processes suggests that prior episodic memories facilitate the parsing of present events with these characteristics (action to fact sequences, observing perspectives, and cognitive feelings). In combination with selection for cycles of equilibrium-disequilibrium-equilibrium and action to fact structures based on value dynamism(s), the relation between episodic memory and event processing suggests that our experiences are (often, at least) structured in terms of meaningful temporal strands available for combination and redeployment in other cognitive activities.

6.6   WEAK NARRATIVITY AND EVENT EXPERIENCES

Why hypothesize about a synthetic concept like weak narrativity rather than, as most quantitative work has done, identifying more limited, discrete processes? For some researchers, understanding the cognitive capacities deployed in processing narratives is a key to understanding the simulative function of memory and the Default Mode Network. What, in other words, does our capacity for narrative processing demonstrate about our ordinary cognition?

Schacter, Addis et al. (2012) emphasize the need for further study of narrative processing, particularly its contributions to memory and imagination. Specifically, narrative processing may help explain functions which share a common neural basis, including prospection, scene construction, autobiographical memory, and self-projection (see Spreng, Mar, Kim).

Recall our working definition of narrative processing: ongoing meaning-directed generation and processing of emergent temporal structures consisting of related value-dynamic sequences involving value-dynamic selected agents, mediated by socio-cultural contexts. Narrative processing involves, then, selection, concatenation, determination of time boundaries, determination of changes in agents relative to other agents, their own condition, and selected objects and phenomena. This determination is inseparable from valuing (itself a multi-dimensional or synthetic form of processing).

My hypothesis, developed further in the next chapter (on affect and cognition), is that this synthetic valuation activity is core to ordinary experience. It is in part responsible for selection and boundary definition, as well as mediating socio-cultural pressures, gist processing, and meaning. Indeed, valuation describes ongoing syntheses of these elements that lead to the key elements of Zacks's definition: time segmentation, location, and beginnings and ends.[19] In other words, valuation reflects the subject's ongoing tracking of value dynamics within the continuous flow of experience, and meaning-laden phenomena (like beginnings and endings) as well as more apparently objective phenomena (temporal span and location) emerge from this processing.

This view conflicts with naturalistic assumptions about the "givenness" of certain features of events, as well as how events became familiar; on the other hand, it has certain explanatory advantages. So, is bringing narrativity into event processing parsimonious? Does introducing narrativity create a new, non-empirical speculative layer of processing unnecessarily?[20]

The case for the necessity of weak narrativity is strengthened by the emergence of predictive processing models of cognition. Once basic cognition is viewed as predictive, we must seek to understand how prediction relates to the anticipatory quality of many of our experiences. Further, once these predictions are viewed as intentionally weighted, we must seek to understand why the time signatures and changes in valuations of selected elements of experience seem freighted with meaning. In the next chapter, I'll hypothesize that the coordination of time signatures and patterns of valuation dynamics includes affectively charged *relational* valuation dynamisms (i.e., valuations of elements that emerge from their relation to other salient elements of experience).

These involve early developing value schema that accommodate temporally extended patterns of moving objects and agents, as well as the observer's subjective, affective response to the event as a whole from an initial state to a concluded state, or as Conway describes episodic memories, from actions to facts (or stable evaluations and/or responses). Taken together, the event processing and affective dimensions of experience create a sense of weak narrativity as basic to some experiences.

This view seems to be at odds with Zacks' model of event boundaries predicated upon failures of predictions and the instantiation of new predictions. That the experiences drawn upon (episodic memories) themselves have action→fact structures and are themselves viewed as guiding attention and executive functions suggests that attending to and coordinating these relational valuation dynamisms is sensitive to the amplitude of particular dynamisms, which wax and wane until a second equilibriar state is reached or anticipated, and the experience becomes a 'fact' (an outcome). At this point predictions about these relational valuation dynamisms may fail, but equally likely is that they no longer hold interest. Thus, the event segmentation may correspond to the emergence of a new set of predictions that reflects new foci for cognition (it may also, as Zacks theorizes, reflect a failure to understand what's immediately happening, but given the prior success of the predictions, this kind of failure seems counterintuitive).

The explanation of event experiences through predictive processing drawing on episodic memory processes creates a model of present experience in which top-down processing is broader than, though directed by, goals with immediate utility to the subject. Bottom-up information causes a continual recalibration of the predictive response and affective valuing of individual elements and of the whole. A felt experience is dynamic and sensemaking, by which I mean affect normatively contributes to and shapes perception by directing attention and weighting dynamic information in relation to goals (and 'proxy-goals,' as in the example of Theory of Mind in disinterested spectatorship). It is in the context of understanding these dynamics that the definition we've considered of narrative processing begins to correspond to the way we experience the world.

6.7   PHILOSOPHICAL PERSPECTIVES ON WEAK NARRATIVITY IN LOW-LEVEL COGNITION

This chapter has considered some ways in which low-level, or first-order, cognition might involve narrative processing in the chunky messiness of temporal experience, particularly in how events emerge as basic structures of experience. However, as the 'narrativist' positions reviewed in earlier chapters imply, this is a counterintuitive claim: narrative seems most obviously to be a *post hoc*, linguistic configuration of experiences which is subsequently summarized, synthesized with other narratives and facts, and applied to make sense of novel experiences. Yet there are also signs that we don't feel these *post hoc* acts of configuration sufficiently explain the origins or nature of narrative. Take, for example, philosopher Judith Butler's description of this configuration: "My narrative begins *in medias res*, when many things have already taken place to make me and my story possible in language. I am always recuperating, reconstructing, and I am left to fictionalize and fabulate origins I cannot know" (p. 39). For Butler, narrative *enables* story but is not coextensive with it.

Richard Menary, one of the leading thinkers challenging top-down views of how narrative might affect cognition, offers the following observation about how narrative structures pre-exist narrative configuration:

> It is not narratives that shape experiences but, rather, experiences that structure narratives. Experiences are the sequence of events that give structure and content to narratives. There may be additions and elaborations to this embodied sequence at a later time, after reflection, but the temporal ordering, the structure is already there in our lived, bodily experience. The mistake is again to suppose that a narrative conceived in abstraction could be brought to bear on a sequence of experiences, ordering them and giving them meaning. (p. 79)

From this perspective, the autobiographical approach to narrative as part of cognition (see Chap. 2, Sect. 2.4) is difficult to square with a predictive processing model and with recent research on the nature of episodic memory. While notions like the 'teller effect' will be considered in the final chapter, autobiographical mental work does not provide a good model for understanding the dynamics in mental action that cause episodic memories to form. Menary's view is that experiences "are ready to be exploited in a narrative of those experiences" (p. 75).[21]

As this chapter (and the next) describe, sequential associations inherently reflect different types of selection, which are likely generated through multiple distributed processes. What Menary calls 'pre-narrative fodder' may be highly structured, selected for and embedded with a variety of elements, including:

- for-me-ness (subjective perspective, self-not-self boundary definition);
- event segmentation (temporal boundaries);

- sensemaking (i.e., association of dynamics, objects, other phenomena to varied causal and analogical phenomena (categorization, intention-reading, prediction, etc.);
- relevance (active attention, signal/noise, and equilibriar monitoring functions);
- valence (affect);
- concatenation (forming temporally based associative sequences that integrate various elements, including 'unlike' elements, via varied criteria including causation).

These elements contribute to experiences ripe with sequential associations characterized by perspective, segmentation, causality, analogy, rich temporality (including memory and prediction), relevance, and valence.

We've considered theories of event processing in some detail in this chapter. The idea, simplified, is threefold: weak narrativity could exist in linkages between events, in the internal features of events, or in the processes that shape experience into events. First, if meaningfully linked events comprise narratives, and our basic experience is unconsciously and consciously 'chunked' into events, there is a possibility of weak narrativity in experience. Also, if event experiences are dependent on internal features that make them internally narrative or ripe for meaningful linkage to other events, there is a possibility of weak narrativity in experience. Third, the processes behind event definition include selection, boundary delimitation, and internal dynamism that accounts for coherence and meaning while parsing condition changes. If these processes are based upon making sense of the present via meaningful temporal and relational patterns, and if they result in experiences that are shaped according to these patterns, and if these patterns have recognizably narrative elements (such as equilibrium-disequilibrium-equilibrium structure and action→fact structure), then there is a weak narrativity in experience.

What is rich about event recognition that is not adequately captured in current models of events? First, a narrative logic may be more useful, or at least a crucial supplement, to action-orientation logics when making sense of events that the subject has no particular stake in, including events whose demand for attention exists outside of any immediate goals other than interest. Simply, the fuzziness of events points to their inextricability from ongoing processing, which includes the 'sentinel' functions, higher order cognitions (including reflection, confabulation, and the like), and other event processing. That is to say, event processing is never fully discrete, and the location of individual event processing within an ecology of sense-making and higher order functions points to a linking process between events that draws upon semantically laden predictions. To describe this messy ecology, the language of 'script' seems inadequate because a script seems directed toward discrete, unrelated events. To invoke narrativity, then, is to suggest that at a basic level of experience our sensemaking and anticipatory faculties are continually engaged in event processing activities that emerge from and are re-sublimated within this messy ecology via linkages between experiences, present, remembered, and anticipated, that are essential to the dynamics of event selection, boundary definition, and internal parsing. Sense doesn't emerge from non-sense immediately. Instead, it emerges from a messy ecology of partial, inchoate, iteratively parsed, ongoing sensemaking. Scripts, event schemata, and other sense-making cognitive resources likely are key to the emergence of sense from this messy ecology.

Our experience of an event is a defining of the event in deep relation to like and proximate events. Events exist in a half-light, generated out of the mess of experience in relations of value to other events and features of experience, and gaining fuller definition under the scrutiny of reflection and communication. Event definition is a processing that emerges and fails continually. An event is defined as singular, and thus detachable from the flow of experience and rememberable as a model for future experience once it achieves a certain sense of stable structure, as indicated by the equilibrium-disequilibrium-equilibrium and action→fact vectors described above. Once 'stabilized' (see above for commentary on event and episodic memory stability), the traces of its roots in the messy, and possibly narrative, ecology of experience are invisible because they have been built into the structure of the event. The event-object, as far as it exists, is structured by its linkages to other events.

Events are also deeply conditioned by the kind of attention higher order concepts cause us to pay. Take the example of sitting in your seat when a woman standing before you points a gun directly at her head. If you are not expecting this, it is sure to provoke a visceral response.

However, if you are not expecting it but you are watching a play and you believe the woman is an actor, the visceral nature of the response is muted. And of course if you are expecting it—say you've seen the production before—you are unlikely to have much of a visceral response at all. That is, our immediate experience is deeply conditioned by 'higher order,' conditional understandings.

The messy ecology/narrative processing view exists in some contrast to, on the one hand, Richard Menary's view; and on the other, to the view expressed in Zacks et al. Note that these two views themselves are challenges to classical models, of narrative in experience on the one hand (see Chap. 2, Sect. 2.3 and Chap. 3, Sect. 3.3), and of cognition and event processing on the other.

In concluding this chapter I want to return to the premise of this book: to argue that weak narrativity is generated in cognitions of ordinary experiences, and to help dispel some unhelpful ideas about narrative and cognition in light of emerging contemporary research into how certain features of cognition operate. Philosophers have long posited that experience is meaningful—that is to say, conscious experience comes preprocessed with meanings, rather than raw. Normative conscious experience involves navigating meaning-laden environs, relations, and situations, rather than taking meaningless percepts and deriving or weaving meanings out of them.

The hermeneutic tradition foregrounds meaning in experience, emphasizing the interpretive nature of our interface with the world. As Meretoja (2013) notes, "in the Heideggerian-Gadamerian [tradition of] hermeneutics … understanding is the fundamental structure of our being in the world,… all experience has the structure of interpretation, of 'understanding something as somethings'" (p. 99). Hermeneutics offers several descriptions of experience that resonate with the narrative features I am describing. First, it distinguishes itself from the phenomenological tradition, which leaves open the possibility of naive (i.e., unprocessed) experience. The hermeneutic perspective, by contrast, views experience as a form of interpretive processing. Interpretation is in this view ontologically significant, in addition to being an epistemological tool (Meretoja 2013, p. 93). Views of narrative within hermeneutic analyses are similarly themed and similarly varied: narrative is seen as fundamental to interpretation, as a kind of commentary, as a "human way of shaping experiences into a meaningful temporal continuum" (Meretoja 2013, p. 103), and as crucial to meaning and ethical reflection. Within conversations in hermeneutics, the makeup and function of narrative vary along axes including representation/epistemology, action/ontology, instrumentality/ experientiality, embodied/mental, hindsight/immediacy, and self-focused/ outwardly focused. A central tenet of Gadamer's hermeneutics is 'linguisticity,' or the necessity of language for interpretation.

Paul Ricœur is a foundational figure in linking hermeneutics to narrative. Working in the phenomenological and hermeneutical traditions,

Ricœur views temporal experiences as thick with an evolving present suffused with the impacts of previous moments and with anticipation of future instances. Ricœur's argument, in the magisterial *Time and Narrative* and subsequently in *Oneself as Another*, points to the importance of a language-based, reflective narrative identity that develops in response to lived experience. Many of Ricœur's readers have concluded that Ricœur sees a discontinuity between narrative and lived experience. Yet according to Lewis, Ricœur is not fully committed "to the notion that lived experience is devoid of narrative structure" (p. 13). Instead, both lived experience and its narrative structuration are subject "to the dominance of mediation" (Lewis 13).

As the research reviewed earlier on episodic memory suggested, episodic memory shares experiential and processing bases with event segmentation. It includes multimodal (non-linguistic) inputs, but may be linguistically mediated as well. It also specifies autobiographical memory and contributes to our ongoing, continuous feeling of future-orientedness. As such, the episodic memory/event segmentation relationship seems fundamental to empirical support for a hermeneutic perspective. And as we've seen, narrativity—but not artifactual narrative—is plausibly component to each. Viewing weak narrativity as a way to describe Ricœurian mediation (via the production of temporal strands with semantic features) helps explain how narratives refined in higher level thinking could ever impact our immediate experiences or even the concepts and values that guide those experiences. For our concepts and values are products of iterative learning, which involves processes of abstraction from experience such that habitual lived experiences are increasingly mediated by perspective.

Ultimately, what's at stake is an effort to more richly describe the cognitive dynamics that produce experience. Conceptually, weak narrativity describes event segmentation and episodic memory in terms of specific, sensory–perceptual–cognitive–affective details (some of which are dynamic) and self-reference, and a tendency toward 'condition→action→fact/valuation' sequencing. Conceived in this way, experiential processing likely to result in episodic memory reflects a dynamic associative process of potentially 'unlike' details for defining event markers that are meaningful. By meaningful, I mean they (a) are employed to construct a form that none of the detail elements represents on its own; (b) regulate the shift from Default Network processing to active attention and back again; (c) employ valuation processes drawn from affective, sensory, and cognitive facilities that mediate self-reference; (d) result in episodic memories structured as 'condition→action→fact/

evaluation' sequences. Together, I've described these aspects of lower order cognition as constitutive of basic 'narrative' processing. It is suitable for more complex narrative processing in which social and personal narratives/narrative-embedded valuations might figure. In the next chapter, we'll consider the role affect plays in making experience 'hot' and meaningful.

Notes

1. The shape of temporality depends on a combination of perceived social construction, individual intentional behavior, and unconscious processes. There is not space here to review the range of debates about this issue, particularly in process philosophy, but along with James, John Dewey and Henri Bergson offered divergent perspectives on the nature of structure in time and its relation to the felt experience of meaning.
2. Events grasped in presence also reflect semantic memory. For example, a savvy health practitioner can quickly grasp the onset of anaphylaxis in a patient allergic to latex. In this case, immediate grasping of events depends upon deep knowledge: Her knowledge of the patient, and her knowledge of the symptoms, triggers, and progression of anaphylactic shock, are inseparable, in all likelihood, from regimes of more and less optimal intervention (reflecting the doctor's goal of treating the patient with minimum risk of harm and maximum optimization of the patient's immediate and long-term well-being).
3. It seems highly likely that the shift in attention is not so clean, moving from one locus of activity to a new set of environmental circumstances. Instead, it seems likely that 'attending' becomes diffuse, moving from a near-total focus on the dynamics of the falling tree to a partial attention to settling noises accompanied by gradual awareness of the new environmental circumstances the event has created.
4. The notion of a 'disruption' of order may not seem to apply to the 'getting ready for work' example. However, we might think of transitions between goal-directed activities as involving the interruption of a goal upon whatever else occupies the subject's cognition, followed by the pursuit of the goal via the various subordinate activities described earlier, to resolution, as if the goal is 'checked off' on one's to-do list.
5. This is a primary way in which the influence of sociocultural values impacts low-level event processing.
6. Hommel updates the theory in 2019 to claim that representation may not be central: "recent theoretical developments provide the basis for a more

integrated view consisting of both the codes that are shared between perception and action in the control processes operating on these codes. Four developments are discussed in more detail: The degree to which the integration and retrieval of event files depends on current goals, how metacontrol states impact the handling of event files, how feature binding relates to event learning, and how the integration of non-social events relates to the integration of social events" (p. 2139).

7. See the examples above for a sense of what this might entail; also, consider the commentary on value in Chap. 7.

8. This will be counterintuitive for readers who think of, say, reading a novel as an apt illustration of experiencing narrativity. The reader opens a container that bounds the narrative, and maybe encounters an internal container (think of framing narrators and the distinction between story and discourse). The dynamic elements are set into motion by elements at the boundaries. If we want to understand narrative features of experience (or, more simply, if we believe experience has a narrative character), however, we have to grapple with how false the 'reading a novel' analogy is. Instead, reading a novel might be best understood as a way to encounter narrativity in experience. It is not itself a narrative experience, but an experience of a highly wrought narrative. At the same time, 'inside-out' and 'container' theories are not logically diametrically opposed—that is, structure could emerge from both the inside-out and imposed external scripts simultaneously.

9. Here I am not addressing the retrospective configuration of many events. For sports fans, consider when a team goes on a 'run'—that is, it has an extended string of successes. If this composite of events is itself an event, then the recognition of the event is *post hoc*. This is related to Meretoja's second level of interpretation.

10. Bar's theory depends on rapid 'gist' processing of essential details from a situation. For more on 'gist' processing, see Chap. 8, Sect. 8.4.

11. In this view, 'what it is like'—that is, the phenomenology of an experience—is a synthesis of diverse intentional weightings, perceptual selections, perceptual capture, and cognitive processing.

12. See Chap. 3 for Herman's 'gradient' conception of narrative and Currie's notion of narrativity.

13. EST claims that "event segmentation is a spontaneous concomitant of ongoing perception, happens simultaneously on multiple time scales, and depends on change" (15).

14. To effectively predict the unfolding of ordinary events, event models "need a particular type of dynamics: stability punctuated by phasic transitions [which]…segment ongoing experience into a succession of events represented by successive working models" (966).

15. The research on event segmentation opens up/creates boundary spaces for fill-in explanations, and that these spaces are where weak narrativity, if it exists, is likeliest located. Weak narrativity makes sense if it describes dynamics necessary for event processing to proceed or be utilized.

16. Hill and Emery argue that "Working Memory contributes to the construction of a single, coherent, future event depiction, but not to the retrieval or elaboration of event details" (p. 677).

17. See also Mullally and Maguire 2013 "Memory, Imagination, and Predicting the Future."

18. 185. For example, Tsuda et al. (2015) find that "a constructed memory itself does not represent an input; rather it represents input/output relationship via bifurcations. The associated dynamics was chaotic itinerancy" (Tsuda et al. 2015).

19. Beginnings and endings are an important consideration—for EST, they reflect the breakdown of predictions and the installation of new models. In narrative, beginnings and endings reflect the initiation and completion of sequences with narrativity. This reflects EST's focus on continuous experience, and the event as a structuring of that experience. In narrative, beginning and ending are oriented toward the continuity of the sequence as a coherent whole. The question for EST, and where 'weak' narrativity comes in to play, is whether the orientation toward structuring continuous, flowing experience can really focus on the 'dynamism' or 'disruption' that causes a breakdown in prediction. To accommodate dynamism-in-continuity, the event segmenting approach must involve some metrics of anticipated dynamisms (appropriate-to-the-event dynamics, vs. not appropriate). This means that anticipation of change must itself entail expected sequences of change. These 'ends' undoubtedly encode information about agentive goals and their realization as well as about the emergence of static conditions after dynamic conditions (whether physically, relationally, or otherwise). So, information about endings may be part of predictive processing, as well as cued by disruptions.

20. An alternative might be simply to stick with 'episodicity.' However, thinking only of episodicity misses how episodicity can be emergent in the context of enchained episodes. That is, the episode definition is conditioned by ongoing weakly narrative event concatenation.

21. Menary is a realist about experiences, rather than adopting the predictive processing and affective constructivism considered in this and the next chapter.

REFERENCES

Andrews-Hanna, J. R., Reidler, J. S., Sepulcre, J., Poulin, R., & Buckner, R. L. (2010). Functional-Anatomic Fractionation of the Brain's Default Network. *Neuron*, 65(4), 550–562. https://doi.org/10.1016/j.neuron.2010.02.005.

Bar, M. (2007). The proactive brain: Using analogies and associations to generate predictions. *Trends in Cognitive Sciences*, 11(7), 280–289. https://doi.org/10.1016/j.tics.2007.05.005

Barsalou, L. W. (1999a). Perceptions of perceptual symbols. *Behavioral and Brain Sciences*, 22(4), 637–660. https://doi.org/10.1017/S0140525X99532147.

Barsalou, L. W. (1999b). Perceptual symbol systems. *Behavioral and Brain Sciences*, 22(4), 577–660. https://doi.org/10.1017/S0140525X99002149.

Barsalou, L. W. (2008). Grounded Cognition. *Annual Review of Psychology*, 59(1), 617–645. https://doi.org/10.1146/annurev.psych.59.103006.093639.

Barsalou, L. W., Kyle Simmons, W., Barbey, A. K., & Wilson, C. D. (2003). Grounding conceptual knowledge in modality-specific systems. *Trends in Cognitive Sciences*, 7(2), 84–91. https://doi.org/10.1016/S1364-6613 (02)00029-3.

Bauer, P. J. (2006). Constructing a past in infancy: A neuro-developmental account. *Trends in Cognitive Sciences*, 10(4), 175–181.

Buckner, R. L., Andrews-Hanna, J. R., & Schacter, D. L. (2008). The Brain's Default Network: Anatomy, Function, and Relevance to Disease. *Annals of the New York Academy of Sciences*, 1124(1), 1–38. https://doi.org/10.1196/annals.1440.011.

Buckner, Randy L. (2010). The Role of the Hippocampus in Prediction and Imagination. *Annual Review of Psychology*, 61(1), 27–48. https://doi.org/10.1146/annurev.psych.60.110707.163508.

Buckner, Randy L., & Carroll, D. C. (2007). Self-projection and the brain. *Trends in Cognitive Sciences*, 11(2), 49–57. https://doi.org/10.1016/j.tics.2006.11.004.

Butler, J. (2009). *Giving an account of oneself*. Fordham Univ Press.

Conway, M. A. (2005). Memory and the self. *Journal of memory and language*, 53(4), 594–628.

Conway, M. A. (2009). Episodic memories. *Neuropsychologia*, 47(11), 2305–2313. https://doi.org/10.1016/j.neuropsychologia.2009.02.003

Daiute, C., & Nelson, K. (n.d.). *Making Sense of the Sense-Making Function of Narrative Evaluation*. 5.

Davachi, L., & DuBrow, S. (2015). How the hippocampus preserves order: The role of prediction and context. *Trends in Cognitive Sciences*, 19(2), 92–99. https://doi.org/10.1016/j.tics.2014.12.004.

Djalali, A., & Potts, C. (n.d.). Synthetic logic characterizations of meanings extracted from large corpora. *David Lewis*, 80.

Faber, M., & Gennari, S. P. (2015). Representing time in language and memory: The role of similarity structure. *Acta Psychologica, 156*, 156–161. https://doi.org/10.1016/j.actpsy.2014.10.001.

Graziano, M. S. A., & Webb, T. W. (2015). The attention schema theory: A mechanistic account of subjective awareness. *Frontiers in Psychology, 06*. https://doi.org/10.3389/fpsyg.2015.00500.

Hommel, B. (2004). Event files: Feature binding in and across perception and action. *Trends in Cognitive Sciences, 8*(11), 494–500. https://doi.org/10.1016/j.tics.2004.08.007.

Hommel, B. Theory of Event Coding (TEC) V2.0: Representing and controlling perception and action. *Atten Percept Psychophys* **81**, 2139–2154 (2019). https://doi.org/10.3758/s13414-019-01779-4.

James, W. (1899). The stream of consciousness. In W. James, *Talks to teachers on psychology—And to students on some of life's ideals* (pp. 15–21). Metropolitan Books/Henry Holt and Company. https://doi.org/10.1037/10814-002.

Kim, H. (2010). Dissociating the roles of the default-mode, dorsal, and ventral networks in episodic memory retrieval. *NeuroImage, 50*(4), 1648–1657. https://doi.org/10.1016/j.neuroimage.2010.01.051

Lewis, K. (n.d.). *Narrative and the Long Route to Ontology.* 1–15. https://d1wqtxts1xzle7.cloudfront.net/31296501/Narrative_and_the_Long_Route_to_Ontology.pdf?1369399511=&response-content-disposition=inline%3B+filename%3DNarrative_and_the_Long_Route_to_Ontology.pdf&Expires=1591262937&Signature=fkwQQWBOjT9A-n5kLGEvb15iUsI7-40-ylX~R5-5AesuQxoFEXBFOzTYBZCTnUyfzwNqDiJG4Ctpa3hyhGLeqbo9Jnlyu57GzauEnJfvHyqZ8y4kB4urhh-vvilNGK-NOkRdIFuIVKHfqRh-v83B8Lb1EerG8bcrxkDec03tJxveo4Mb9twi06oU4iVCEh2TeifvL9ZVBEzSXE8-X-Wg3yXoONgn~O9dRIS9A7IbjKGLrfGN9TVOqd7uTGaeCIddmI5IB0h2~vjiAV~7AS8QungFHFxRN-angxZwUYOHAt-QucM6tnjED1lBBo6h09hu0fUw-QnKvDNg-fFFAerwDw&Key-Pair-Id=APKAJLOHF5GGSLRBV4ZA.

Memelink, J., & Hommel, B. (2013). Intentional weighting: A basic principle in cognitive control. *Psychological Research, 77*(3), 249–259. https://doi.org/10.1007/s00426-012-0435-y.

Menary, R. (2014). *Cognitive integration: Mind and cognition unbounded.* Palgrave Macmillan.

Menary, R. (2008). Embodied Narratives. *Journal of Consciousness Studies, 15*(6), 63–84.

Menary, R. (2010). Introduction to the special issue on 4E cognition. *Phenomenology and the Cognitive Sciences, 9*(4), 459–463. https://doi.org/10.1007/s11097-010-9187-6.

Menary, R. (2013). Cognitive integration, enculturated cognition and the socially extended mind. *Cognitive Systems Research, 25–26*, 26–34. https://doi.org/10.1016/j.cogsys.2013.05.002.

Meretoja, H. (2013). Philosophical underpinnings of the narrative turn in theory and fiction. *The travelling concepts of narrative*, 93–117.

Montemayor, C. (2013). *Minding time: A philosophical and theoretical approach to the psychology of time*. Brill.

Montemayor, C. (2015). Trade-offs between the accuracy and integrity of autobiographical narrative in memory reconsolidation. *Behavioral and Brain Sciences, 38*. https://doi.org/10.1017/S0140525X14000247.

Nelson, K. (2003). Narrative and the Emergence of a Consciousness of Self. Narrative and Consciousness. 17–36. https://doi.org/10.1093/acprof:oso/9780195140057.003.0002.

Richmond, L. L., & Zacks, J. M. (2017). Constructing Experience: Event Models from Perception to Action. *Trends in Cognitive Sciences, 21*(12), 962–980. https://doi.org/10.1016/j.tics.2017.08.005.

Ricœur, P. (1992). *Oneself as another*. University of Chicago Press.

Schacter, D. L., & Addis, D. R. (2007a). The cognitive neuroscience of constructive memory: Remembering the past and imagining the future. *Philosophical Transactions of the Royal Society B: Biological Sciences, 362*(1481), 773–786. https://doi.org/10.1098/rstb.2007.2087.

Schacter, D. L., & Addis, D. R. (2007b). Remembering the Past to Imagine the Future: A Cognitive Neuroscience Perspective. *Military Psychology, 21*(suppl.1), S108–S112. https://doi.org/10.1080/08995600802554748.

Schacter, D. L., Addis, D. R., Hassabis, D., Martin, V. C., Spreng, R. N., & Szpunar, K. K. (2012). The Future of Memory: Remembering, Imagining, and the Brain. *Neuron, 76*(4), 677–694. https://doi.org/10.1016/j.neuron.2012.11.001.

Schacter, D. L., Benoit, R. G., De Brigard, F., & Szpunar, K. K. (2015). Episodic future thinking and episodic counterfactual thinking: Intersections between memory and decisions. *Neurobiology of Learning and Memory, 117*, 14–21. https://doi.org/10.1016/j.nlm.2013.12.008.

Schacter, D. L., & Madore, K. P. (2016). Remembering the past and imagining the future: Identifying and enhancing the contribution of episodic memory. *Memory Studies, 9*(3), 245–255. https://doi.org/10.1177/1750698016645230.

Schwartz, R., Events Are What We Make of Them, in Thomas F. Shipley, and Jeffrey M. Zacks (eds.), *Understanding Events: From Perception to Action* (New York, 2008; online edn., Oxford Academic, 1 May 2008), https://doi.org/10.1093/acprof:oso/9780195188370.003.0003, accessed 19 Mar. 2023.

Shipley, T. F., & Zacks, J. M. (Eds.). (2008). *Understanding events: From perception to action*. Oxford University Press.

Shipley, T. F. (2008). An invitation to an event. *Understanding events: From perception to action*, 3–30.

Simons, D. J., & Chabris, C. F. (1999). Gorillas in our midst: Sustained inattentional blindness for dynamic events. *Perception, 28*(9), 1059–1074.

Speer, N. K., Zacks, J. M., & Reynolds, J. R. (2007). Human Brain Activity Time-Locked to Narrative Event Boundaries. *Psychological Science, 18*(5), 449–455. https://doi.org/10.1111/j.1467-9280.2007.01920.x.

Spreng, R. N., Mar, R. A., & Kim, A. S. (2009). The common neural basis of autobiographical memory, prospection, navigation, theory of mind, and the default mode: a quantitative meta-analysis. *Journal of Cognitive Neuroscience, 21*(3), 489–510.

Tsuda, I., Yamaguchi, Y., Hashimoto, T., Okuda, J., Kawasaki, M., & Nagasaka, Y. (2015). Study of the neural dynamics for understanding communication in terms of complex hetero systems. *Neuroscience Research, 90*, 51–55. https://doi.org/10.1016/j.neures.2014.10.007

Tversky, B., & Zacks, J. M. (2013). Event perception. *Oxford Handbook of Cognitive Psychology, 1*(2), 3.

Yarkoni, T., Speer, N. K., & Zacks, J. M. (2008). Neural substrates of narrative comprehension and memory. *NeuroImage, 41*(4), 1408–1425. https://doi.org/10.1016/j.neuroimage.2008.03.062.

Webb, T. W., & Graziano, M. S. A. (2015). The attention schema theory: A mechanistic account of subjective awareness. *Frontiers in Psychology, 6,* Article 500.

Wittmann, M., & Butler, E. (2016). *Felt time: The psychology of how we perceive time*. MIT Press.

Zacks, J. M., & Tversky, B. (2001). Event structure in perception and conception. *Psychological Bulletin, 127*(1), 3.

Zacks, J. M., Speer, N. K., Swallow, K. M., Braver, T. S., & Reynolds, J. R. (2007). Event perception: A mind-brain perspective. *Psychological Bulletin, 133*(2), 273–293. https://doi.org/10.1037/0033-2909.133.2.273.

CHAPTER 7

Affect and Weak Narrativity

Recall the definition of narrative processing articulated at the end of Chap. 4: ongoing meaning-directed generation and processing of emergent temporal structures consisting of related value-dynamic sequences involving value-dynamic selected agents, mediated by socio-cultural contexts. In the previous chapter, event processing is characterized as a locus of emergent weak narrativity. What's missing from this model, however, is a theory of dynamic valuation shaping this emergence.

This chapter considers the role affect and emotion play in the valuation processes that shape event perception. This may seem odd, given that historically researchers have drawn a bright line between cognition and emotion.[1] However, recent research describes how affect and emotion work in relation to, and as integral to, cognition.

Affect and emotion are crucial to weak narrativity in event processing because they are strongly associated with how we attribute value and meaning to our experiences. For example, Cromwell and Panksepp (2011) associate affect with valuation, and cognition with information. These ideas, key to defining weak narrativity, will provide a basis for a robust model of how concatenation, temporal extension, and agency are mediated by personal, social, and cultural contexts.

A number of theorists of narrative have linked narrative to affect and emotion. For example, Meir Sternberg (2003) describes curiosity, anticipation, and surprise as narrative universals (see Chap. 4., Sect. 4.1). David

© The Author(s), under exclusive license to Springer Nature
Switzerland AG 2023
B. Miller, *Narrativity in Cognition*,
https://doi.org/10.1007/978-3-031-40349-1_7

Velleman (2003) points to emotional cadences, rather than other forms of coherence or explanation, as the key to narrative's power. In *Affective Narratology* (2011), Patrick Colm Hogan ably reviews his antecedents in this area, including Aristotle, Labov, Bordwell, Bortolussi and Dixon, Tan, Eder, Palmer, Herman, Stockwell, Keen, Oatley, Miall, Todorov, Bremond, Greimas, Bruner, Propp, and Kafelnos (see pp. 10–15 and pp. 77–80).

Hogan's approach to narrative and affect is structural. That is, he argues that story structures are "shaped and oriented by emotion systems," and that this structuring has natural correlates in the way we experience ordinary time and space as subjectively meaningful (p. 1, pp. 29–31). Hogan describes how emotion contributes to structuring time in nested units. He begins with *incidents*, which are marked by sudden increases in emotion, and which shape our orientation toward experience in the near future, including where attention is directed. The cognitive processing of incidents in relation to the past, the anticipated future, causal explanation, and the like extends incidents into *events*, primarily in working memory. In turn, these are developed into associated *sequences of episodes* with patterns of deviation from and return to normative conditions (pp. 66–7). Thus, narrative units reflect emotional markers. Likewise, experience features the selection and marking of space and particular agents by emotional systems for significance in a way that reflects narrative structure.[2]

The definition offered here of narrative processing does not rise to the level of Hogan's 'story.' Specifically, Hogan distinguishes stories from ordinary experiences in terms of goal-orientation and closure (pp. 121–2):

> To have a highly prototypical story, we need occurrences that are not routine, ideally events that are emotionally significant. These events should be mutually emotionally relevant and causally integrated not only at the level of episodes but also at the level of highly elaborated appraisal. Such appraisal involves a broad range of causal relations beyond mere entailment and a range of emotional relations not confined to congruence. (p. 76)

If our task is to understand first how emotion systems help structure experience in ways that have narrativity, then 'highly prototypical' stories emphasize a gradient degree of emotional and causal coherence between selected elements as well as a meaningful, unfolding temporal structure. Ordinary experiences are structured by the same emotional and cognitive systems, and thus may be understood to reflect narrativity to a gradient degree, including extremely weak or no narrativity.

On the other hand, a key feature of prototypical stories is 'highly elaborated appraisal.' Hogan addresses this issue robustly in *Affective Narratology*, relating the structure of evaluation implied in narrative endings to theories of emotion that attribute an 'appraisal' quality to elicited emotions.

Appraisal sounds like a *post hoc*, ruminative activity, but Hogan describes an ongoing synthesis of the perceptual and the reflective:

> even in cases where the perceptual account applies most obviously to a focal emotion-eliciting perception, there is still a penumbra of appraisal-like thought that bears on the ways in which the emotion is sustained, enhanced, inhibited, and so forth. That appraisal-like thought continually incorporates perceptual and related emotional elements. (pp. 47–8)

Thus, Hogan argues that perception elicits emotion, and appraisal both draws on and sustains emotion. In observing this, Hogan begins to reconcile 'perceptual' and 'appraisal' views of emotion, which we'll examine shortly.

In the argument that follows, I develop Hogan's effort to reconcile perception and evaluation to argue for how affect and emotion influence event perception and concatenation to generate a weak narrativity in our experiences. My hypothesis is that the emergent models of cognition introduced in the previous chapter, along with new research programs on affect and emotion, effect this reconciliation in granular and varying ways. In so doing, they bolster the case for weak narrativity in our experiences. Several factors support this hypothesis: evidence that affect is a constant feature of experiences (rather than *only* being triggered by resonant incidents); that causal and emotion-based appraisals are key components, but not encompassing of, emergent, dynamic salience networks based on *relationality*; and that affect and emotion are crucial to the anticipatory, or predictive, structure of cognition.

7.1   THEORIES OF EMOTION

In the Western philosophical tradition, theories of emotion emerged at least as early as Aristotle and Plato, and crucial early touchstones include Descartes, Spinoza, Hume, Montaigne, Hobbes, Kant, and others.

Psychology's emergence as a discipline autonomous from philosophy and (at least partly) defined by empirical study in the nineteenth century led to a number of relatively well-defined tracks in models of emotions: Charles Darwin, Herbert Spencer, William James, William Wundt, and others promoted various understandings of emotion that anticipate the models we continue to hold today. Contemporary interest in emotion is linked to Bedford, Kenny, Arnold, Schacter and Singer, Tompkins, and others.

One of the philosophical fault lines in theories of emotion involves the difference between 'feeling theories,' which focus on emotions as sub-personally triggered physiological events, and theories that grapple with the intentional nature of emotions (that is, that emotions are typically about something, whether it be an external entity or property or an interior state, belief, desire, etc.). One way to approach this difference is to consider that they both understand affect/emotion as a form of valuing. In feeling theories, the feeling is itself the value, as in "I feel happy" or "I feel depressed." In appraisal theories, affect/emotion is similarly a personal feeling (again, "I feel happy or depressed"), but it is coupled to an appraisal of some kind ("That charging bull is scary"→"I feel scared").

Contemporary psychology features three prominent approaches to emotion—the Basic Emotions approach, the appraisal approach, and the constructivist approach. These approaches differ regarding whether emotion and cognition are separate brain systems, tightly integrated, or somewhere in-between. They can be distinguished from one another by considering the place of emotion in perceptual processes, rather than reflective cognition. The Basic Emotions approach describes a set of fundamental emotional responses that have adaptive value and their own distinctive neural pathways. The appraisal approach views emotion as a form of judgment: the subject's evaluation of perceptual stimuli includes emotion, which colors higher order thinking. The third approach—constructivism—views emotion itself as a product of sensory inputs and top-down, higher order concerns.

There are some key differences between these models—where the Basic Emotions approach views emotions as products of neural systems distinctive from rational cognition, the constructivist approach views emotions and rationality as emerging from common or robustly integrated sources. Where basic emotion approaches see a distinctive taxonomy of emotions, constructivist approaches offer dimensional models emphasizing valence, arousal, and sometimes other factors (such as intensity and dominance). Where basic emotions approaches and appraisal approaches tend to emphasize either the modularity of emotions, or a 'two-speed' system of fast and slow processing, constructivist models do not make such a distinction (and, as we'll see, are conducive to integration with the predictive processing model of cognition explored in Chap. 6).

7.2   AFFECTIVE COGNITION

These differences turn upon the relationship between emotions and rationality, which is widely debated in philosophical discussions of affect and emotion. There are several strong threads within this discussion, but two prominent sub-discussions consider (a) whether emotion is an instrumental support of human rationality and (b) whether emotion generally, or particular emotions, are modular systems characterized by limited information 'packets' or streams that render them distinctive from rational processes (Fauchet and Tappolet 2007; de Sousa 2006; Jones 2006). Some theories consider the effects of general affective states—mood—on evaluative judgment (Forgas 2008).

Contra belief in a 'two-track' system, where emotion and cognition are disassociated, a growing body of research suggests they commonly, and even typically, mutually impact one another. These impacts come in different forms. For example, in Joseph Forgas's Affect Infusion Model "emotions infuse into a cognitive task, and influence memory and judgment depending on the extent to which the task depends on complex and constructive processing, or on matters that depart from prototypes" (Forgas 2001, p. 123). Bower builds upon this model in his emotional congruence account, which argues that we should be able to learn new material that is congruent with our current memory (Oatley, p. 264).

Conversely, emotions have been conceived as the result of appraisal, dating back to Magda Arnold's and Richard Lazarus' pioneering work in the 1960s. Klaus Scherer (who conceived the component process theory of emotions) and Phoebe Ellsworth note that

> the basic premise of appraisal theories is that the organism's evaluation of its circumstances (current or remembered or imagined) plays a crucial role in the elicitation and differentiation of its emotions ... some of the central dimensions proposed ... [include] novelty, intrinsic pleasantness, certainty or predictability, goal significance, agency, coping potential, and compatibility with social or personal standards... (p. 573)

Oatley offers a thorough review of this work in *Understanding Emotions*, noting that "The literature on emotion-related appraisal … suggests that emotions are often the product of rather complex beliefs about real events in the world" (p. 259). For example, Robinson and Clore argue that feelings are information, and are used when we make judgments (Oatley; see Cromwell and Panksepp (Chap. 8, Sect. 8.5, also Sect. 7.5), to note how this is distinctive from their views).

Other notable models view the integration of emotion and cognition as partial. The SPAARS model created by Power and Dagleish modifies the two-system modularity of emotion and cognition by envisioning two paths to emotion, one aligned with the pre-conceptual 'basic emotions' framework and a second based upon appraisal. Klaus Scherer's (2009) component process model (CPM) describes both cognitive and physiological components of emotion:

> the CPM suggests that the event and its consequences are appraised with a set of criteria on multiple levels of processing. The result of the appraisal will generally have a motivational effect, often changing or modifying the motivational state before the occurrence of the event. Based on the appraisal results and the concomitant motivational changes, efferent effects will occur in the autonomic nervous system (ANS; in the form of somatovisceral changes) and in the somatic nervous system (in the form of motor expression in face, voice and body). All of these components, appraisal results, action tendencies, somatovisceral changes and motor expressions are centrally represented and constantly fused in a multimodal integration area (with continuous updating as events and appraisals change). (p. 3462)

Scherer's model integrates cognitive, bodily, motivational, expressive, and subjective components into the production of an emotion. Scherer's model views emotion as a dynamic, feedback-oriented form of appraisal.

Antonio Damasio's somatic marker hypothesis similarly views emotion as the product of a variety of systems. For Damasio, learned bodily reactions in relation to particular stimuli create anticipation about the results of particular choices. Thus, emotional processes guide behavior by seeding predictions with particular sorts of feelings.[3]

Ronald de Sousa's *The Rationality of Emotions* considers whether, given theories like Scherer's and Damasio's, emotions need to be thought of as modular systems. For de Sousa, theories like this might seem to identify a limited set of 'emotion programs' that can subsequently be integrated into cognitive processes. However, de Sousa argues against this model of 'modularity' by noting the particularity and complexity of the experiential field about which appraisals are made, and by implication the "wealth of specific meanings enriched by an immensely large class of contrasts" (p. 16). This wealth of meanings constitutes the field of experience as a rich fabric of diverse meanings, which he describes as "the polychrome vision of the emotional field" (p. 16).[4]

7.3   Emotion and Perception

A number of prominent theories describe emotion as integral to perception. Christine Tappolet, writing in 2000, argues that "les emotions sont des perceptions des valeurs" (roughly, "emotions are perceptions of values") (p. 169). By this, she means that emotions are a form of non-conceptual perceptual cognition. Robert Roberts' construal-based account integrates perception of exterior objects and events with care and action readiness. Thus, emotions are perceptions of the impact of some entity or event upon something cared for, along with action readiness to act in a relevant way. Interestingly, Roberts' examples of concern extend beyond the biological organism to objects of concern in the world (a paradigmatic example is one's child and the emotions that commonly emerge in the parent when that child is endangered).

Jesse Prinz argues, in his 2004 book *Gut Reactions*, for emotions as 'embodied appraisals.' For Prinz, emotion is the experience of physiological changes, which alert us to relevant features of experience (such as threats). While in *Gut Reactions* Prinz supports the notion of emotional modularity, in a 2006 article he modifies his view by rejecting 'informational encapsulation.'[5] Further, he argues that "perceptual representations can represent complex relational properties that have no intrinsic morphological unity," a point that forces us to consider the nature of the processing of relationality and, moreover, the processing of dynamic relationality (how relations change over time, and how the nodes in a relational network themselves change).

In *The Cognitive-Emotional Brain* (2013), Luis Pessoa notes that "cognition and emotion have been traditionally described as mutually antagonistic, the one interfering with the other and vice versa" (p. 251). In this 'standard hypothesis,' emotion is a primal, fast, automatic, and modular (read: insulated) rapid detection system. In addition, emotional processing is conceived as "preattentive," "automatic," and "unaware" (p. 81).

As he puts the matter, "The standard hypothesis has influenced both basic and applied research and, at first glance, has intuitive appeal. Emotional reactions can be fast and relatively impervious to top-down effects when task demands are not high. Nevertheless, a host of problems plague the hypothesis in its basic form" (p. 61).

Pessoa is doubtful of empirically establishing the standard hypothesis:

> the question of whether there are two systems in dual process models is not an entirely empirical one. This is because no single critical experiment can provide a final, definitive answer. In the end, however irresistible dichotomies are to the human mind (Kelso and Engstrøm 2006; Newell 1973), dichotomizing implies oversimplifying (Keren and Schul 2009; Kruglanski et al. 2006). A continuous framework is better, albeit more complex (Kruglanski et al. 2006). (p. 251)

Pessoa argues that emotion and cognition are not conducted through modular, separate neural systems. Instead, brain areas identified with emotion and/or cognition serve a wide variety of roles: "emotion and cognition not only strongly interact in the brain, but ... they are often integrated so that they jointly contribute to behavior" (p. 148).[6] Specifically, so-called cognitive regions of the brain, like frontal cortex, are integral to emotion, while 'emotional' regions, like the amygdala, serve a variety of cognitive functions.

While he is not arguing the brain is monolithic, Pessoa contends that alternative views that account for network dynamics, specifically reciprocal interactions between brain areas, lead to a greater appreciation of how emotion and cognition function in relation to one another. His view accommodates both the notion of cognition-emotion 'push-pull' (or competition for resources) and processes that draw widely from different regions and apparent functions. In this, he is supportive of Josef Parvizi's proposal that "subcortical regions play much more prominent roles in complex behaviors: 'higher' functions of the brain might in fact depend on signals from subcortical to cortical structures rather than the other way around" (p. 240, Parvizi 2009, p. 358).

Based on the notion that the brain operates through distributed, networked regions, Pessoa believes network dynamics, rather than stepwise, hierarchical, and functional pathways are the key to understanding the relations between emotion and cognition. He offers a 'multiple waves model' involving rapid processing of affective information and feedback as an alternative to the 'high' and 'low' road models of cognition popularized by figures like Daniel Kahneman.[7]

Pessoa's model envisions cognitive-emotional integration via a number of shared processes that in some cases require reconceptualization: the notion of unconscious cognitive activity, mechanisms of selection of features of experience for additional processing, including attention and motivation, value representation, and salience.

The multiple waves model is consonant with views of unconscious processes as "sophisticated behavioral tendencies" in relation to subliminal influences and effects of triggering stimuli (of which the subject is aware) (Barrett and Mesquita 2008). This view differs from the notion of unconscious processes in priming literature, which suggests that the subject is unaware of the stimuli themselves. One consequence of this alteration is that it locates unconscious processes directly in relation to the perceived world, not as passively received, but as encountered and processed actively and continuously. But what do these processes do? For Morsella and Bargh, there are "sophisticated, flexible, and adaptive unconscious behavior guidance systems" at work, as is particularly evident when we mentally time travel (p. 8).

These guidance systems profoundly shape our experiences: perception is heavily mediated by emotion and motivation. Whereas the standard models exempt early sensory processing from value-based modulations, Pessoa sees affective and motivational influences throughout all forms of sensory processing (p. 256): A "common effect of emotion and motivation is to confer enhanced salience … Thus task-relevant items are detected better, whereas task-irrelevant items act as more potent distractors" (p. 252).

This view of emotion and salience—understood in this context to mean prominence (visual, for Pessoa)—is rather profound, though subtle: emotion and motivation, by directing increased attention to particular features of experience, render experience in terms of significance.

Pessoa cites the work of Goldberg and colleagues, who have argued for a "salience map" that corresponds to attention to elements of the visual field. Pessoa proposes that emotion and motivation activate evaluative sites in the brain to "prioritize processing based on the emotional value of a sensory stimulus": "affective significance determines the fate of a visual item during competitive interactions by enhancing sensory processing. In such a manner, the amygdala helps separate the significant from the mundane" (p. 164).

7.4   Valuation in Different Cognitive Processes

Coding value—or 'valuation'—is thus not as simple as assigning a number or quality (e.g., "that dog is an 8/10 on the health scale" or "that person is intelligent but elusive"). Instead, 'valuation' is intrinsic to perception—a compound of abstractable, semantic qualities, affective significance, and attentional resources. In addition, there is evidence that valuation shapes both intentional and sub-personal cognitive processes.

Pessoa sees a crucial linkage between valuation processes and task-oriented processes. Neural research reveals "direct pathways between task and valuation networks," and "cognitive-emotional interactions rely on the communication between 'task networks' (e.g., the attentional network during attention tasks) and 'valuation networks,' which involve both sub-cortical regions … and cortical ones" (p. 175, p. 174).

Finally, attention and valuation can function as predictive mechanisms that drive learning and shape experience:

> expectation-dependent modulation of responses resembles "prediction error" signals that are central to formal models of learning (Pearce and Hall 1980; Rescorla and Wagner 1972; Sutton and Barto 1988). Whereas, in some models, prediction errors drive learning directly, in others they do so indirectly, determining the amount of "event processing," which then influences the rate of learning—a process that can be viewed as an attentional function. In this regard, a connection between prediction errors and attention in learning has been revealed for the rat basolateral amygdala. (Roesch et al. 2010) (Pessoa, p. 15)

The nature of value representation supports its role in predictive coding. Valuation draws upon "highly processed information," is directed toward properties that demonstrate continuity, and is tracked 'moment to moment' for change.[8] These findings suggest that the amygdala encodes predictive reward value. This prediction mechanism, according to Pessoa, can be particularly useful for detecting 'surprise' events in experience (p. 15).

Valuation, then, is central to arguments that emotion is integral to cognition. The terms 'value' and 'valuation' can be construed in a number of different ways. In common parlance, a 'value' is tantamount to an ethical belief, and the verbal form—"to value"—is to appreciate, recognize the worth of, and/or to assess a particular entity or property. In philosophical discussions of emotion, the relation of emotion and value often concerns the relations of emotions to morality. But some thinkers have considered how emotional experiences involve implicit valuing of features of or relations within experience (see Tappolet 2000).

In thinking of present experience-level affect, value and valuing can be a way of describing non-propositional, and even non-conceptual, features of experience (that can be integrated with propositional, conceptual thinking at various levels of cognition). In ordinary speech, we use the term value to indicate a way to compare a particular property or entity to others (see 'amodal perception,' Chap. 6.2). Thus, we have Marx's famous 'exchange value,' but we also have the redness of one rose juxtaposed to another, one student's exam score juxtaposed to the class's, and the like. In some cases, such as the Fahrenheit and Celsius scales for temperature, value is calculated based on a particular or a particular pair of set reference points. Nevertheless, though empirically verifiable, it is still ultimately based upon a *relative metric* (in this case, 'degrees' above or below set points).

There is a second important, but similar sense of the term 'value'—to mean the significance of something. Most often, this significance entails the relatedness of the selected entity or property, usually to the agent, but often not to the agent. This is easiest to understand in terms of words like 'mother,' 'father,' 'sister,' and 'brother,' but this relational form of significance takes on wide-ranging, varied forms.[9]

Value is often treated in the psychological literature in a narrower sense, as biological or evolutionary value, which emphasizes reproduction and survival (though not exclusively). In these formulations, value is conceived as immediately value-for-self in terms of the reward or threat (in terms of pleasure, survival, or reproductive efficiency) estimated to reside in a particular property or entity, and it triggers 'approach/avoid' tendencies. In addition, this type of 'value' can be a potential relationship between the subject and the property or entity. Some theorists of cognition emphasize how perception is related to 'affordances'—the potential for acting-upon is embodied in neural and physiological action readiness, which is itself affective. The differences between these sorts of 'value' might help account for the relationship between responses to entities or properties that immediately threaten or promise to sustain the subject (say, tasty food), and entities or properties where the immediacy of reward or threat is less obvious (say, in aesthetic pleasures like enjoying classical music).[10]

7.5   THE ANOETIC SUBSTRATE AND VALUE

In the previous section, we noted the distinction between 'noetic' and 'autonoetic' consciousness in relation to memory. In addition, researchers hypothesize the existence of 'anoetic' consciousness, which is comprised of "both automatized and unexperienced perceptual-sensory and procedural information-processing, as well as raw experiences such as affective feelings" (Vandekerckhove and Panksepp 2009, p. 1022). In Vandekerckhove and Panksepp's model, these components emerge unconsciously, are non-conceptual and phenomenal, and are 'balanc[ed]' into a continuous stream of experience[11] (p. 1022).

Functionally, anoesis involves "intrinsic valuative processes of the brain (emotional, homeostatic, and sensory affects) that become continuously part of actual information processing and … perception of the world" (Vandekerckhove et al. 2014, p. 6). These valuations mediate between environmental stimuli and the individual's needs, including primal responses and "various social processes" (p. 1022).

Anoetic consciousness serves as a bridge between 'raw' affective valuation and information processing and higher order cognitive processes: "anoetic consciousness is heavily linked not only to raw sensorial and perceptual abilities but to various subcortical emotional and motivational process intrinsic affective value structures, and hence is associated with the intrinsically more implicit free-flow of affective consciousness" (p. 1026).

Anoetic consciousness thus anchors the continuous flow of conscious experience and "may be the basis of all thoughts and actions" (p. 1022). Vandekerchove and Panksepp describe higher order thinking as a 'concatenation' of elements drawn from selected (presumably temporal) segments of experience and from high-level information processing:

> Higher order thinking, such as doubting during an important personal decision-making process, presumably results from a variety of lower affective state-control and higher information processing reflecting a concatenation of implicit and explicit internal feelings, beliefs, desires and thinking processes. It requires selection of restricted segments of experience from the ongoing stream of anoetic experience. This selection process, embedded in a rich perceptual–sensorial self-awareness, may also inhibit our capacity to experience the flow of more primitive anoetic-affective processes. The limited capacity of all forms of noetic and autonoetic consciousness may have caused great mischief in conceptualizing the nature of the unconscious.

What may be potentially experienced at the anoetic level may often be unconscious at higher, more effortful levels, but may re-emerge spontaneously when one abdicates higher control, as in dreams and meditation. (2009, p. 5)

This form of consciousness, its selection and concatenation into meaningful, analytic higher thought, and its emergent nature in dreams, is suggestive of several aspects of our definition of weak narrativity. In particular, the 'selection' from anoetic experience brings together two aspects of the subjective temporality Hogan foregrounds: first, boundary definition of selected temporal units; and second, an experiential unfolding intrinsic to the selection process. How these features are related, and how this relation reflects dynamic and relational affective valuation, is a key to weak narrativity.

To return to one of the goals for this chapter, anoetic consciousness specifies an integration of perception and appraisal. Vandekerckhove and Panksepp's model is based on research indicating that individual emotion systems (SEEKING, RAGE, FEAR, etc.) are responsible for the generation of emotion. Within this context, the synthetic work of integrating affective valuations and perception, and the bridging work of linking primary processing to reflective processing, happen at intermediary levels.

Views of perception based on Bayesian prediction differ from this framework, describing affective valuation as integral to perception. The next section explores this model, and in so doing elaborate two more detailed models of how affective valuation contributes to weak narrativity. The subsequent section considers a final model, the Higher Order Theory of Emotional Consciousness, which seems conducive with the role of affective value in these models.

7.6   THE PREDICTIVE MIND
AND CONSTRUCTED EMOTION

Anil Seth writes "there is now a consensus that emotions are psychological states that encompass behavioural, experiential, and visceral changes [23, 26–28]. This view refers to several contemporary frameworks for understanding emotion and its relation to cognition and self [11–13]" (p. 567). Of these frameworks, the Bayesian approach to Predictive Coding has emerged as one way to explain how the various elements of valuation are coordinated in making experience meaningful.

In this model, emotions are produced through highly iterative feedback loops that operate in what Critchley and Garfinkel (2017) describe as a 'reverberating causality': top-down predictions about endogenous and exogenous states, and changes are affirmed or disaffirmed by sensory and interoceptive data, resulting in emotion states.[12] For Critchley and Garfinkel and other thinkers, the predictive mind evaluates the world as part of sensing it. Put another way, "sensing" is a predictive operation that identifies portions of experience through affective processing (of valence and arousal). Predictions identify features of the environment, and they manage change and salience detection. They manifest as models/simulations that anticipate predicted allostatic needs and events in the sensory environment.

Lisa Feldman Barrett, along with a host of collaborators, offers an empirically grounded constructivist model of emotion based upon a predictive processing framework. She embraces the

> increasingly popular hypothesis ... that the brain's simulations function as Bayesian filters for incoming sensory input, driving action and constructing perception and other psychological phenomena, including emotion. Simulations are thought to function as prediction signals (also known as 'top-down' or 'feedback' signals, and more recently as 'feed-forward' models) that continuously anticipate events in the sensory environment.) (2016, p. 10)

Her theory is that "using past experience as a guide, the brain prepares multiple competing simulations that answer the question, 'what is this new sensory input most similar to?'" (see Bar 2007, 2009) (2016, p. 7). The answers are determined "using Bayesian logic ... to decide among simulations and implement one of them (Gallivan et al. 2016), based on predicted maintenance of physiological efficiency across multiple body systems" (2016, p. 7).

Moreover, prediction-based evaluation is not passive or abstract. Instead, "predictions are categorizations that maintain physiological regulation, guide action and construct perception. The meaning of a sensory event includes visceromotor and motor action plans to deal with that event" (Barrett 2016, p. 7).[13]

One of the implications of this model is that predictions about the nature of experience make acts of perception meaningful. Predictions are not holistic; that is, they do not manifest as a result of analyzing static batches of data that encompass the subject's environs. Instead, they are provisional and based upon changes in salience in environmental inputs as they relate to allostasis (i.e., processes for achieving stability). This affectively loaded sensing is "driven by regions of the brain that are responsible for implementing allostasis" (Barrett 2016, p. 9)).

This requires a more integrated and gradient view of affect: rather than thinking of emotions as derived from a limited set of basic emotions, constructivists conceive of a dynamic dimensional model of emotion. Sensory inputs are shaped by arousal—the degree to which they excite attention and further processing—and valence (the 'pleasure and displeasure' the brain predicts will be associated with this input, "constitut[ing] a neuropsychologic barometer of the individual's relationship to an environment at a given point in time" (p. 6)). Valence and arousal are not separate factors but are coordinated into the relative "pressure" (to adopt Barrett's barometer metaphor) of the environs as well as prospective responses. As Citron (2014) puts it, "Human emotions can be conceptualised within a two-dimensional model comprised of emotional valence and arousal (intensity). These variables are at least in part distinct, but recent studies report interactive effects during implicit emotion processing and relate these to stimulus-evoked approach-withdrawal tendencies" (p. 79).

The individual's relationship to the current environs is registered as 'core affect,' which Barrett, borrowing from Spelke, describes as "a form of affective responding that functions as a kind of core knowledge about whether objects or events are helpful or harmful, rewarding or threatening, calling for acceptance or rejection" (Barrett et al. 2007, p. 5). This core affective state is produced by "the coordination of sensory samplings and somatovisceral allostatic predictions, which] leads to a 'core affective state' that is the basis of what we experience as emotions." This coordination is tuned by a neural 'salience network' that identifies what prediction errors to pay attention to.

The salience network is dynamic and facilitated by physiological changes, such as increases and decreases in heart rate, known as 'interoception.' Interoception is the basis for emotional feeling states. As Critchley and Garfinkel put it, "Interoception describes the afferent signaling, central processing, and neural and mental representation of internal bodily signals" (p. 7). Anil Seth proposes that "interoceptive predictive coding," or "interoceptive inference," "determine[s] [emotional content] ... by active inference on the likely internal and external causes of changes in the physiological condition of the body" (p. 567). In Seth's model, "interoceptive inference involves hierarchically cascading top-down interoceptive predictions that counterflow with bottom-up interoceptive prediction errors. Subjective feeling states—experienced emotions—are hypothesized to depend on the integrated content of these predictive representations across multiple levels" (p. 567).[14]

This unites 'affective' and 'cognitive' areas of the brain:

> The function of this circuitry is to link sensory information about a stimulus with a representation of how the stimulus affects the person's internal (somatovisceral) state (Barbas, Saha, Rempel-Clower, & Ghashghaei, 2003; Ghashghaei & Barbas, 2002; Kringelbach & Rolls, 2004; Ongur, Ferry, & Price, 2003; Ongur & Price, 2000). This circuitry involves areas of the brain that are traditionally considered to be "affective" (e.g., amygdala and ventral striatum), along with anterior portions of the cortex that have traditionally been considered cognitive. (Duncan and Barrett 2007, p. 3)

Value is integral to models and simulations (predictions that shape the perception of a stimulus).[15]

So, the new predictive models conceive of a valuation-based form of representation linked to prior context. Indeed, representation *is* predictive simulation linked to action-orientations. Further 'downstream,' perception is a predictive coordination of sensory inputs with core affective states in Bayesian error minimization loops. Thus, Barrett claims that "the brain constructs an on-line concept of happiness, not in absolute terms, but with reference to a particular goal in the situation (to be with friends, to enjoy a meal, to accomplish a task), all in the service of allostasis" (Barrett 2017, p. 11).

These models contribute to the felt quality of meaning being imbued in our experiences. Barrett and Mesquita assert that these 'mental representation[s] of emotion' are experienced as caused by the stimulus, and that the representation and perception of stimuli "constrain one another, rendering perceptions of physical actions instantly into psychologically meaningful acts" (Barrett and Mesquita, p. 12). Thus, perception at the basic level of stimuli that impact allostasis is inherently psychologically meaningful, not in a stepwise, processing manner in which sensory inputs are processed and coded for psychological meanings, but immediately as part of the perception itself.

7.7   SYNTHESIS, TEMPORAL EXTENSION,
AND NONPERSONAL MEANING

These models of perception and emotion begin to account for the meaningfulness that seems immanent in our experiences. However, they also raise questions about the coherence and scope of our experience, including:

1. how does synthesis work? that is, if the sensory field is strewn with arousing, valenced objects, how is a 'core affective state' generated?
2. the model seems appropriate for static objects—how do changes in valence and arousal complicate this synthesis?
3. valence and arousal are tied to allostatic conditions, but we may not value and attend to experiences not bound directly to our potentialities for action. How are context and non-self-directed significance accounted for?

Synthesis is facilitated by capacity limits on attention and the accompanying need for selection and prioritization, along with top-down goals. One important implication of Barrett's model is that the core affective state is dynamic, continuous, and continually updated. Thus, because of capacity limits, fixation upon particularly arousing stimuli can make the core affective state recede into the background, where it is experienced as "a property of the external world" rather than as a representation available for reflection (Barrett and Mesquita, p. 16).

Moreover, affective predictive processes directly influence what's selected for our conscious attention.[16] This occurs within an attentional matrix that cues additional processing for selected sensory stimulations.[17] Both regulatory selection and the attentional matrix draw upon forebrain systems associated with goals and planning, which provides context driven by personal goals. Meaningful temporal extension emerges in part through dynamics in which core affective state is updated by monitoring not only the emergence of new stimuli, but also changes in stimuli (through top-down contextualization and bottom-up monitoring processes). Through 'affective working memory' and the 'remembered present,'[18] time begins to take shape in terms of emotional processes and the processes in the world being affectively tracked. This combination, along with the ongoing effect of predictive processing, contributes to the qualities of 'protention' and 'retention' Husserl associated with present experience. Top-down predictions about the situation, based upon goals and schema derived from prior experiences, shape perceptions of meaning in these emerging temporal shapes.

Meanwhile, core affect constrains how situation is construed.[19] Affect is episodic, created by condition changes from allostatic 'set points' to increased disharmony and/or volatility and back toward set points. This contributes to the experience of meaningful affective temporal structures and is one of several networks used to generate emotional episodes (Barrett 2016, p. 11).

What about properties and entities in experience not directly tied to allostasis? Citron (2014) notes heightened perceptual processing of "emotionally salient stimuli" and "emotionally incongruent information" during reading (which is, of course, a language-mediated experience rather than a direct perceptual experience) (p. 87). Moreover, there is some research which finds that emotional cognition, while emerging from core 'allostatic' processing, is the basis of our aesthetic sensibilities. Brown et al. (2011) argue "aesthetic processing is, at its core, the appraisal of the valence of perceived objects. This appraisal is in no way limited to artworks but is instead applicable to all types of perceived objects. Therefore, one way to naturalize aesthetics is to argue that such a system evolved first for the appraisal of objects of survival advantage, such as food sources" (p. 3).

However, the 'object' orientation of Brown and Gao's perspective doesn't account for (a) temporal extension, (b) the coordination of multiple objects, (c) valuing of agents, or (d) a, b, and c together. When we combine Brown and Gao's insights with the ideas about 'selection' and 'attentional matrices' reviewed above, we move toward a natural aesthetic appraisal that starts to meet the definition of 'narrativity' established earlier in the book.

7.8   Forms of Significance in Emergent Meaningful Experience

The processes described above illuminate the dynamics through which experience takes on meaningful temporal shape. But what of the nature of the contents that manifest these meanings, and how are they related to narrativity? In the constructivist-predictive model of affect, synthesis, temporal extension, and non-self-directed significance are fostered by several features and processes, including relational valuation, situational valuation, contextual valuation, and theory of mind.

Relational content, according to Barrett and Mesquita, is "the content in an emotion experience that represents the emoter's relationship to another person. In many cases, a mental representation of emotion incorporates the proximity or status of an individual with respect to other individuals present or imagined. Cultural models of relating tend to influence relational content" (p. 8). In addition, "… people report experiencing content related to dominance or submission" (Barrett et al. 2007, p. 8; also, see below).

Relational dynamics contribute to predictive modeling of the whole of an experiential field, but affective contents are specific to the agents involved. The whole is modeled as a 'situation.' Situational content, according to Barrett, is "the meaning of a situation, particularly as it relates to the perceived cause of core affect. Situational content has been mapped using several appraisal dimensions but likely goes beyond these dimensions to reference cultural meanings and practices" (p. 8). For Barrett and Mesquita, "A situation is also experienced as calling for some maintenance or change in the behavioral stance (action readiness) where the parameters for actual action are probabilistically certain to some degree" (p. 8).

Situations include both physical surroundings and sociocultural contexts: "instances of experience that are categorized as the same emotion, such as anger, are constituted by a variety of experiences of both the physical surroundings and the sociocultural context (Mesquita and Leu 2007)" (p. 8). Cross-cultural differences, particularly around notions of selfhood and social relations, significantly impact emotional experiences. These differences could extend to the dimensions (valence and arousal) that constructivist researchers use to assess emotion. There is considerable social constructionism at work, in other words, even at the level of immediate emotional and perceptual experience.

A starting point for understanding how situations 'chunk' time is to consider how the constructivist perspective understands allostasis in terms of equilibriar levels of valence and arousal. Situations emerge and resolve through patterns of changing arousal and valence between conditions of 'harmony' and 'disharmony.'

In the Fig. 7.1 above, Bakker and de Boon illustrate how particular extremes of valence and arousal create experiences of 'disharmony.' Disharmonious conditions spur the recruitment of heightened attention to elements of the experiential field, as well as response mechanisms such

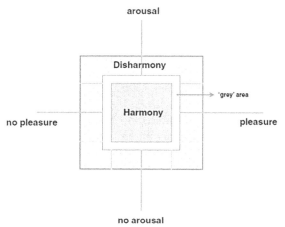

Fig. 2 Pleasure and arousal as indicators for harmony and disharmony in the physical environment (Bakker and de Boon 2012)

Fig. 7.1 From Bakker and de Boon: Pleasure, Arousal, and Harmony

as action plans to bring the subject to a new harmonious state. Meaningful temporal extension emerges through state changes from 'harmony' to 'disharmony' and back again. In other words, episodes are created by condition changes from allostatic 'set points' to increased disharmony and/or volatility and back to set points. Prior episodes (immediate, but also further in the past) influence the 'set points,' and this pattern of influence-modulating predictions creates a meaningful affective temporal structure of linked episodes (Fig. 7.2).

The linked episodes we associate with narrativity (see Chap. 6), taken individually, are not necessarily characterized by initial stasis, followed by dynamism, and succeeded by a return to stasis. Narrativity involves harmony-disharmony-harmony dynamism across episodes (narrative theorists describe the plot arc in these terms, for example). This implies that individual episodes must themselves be continuously characterized by some form of dynamism (conceived as a relatively high level of prediction activation). The second figure helps explain this by emphasizing the importance of a limited range of dynamism in experience. Here, the 'set point' (or 'harmony') focuses on degree of order, but also the amount of 'variation' attended to. Harmony is not stasis—instead, it is a dynamism unfolding through time that involves variation, including changes within

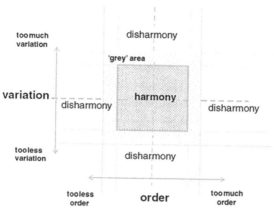

Fig. 3 The degree of order and variation as indicators for harmony and disharmony in the physical environment (Bakker and de Boon 2012)

Fig. 7.2   From Bakker and de Boon: order and variation

a range of acceptable orderliness. If the first figure suggests temporal markers emerge from dynamic flights away from and back into set points, this figure supplements this notion by emphasizing the way dynamism is built into set points. Therefore, equilibriar states of the environment are valued, changing states, but changing within a non-disruptive range.

Taken together, temporal boundaries set by harmony-disharmony-harmony patterns generated around set points attuned to immediately prior and longer durée past experiences, and characterized by relative dynamism, provide a framework for emergent episodicity. The meaningfulness of an episode is tied to these temporal forms in any of at least three ways: first, the new 'harmony' condition stimulates a particular core affective state as well as higher order reflection; second, the difference between the initial and new harmony conditions may itself have significance; and third, questions about the causes of disharmony may prompt reflection.

The emergent meanings attached to episodes facilitate the entrainment of episodes into meaningful concatenations. In other words, these emergent temporal shapes provide an affective framework in which weak narrativity can emerge. In what follows, I propose how care, higher order goals, and attention to dominance provide principles which structure our attention and contribute to organizing time into meaningful episodes.

7.9   CARE, HIGHER ORDER GOALS, AND DOMINANCE AS SOURCES OF RELATIONAL DYNAMISM

7.9.1   *Situation Boundaries*

Recall that relational content is "the content in an emotion experience that represents the emoter's relationship to another person." In this framing, relationality is dyadic and self-related. That is, the subject's core needs drive relational valuative processes. This certainly makes sense as a way to conceive of relationality. If, say, a bear walks into one's campsite while one is looking through a vent in one's tent, one might reflexively try to remain silent to avoid the bear's attention. One's mental schema related to bears would help direct attention toward whether the bear senses one because of the clear personal threat. Action-planning, perhaps recruiting abstract knowledge about ways to confront bears, would be stimulated as the bear is observed. A meaningful episode—of noticing the bear, observing its movements about the campsite, and watching it wander back into the woods—conceivably emerges as an apparently natural form of this experience, and follows the patterns described in the previous section.

We are (fortunately) rarely confronted by bears at campsites, but the description of relationality regarding other people is similar. For example, you might see a highly attractive stranger walking in a park and have an affective experience related to sexual arousal with episodic parameters, perhaps even stimulating a fantasy (itself with episodic parameters). Our affective experiences still reflect our perceived relationship and potential relationship to the other person. However, this view of relationality, while rightly pointing to the centrality of how another person relates to our needs, needs to be expanded to account for the complexities of our encounters with the world.

Consider the following extension of our example to demonstrate how care is extended beyond mere 'approach/avoid' tendencies. You see a highly attractive man walking in the park with another. The sight of this man stimulates arousal and increased attention. So far, your attention is trained entirely on a single stimulus. However, you notice that he and the other man are holding hands. Now, the stimulus shifts, though it still plausibly fits within a definition of relationality in terms of a self-relation to another person. Your feelings shift to jealousy, and it stimulates increased interest in the other man. As your attention to the other man increases, you recognize him as your sisters' husband, though he is consciously averting his gaze in the hope, you speculate (via theory of mind), of not being recognized. In this melodramatic example, the 'other man' initially lacks salience for you, but develops salience in relation to his apparent relation to the man you desire, and heightened salience as he is recognized. This secondary recruitment leads to increased scrutiny and recognition, as well as affect regarding the *relation* between the two men.[20] Further, networks of relation are immediately recruited into your affective response. Your sister, though not physically present, shapes your core affective experience of the scene.

In describing 'situations,' Barrett and Mesquita argue that "core affect is foregrounded and bound to conceptions of the situation, and in so doing, transforms affect into an intentional state by allowing an attribution about its cause. The resulting experience is an emergent gestalt that corresponds to the colloquial notion of having an emotion" (p. 14). The networked view of relationality described above helps us understand how care shapes situation-construction. Focal (i.e., cared-for) agents can be the building blocks of situational understanding.

In our example, an emerging network of relationality is mediated by dynamic affective responses: desire morphs into jealousy and then into censure and worry (for your sister). The recruitment of increasingly distal schema for tuning your affective response, and the increased intensity of the response, may lead you to ignore stimuli that ordinarily you might be attuned to. For example, perhaps a famous celebrity runs by, but you do not notice. In this process, care-based focalization leads to the emergence of a network of agents (who otherwise might not be salient) relevant to the situation. We can think of this process as implicit agentive boundary definition.

Extrapolation from this relational example helps us understand how synthetic valuations (or, in Barrett's terms, a gestalt) of a scene emerge. From relational logics centered upon stimuli imbued with more or less care emerge relational, limited networks that temporarily define situations as wholes. Via these networks, the boundaries of agents (who is included in the scene, who receives attention) are defined. Put another way, raw experience is shaped by the emergence and dynamic economies of these relational networks, such that raw experience is never actually raw. Consider, here, an analogy from theater—through relational networks, experience is 'cast' with a particular group of figures of concern. In fact, non-present members of this relational network may shape the affective tone of experience as well (as, for example, does your sister in the situation recounted above).

Valuation processes are particularly complicated in relation to other people. Encounter with others is *ipso facto* meaningful encounter. When the subject encounters other agents, valence and arousal may be heightened by higher order processes such as care, identification, desire, socio-culturally derived beliefs, and the like. In these cases, another agent may become a dynamic focal point around which experience is in part structured.

The presence of other thinking agents also strongly impacts how the subject constructs emotional experience. In Theory of Mind processing, according to Saxe and Houlihan,

> observers attribute specific granular emotions to another person based on inferences of how she interprets (or 'appraises') external events in relation to her other mental states (goals, beliefs, moral values, costs). These attributions share neural mechanisms with other reasoning about minds. Situating emotion concepts in a formal model of people's intuitive theories about other minds is necessary to effectively capture humans' fine-grained emotion understanding. (2017, p. 15)

In combination with the accretion of dynamic relational networks based upon care, theory of mind leads to finely tuned, multivariate affective responses. As opposed to encounters with the world being modulated by an overwhelming, undifferentiated 'core affect,' in this model affective experience is more like the 'polychrome' field described by de Sousa, which the predictive imagination continuously works to resolve toward a synthetic appraisal.

These emergent relational networks are continuously mediated by distal higher order goals and ongoing narratives about the self and others and are shaped for evaluation in terms of these goals and narratives. Here's an anecdotal, quite ordinary example of how we think of our experiences in terms of clear agentive and spatial boundaries, inter-agentive dynamics, and temporal markers that emerge as a result of the achievement of a relative stasis of inter-agentive dynamics: I confront my 11 year son, who has lost the form he needs me to sign to attend a school field trip—it is the second time this has happened. Choices offer themselves—do I (a) tell him he can't do the activity that he needs the form signed for, (b) explode in frustration at his lack of responsibility, (c) go to the school and sign a copy there, (d) have him bring home a new copy for me to sign, or (e) some combination or different set of reactions. After the choice is made, what happens next? Do I reflect with him on the need to be more responsible? Laugh it off as the temporary condition of a mind more consumed by the excitement of swear words and fart jokes than the boringness of school bureaucracy?

What outcome do I most wish for? What different balancing priorities are there, such as facilitating an exciting co-curricular experience for my son versus teaching him a lesson? How would he tell his friends, brother, or mother about this? How would one or another choice affect any of the following larger concerns: From how this relates to how I've raised him, to who I want him to be, to who I think he is becoming? To what would my wife think of my behavior and her evaluation of how I've evolved as a parent?

In this ordinary decision, my choices can be formulated as a higher order dichotomy or cascade of dichotomies of values drawn from my understanding of good parenting, my self-image as a parent, and the like: the value of an enrichment experience versus the value of a lesson about responsibility; the impact of either choice on the value of my parenting, etc. In this example, the immediate is linked to larger questions I have about myself and my son, and these larger questions are likely to emerge in relation to the present (How this set of errors reflects the contexts of the moment in which they occurred as well as the pattern of my son's development?).

But these higher order dichotomies emerge only as a result of an underlying process of framing the situation in ethical terms. This requires the selection of a variety of parameters and the abstraction of ethical dichotomies from sequences of events defined via these parameters. For example, the example has two characters—myself and my son—with a third (my wife) brought in. What principles undergird the selection of these two characters, and why not others? For example, what if I saw my son's rascally friend Tony, who fills his head with all the latest swear words, as a threat to my son's growth and to the integrity of our relationship? But the dyad of myself and my son presents itself to me—in unfolding time—as the natural form of this experience.

Second, the story has implied spatial parameters—the school and the home—and temporal parameters—the initial loss of a form, the second loss of a form, and the present. Along with these temporal parameters, there are future-oriented parameters that extend from the near future to the length of my son's life. The obvious question is, what selects these parameters? There are a number of commonsense ways to explain these selection processes. For example, the signing of a form is one of a number of typical events, and thus the narrative forms around the sequence of uncompleted typical events along with decision processes about completing it in relation to other priorities. Another is that the events in the present fit with an ongoing narrative (e.g., my formerly responsible son has become less responsible of late).

However, these answers work at the level of higher order reflection—they require further explanation if we are to understand how experience itself seems to emerge in these forms. For example, if schema are deployed to help tune predictions, it is relatively easy to comprehend how the emergence of, say, an individual threat might trigger schema for predicting behaviors and outcomes. But how do natural parameters and 'top-down,' schematic parameters shape presence in terms of meaningful dynamisms within relational networks?

Present experience typically involves an immediate, foregrounded space, along with a backgrounded space (see Jacobs, Chap. 4, Sect. 4.1). For example, as I sit here writing on a Saturday morning, I am immediately conscious only of the room in which I am working, which is rather messy and distracting. In the background, my wife, sons, and their friend are eating an early lunch, and I can faintly hear their repartee. As soon as I reflect upon the spatial boundaries that frame my present, they dissolve as I mentally travel—first, to the gym where I was a couple of hours ago, then to my home town. The progress of these reflections is less important than what they dispel—an unconsciously selected, enfolded spatial boundary system that emerges from my current locus of care (this writing). The point, then, is that our spatial boundaries in experience are partly derived from relational valuations.

As described in the previous section, temporal boundaries emerge through outcome orientation, returns to allostatic set points, relational valuation and the emergence of relational networks. The emergence of temporal boundaries 'naturalistically' (or better, in the course of ordinary experiential processing) can be shaped by many factors. As the previous sections have demonstrated, temporal boundaries frequently coincide with the emergence and dispersal of disharmonious affects. These patterns can be entirely based on fluctuating 'avoid/approach' affective responses to the environment. However, they can also be stimulated by emergent dynamisms within relational networks, or through the emergence and super-imposition of new relational networks.

The role of affect in constructing these dynamics reflects complex combinations of natural and socially constructed parameters. Temporal boundaries can emerge through socially ritualized activities. Consider the temporal boundaries imposed by a sports match and perhaps the extracurricular rituals surrounding a match (rival groups of fans gathering in particular spaces and engaging in drinking and social bonding rituals to heighten each fans sense of belonging and thus of the meaningfulness of the sports event). These social rituals may be related to natural phenomena, such as diurnal rhythms or evolved practices of simulating civil conflict to disperse in-group social tensions. Correspondingly, they may emerge in relation to personal biochemical patterns such as circadian rhythms, which shape the ability to direct low-stakes attention to a particular stimulus or environs. Temporal boundaries may emerge in relation to anticipated outcomes, to shifts in task and goal attention, and in relation to the ebbs and flows of dynamism in particular stimuli and relational networks. With all of these factors potentially at play at once, temporal boundaries, even though they emerge unconsciously, have complex etiologies.

Before we proceed, however, let's consider a derivative model of the care-based valuation model described above, based in this case upon our affective sensitivity to power. When we perceive agency, we are attuned to our own agency in relation to others'. In terms of the predictive-affective model, the predictions we make to simulate the world involve action plans for reacting to dynamisms within it. When these action plans are centered on other agents, predictions about relative power are critical.

Barrett and Mesquita note that dominance and submission are part of people's affective experience (p. 7). Bakker et al. (2014) propose a three-dimensional model of affect, cognition, and conation based around the familiar dimensions of valence and arousal, but augmented by dominance: our perceptions of agency are attuned to hedonic value and to our own agency in relation to others. In terms of the predictive-affective model, the predictions we make to simulate the world involve action plans for reacting to dynamisms within it. When these action plans are centered on other agents, predictions about relative power are critical.

During experience, relations of power are continuously updated and integrated with prediction. The temporal boundaries this creates enfold the dynamics described above into an outcome-oriented dynamic pattern. As an analogy, think of the implicit narrative structure of witnessing a wrestling match—as an observer, you continuously update your valuations of the relative agency and circumstances of each wrestler. These valuations may be high in arousal, even though you (via top-down processing) know that the wrestlers do not pose a threat to you, and that they operate under the bounds of regulatory systems and agents. When the match begins, the valuations are a combination of relatively static physical appraisal, and of how the wrestlers' affect-toward the other seems. If you have knowledge of either wrestler's history, this knowledge shapes predictions.

As the match unfolds, these valuations are updated by modeling of the power relations manifested in the physical interactions of the wrestlers. Toward its end (the end of a round, or of the contest), valuations might shift toward concerns about fatigue, about one wrestler sussing out the others' relative vulnerability, etc. The arc of these valuations, and the conclusion of the match (in a pin, for example), framed within the known schema of match structure, provides a weakly narrative structure. This is just an analogy, of course—life is not a highly ritualized wrestling match of which we are spectators.

However, our attention to power in the world can include dominance/submissiveness processing that coordinates meaning by applying potential, but distant, threat valuations to power assessments that weight relational networks. As time unfolds, the subject updates relational, outcome, and temporal predictions based on revised valuations. Over time, this leads to the emergence of meaningful harmony/disharmony/harmony episodes delimited by shifts in power relations and the movement into stability conditions, all within ritualized patterns. To gain insight into how ritualized patterns create anticipated stability conditions, consider how consciousness of ritual patterns emerges when they are violated: think of scenes in film, for example, when a violent act turns from a 'normal' violent episode into something that 'goes too far' (e.g., a policeman's use of restraint techniques that morphs into a beating that ends up killing or severely maiming the arrestee).

At minimum, certain kinds of sophisticated relational judgments, which seem intuitively to accord with the model of emotion (including interoceptive response) described above, are hard to imagine without semantically rich selection, delimitation, and sequencing.[21]

7.10   OTHER VALUATION MODELS
AND THE CONTRIBUTION OF AFFECT TO WEAKLY
NARRATIVE PERCEPTION

Other models of higher order thought similarly suggest a feedback circuit of anoetic (including affective) and higher information processing in the emergence of meaning. Joseph LeDoux, a leading proponent of dual process theory, and Richard Brown, a leading advocate of Higher Order Theory (see Chap. 8), offer the Higher Order Theory of Emotional Consciousness, which offers a hierarchized, but both 'top-down' and 'bottom-up' theory of how working and long-term memory, secondary perceptual processing areas, and cortical areas produce emotion-inflected self-representations as a continuous tone of phenomenological consciousness.

Ledoux and Brown see overlap between their theory and others reviewed in this chapter:

> Our theory of emotion, which has been in the making since the 1970s (8, 9, 20, 35, 166, 183), shares some elements with other cognitive theories of emotion, such as those that emphasize processes that give rise to syntactic thoughts (169), or that appraise (184–186), interpret (112), attribute (171, 187), and construct (188–192) emotional experiences. Because these cognitive theories of emotion depend on the re-representation of lower order information, they are higher-order in nature. (p. E2023)

This view is not completely reconcilable with the views described above. In particular, Ledoux and Brown's model implies that emotions are always conscious and emerge in General Networks of Cognition rather than at the perceptual level. It also appears to have less flexibility for the kinds of relationality described above. However, emotions trigger schema that shape perception downstream, and the structuring of our active working memory in relation to emotional self-representation plausibly includes some of the same dynamics described above.[22] What the cognitive-emotional schema points to is the possibility of dynamic valuations as essential to cognition. The 'reverberating causality' between perceptual and higher order processes operates within a Bayesian logic of increasingly precise predictions; however, those predictions may need to account for change as well as identification. Through this need, meaningful temporality emerges.

7.11   CONCLUSION

This chapter has considered several models which specify how dynamic relational networks, spatial boundaries, and meaningful temporal structures are shaped by the affective economy of our experiences. Affect is a basis for processes of dynamic valuation at the heart of a model of weak narrativity and can be understood to structure temporality through dynamics regarding relational salience.

These models of affect and emotion offer frameworks for how experience comes pre-structured via factors like arousal, valence, salience, selection, and allostatic set points. From these, we can hypothesize about how valuation processes shape agentive, spatial, and temporal features of 'given' experience into forms that account for meaningful synthesis and coordination of individuated stimuli with synthetic scenes and a coordination of particular experiences with larger executive goals and self-understandings.

That is, when emotion is viewed as a key participant in predictive cognition, valuation dynamics, including those related to stability conditions and anticipated outcomes, structure temporality as we experience the world. This structuring may be described as weakly narrative insofar as prediction draws upon novel or remembered care networks and tracks patterns of value dynamism through them. In this way time is experienced in terms of meaningful concatenations of value-dynamic episodes. However, to understand experience in terms of other characteristics of narrative, we need to consider other elements of basic cognition that make the episodicity of these affective dynamics conscious and meaningful, and which integrate them into higher order reflection.

These examples do not involve a retrospective structuring of experience into particular forms. What's distinctive is that structuring occurs in real time, along with and inseparable from perception, emotion, prediction, and action-orientation. This perspective reflects a modification of previous views of the relationship between emotion and narrative. In proposing an enactivist model, Hutto points to Peter Goldie's view of emotion: as "typically complex, episodic, dynamic and structured" (Goldie 2000, p. 16). Hutto sees an inherent affinity between emotion and narrative:

> Eschewing the object-based schema, on this account, emotions, like acts of perception, are not synchronic occurrences but are extended over time. For this reason, an emotion can constitute part of a narrative—roughly, an unfolding sequence of actions and events, thoughts and feelings, in which

the emotion is embedded. The different elements of the emotion are conceived by us as all being part of the same emotion, in spite of its complex,
episodic and dynamic features. The actions which we do out of an emotion,
and the various ways of expressing an emotion, are part of the same narrative, but are not themselves part of the emotion itself (Goldie 2000, pp. 13,
102). Or, as I would prefer to say, emotions and their consequences have a
kind of structure that is ripe for narration. (Hutto in Menary, p. 17)

Hutto's observation gives emotions roles as components of narrative and
also in the construction of narrative. The inherent meaningfulness of emotions, along with their extension through time, with phases of onset,
extension, and conclusion give emotion structure that fits well into the
meaningful concatenation of 'chunked' experience at the heart of experience, both as parts of narrative and as frameworks upon which narrative
parts are constructed. In other words, the suffusion of affect in experience
provides a baseline of narrative possibility for retrospective construction.

It seems undeniable that emotional experiences are candidates for being
retrospectively turned into narratives. The insights reviewed here from the
empirical literature point to the roles of selection, attention, prior experience, and predictions in valuations that are meaningful, shaped by sociocultural context, and related but not limited to allostatic needs. The
emotion-based case for weak narrativity inverts Goldie's formulation:
rather than emphasizing the narrative structure of emotion, this view envisions emotion, as a form of valuation, as *episode-making*. The final chapter
of the book considers the roles this 'weak narrativity' might play in higher
order cognition, with reference to selfhood and social communication.

Notes

1. Given the pervasive role described in this chapter for value in cognition
   and its relation to emotion, it is worthwhile to consider how the terms are
   deployed and what the various uses of the terms, taken together, might
   entail. First, rather than emotion, we probably are best off speaking of
   affect when we are considering processes immediately engendered by and
   integral to perception. Emotion as typically conceived is more conscious,
   more 'processed,' and more present-to-itself, though the differences
   between the terms can be vague and frustrating. An advantage of using
   affect is that it focuses on empirical literature upon measurable processes.
   Affect is used in psychology, neuroscience, and sometimes in philosophy.
   For humanists, however, this tends to introduce a different set of concerns.

2. This is not an exhaustive survey of Hogan's analysis, which includes larger-scale units, including 'works' and 'genres,' as well as consideration of the narratological concept of discourse, and a variety of other concepts.
3. In Miller 2013 I offered the following summary of Damasio's ideas about emotion and valuation:

> Damasio's belief in the key role emotion plays in cognition is frequently cited in recent literary approaches to consciousness. Damasio views consciousness as a selective, organized system of images constrained by limited "display space" and a "tendency to organize them into coherent narratives" (p. 174). These constraints mark the way in which subjectivity is implicated in the very ordering of the contents of consciousness. The organization of images reflects choices based upon evaluations of positive or negative value choices. As Damasio puts it, "it is about value-stamped selections inserted in a logical frame over time." (p. 72)

> Thus the stream of consciousness is organized for the purpose of securing the well-being of the organism. This is partly the result of the body's role in mediating the representations that enter the mind (p. 91). The brain is intrinsically about the body; that is, it is shaped by an intentional attitude regarding the body (p. 90). Consciousness's primary role is to support homeostasis, or life regulation, through equilibrium states. As such, the "foundations for the processes of consciousness are the unconscious processes in charge of life regulation" and "consciousness is just a late comer to life management." (p. 176)

> Central to Damasio's premise is the idea that notions of value are based on their contributions to healthy and advantageous biological states. It is as the agency mediating biological, then socio-cultural, value that Damasio's central motif, "self comes to mind," occurs. "Self" is the name we give to the "broker," "guardian," and "curator" of value (p. 177, p. 183). It is an evolved capacity, built through coordination of mechanisms for regulating homeostasis at a more primal level.

Damasio's model of self is structured into three tiers that reflect this origin:

> The self is built in distinct steps grounded on the protoself. The first step is the generation of primordial feelings, the elementary feelings of existence that spring spontaneously from the protoself. Next is the core self. The core self is about action—specifically, about a relationship between the organism and the object. The core self unfolds in a sequence of images that describe an object engaging the protoself and modifying that protoself, including its primordial feelings. Finally, there

is the autobiographical self. This self is defined in terms of biographical knowledge pertaining to the past as well as the anticipated future. The multiple images whose ensemble defines a biography generate pulses of core self whose aggregate constitutes an autobiographical self. (pp. 22–3)

Damasio's three-tiered model posits continuity between the functions of the most "primordial" and most abstracted mental operations, around homeostasis. The homeostatic principle applies to symbolic, social equilibria just as it does to "primal" equilibria such as body temperature: "sociocultural homeostasis was added on as a new functional layer of life management, but biological homeostasis remained" (293). Consciousness is itself understandable as an adaptation that "enabled humans to repeat the leitmotif of life regulation by means of a collection of cultural instruments—economic exchange, religious beliefs, social conventions and ethical rules, laws, arts, science, technology" (59). Sociocultural homeostasis emerges from a prereflective dynamic system that continues to shape its dynamics in terms of its contents and temporally.

4. Barrett Feldman offers a strong articulation of this view: "it is very unlikely that perception, cognition, and emotion are localized in dedicated brain systems, with perception triggering emotions that battle with cognition to control behavior" (2017, p. 6). This casts doubt on classical accounts of emotion, which offer a stimulus-response based model of mind.

5. Jerry Fodor's 1983 account of modularity is a touchstone for many of these theorists.

6. Barrett and Mesquita offer a similar view:

the distinction between cognitive activity and emotion experience is probably better conceptualized as more of a gradient rather than two independent systems that can interact with one another. (2007, p. 17)

7. Indeed, Pessoa hopes "to shift the debate away from whether there is a unique subcortical pathway to whether a processing architecture exists that is capable of rapidly transmitting information via multiple pathways" (p. 175).

8. Pessoa proposes that

"highly processed information is important for value representation (see chapter 2) since value may often depend not on superficial sensory properties, but on those showing a fair degree of 'invariance.'" (234). Thus, value involves a top-down form of processing that modulates basic sensory processing. At the same time, value fluctuations are particularly important to subjects—for example, a previously neutral person may become threatening. Thus, "another study reveals that amygdala neurons may help track value moment to moment" (Belova, Paton, and Salzman 2008). (p. 234)

9. For example, a particular property—the creaking sound of an unhinged gateway—might take on particular value if accompanied by the sight of a raging bull charging at you from within its corral. In a social context, an otherwise nondescript looking man in a suit might assume particular salience if it is known that he is the husband of the Prime Minister.

10. Value is not inchoate in features of experience, though it is perceived as such. Valuing is a key part of all models of affect and emotion. Value is assigned via the delineation of and focus upon entities and properties, and value is assigned to entities and properties, often unconsciously. In the case of a stretch of sand at noon on a sunny summer day in Jamaica, the sand is valued as 'burning hot' to one's feet if and only if neural patterns that register pain and activate action responses to it are released. However, that same sand would not register as hot to a glassmaker preparing her materials for the glass-making process. (so, 'burning hot' or 'not hot' is really a contextual and relational value, but it is commonly attributed as a property of the sand itself);

Valuing has cognitive value. That is, affect toward entities and properties plays a role in our reflective cognition, including our capacity for judgment. While this role may intuitively seem like bias, it is nevertheless an important mechanism upon which our rational understandings depend; at the same time, higher order evaluations are not the same as affective valuations.

Valuing produces 'values,' but we need to be precise regarding what constitutes a value. The use of 'value' may be a crutch if it encompasses conscious and unconscious affective activity that shapes and processes incoming sensory data. In much of the literature, psychologists use the notion of 'representation' to describe both the exteroceptive content to which the affect is a response and to describe the affect itself. For humanists, this use of representation is challenging, as it can equally mean ('mimesis') an inner symbolic depiction of events, a libidinal investment that forms feelings, action readiness, and the like, and a synthesis of sensory 'data' and interoceptive and other feelings into a whole. Valuing is meant to convey that what is felt, reflected upon, and remembered is not objective, but instead is highly processed. This view may favor a radical constructivist view, recent versions of which describe perception itself as constructed, in part via affective valuation. Despite this concern, the major models of affect all employ notions that correlate to value.

Value may shape perception, cognition, and the experience of emotion through framing effects (i.e., selection and amplification) as well as through direct value weighting of particular entities and properties. Dynamism in value is important, both individually and relationally. That is, we are attentive not only to the values we assign to particular properties and entities, and we not only select and amplify certain of these for further scrutiny, but our experience involves monitoring for changes in value.

Values, relations between values, value dynamisms, and more complex formations (dynamic relations between value dynamic entities that amplify and mute particular properties of these entities over time, for example) exist and shape the subject's affective/emotional state. There is a synthesis and translation dynamic to account for.

Value is a transductive concept, bridging between pleasure and pain, arousal and intensities, and mentational emotions. How affect and emotion are conjoined and mutually affecting is a baffling, complex question, but one that I will argue finds partial and useful explanations in narrative forms of understanding.

More to the point for the model we'll consider below, 'value' as deployed by Pessoa and other theories of emotion based in the notion of the brain as a prediction machine, is entailed in action plans and deployed as parts of modeling simulations that gauge the nature of experience as part of anticipating how to respond to it and how it will change. In this sense, 'value' contrasts with 'evaluation.'

With such a view of value in place, and with the benefit of the insights into cognitive-emotional interrelatedness we've reviewed, we can tackle the role valuation may play in a predictive processing model that includes emotional cognition, and ultimately that entails weak narrativity.

11. Vanderkerckhove and Panksepp relate anoetic consciousness to the 'stream of consciousness' popularized by William James and to the Freudian unconscious. With regard to the 'stream,' anoetic consciousness provides a 'penumbra,' 'fringe,' or 'psychic overtone' to higher awareness (2009, p. 1019). It is the phenomenological 'going through' of experience.

12. They elaborate:

> The conceptualization of the brain as a 'prediction machine' challenges previous ascription of emotional feelings to cortical representations of viscerosensory afferent information. Instead, there is 'reverberating' causality:
>
> Neural encoding of generative (i.e. top–down) predictions concerning internal bodily state is expressed in drive to the autonomic nervous system (and in endocrine and immune responses). Efferent autonomic responses can thus be viewed as descending 'interoceptive predictions' through their effects on peripheral physiology [3,43,44,45,46]. These are met with ascending interoceptive neural signals that cancel predictions and inform (through prediction errors) a revision of the predicted

state. Autonomic efferents represent means to probe and actively infer the internal state of the body, and both emotions and feelings arise through the interacting representational cascades of ascending prediction errors and descending bodily predictions (autonomic drive). The interoceptive sensing of internal information can thus be built upon higher predictive representations. (Critchley and Garfinkel 2017, p. 12)

13. For Feldman Barrett,

> For a given event, perception follows (and is dependent on) action, not the other way around … Predictions are concepts … Completed predictions are categorizations that maintain physiological regulation, guide action and construct perception. The meaning of a sensory event includes visceromotor and motor action plans to deal with that event. (Barrett 2017, pp. 6–7)

14. In Seth's model, "emotional content is generated by active 'top-down' inference of the causes of interoceptive signals in a predictive coding context" (p. 565).

15. Note that value may be produced via an 'original value' and a 'context-dependent' revaluation:

> connections between the basolateral (BL) complex of the amygdala, which indelibly codes the original value of a stimulus (Bouton 2005), the central and lateral aspects of the OFC, which is necessary to a flexible, experience or context-dependent representation of an object's value (Elliott et al. 2000, Kringelbach 2005, Kringelbach & Rolls 2004, Morris & Dolan 2004), and the anterior insula, which is involved in representing interoceptive cues (Craig 2002, 2003; Dunkley et al. 2005; Wiens 2005). Both the BL and lateral OFC have robust connections with cortical representations of every sensory modality and have strong reciprocal connections (Ghashghaei & Barbas 2002, Kringelbach & Rolls 2004, McDonald 1998, Stefanacci & Amaral 2002), so that they form a functional circuit that integrates sensory (including somatovisceral) information. This information is needed to establish (at least initially) a value-based representation of an object that includes both external sensory features of the object along with its impact on the homeostatic state of the body. One recent formulation argues that the BL complex formulates the predictive value of a stimulus, whereas the OFC participates in generating a response based on that prediction (Holland & Gallagher 2004). (Duncan and Barrett, p. 4)

16. "Pleasure and displeasure are not only mental contents that can be consciously experienced, but also are regulatory factors that play a broader role in selecting the contents of consciousness" (Barrett, Mesquita, p. 16).

17. Barrett et al. (2007) write:

> an "attentional matrix" (Mesulam 2000) within the brain foregrounds particular contents of consciousness (whether core affect and/or beliefs about core affect) by modulating the intensity of neural firing in coalitions of neurons. This attentional matrix includes not only the core affect–driven bottom-up form of attention (supported by the brainstem and basal forebrain; Edelman & Tononi 2000, Parvizi & Damasio 2001), but also a top-down form of attention (supported by dorsolateral prefrontal, anterior cingulate, and parietal cortices) that is entrained by sensory stimulation of sufficient intensity or driven by an individual's processing goals (Crick & Koch 2004, Dehaene & Changeux 2004, Maia & Cleeremans 2005, Naghavi & Nyberg 2005). Whatever the mix of attentional factors, each person has one seamless flow of experience

> that is continually changing and can be more or less infused with some sort of affective content, depending on the focus of attention. (p. 17)

18. Barrett et al. (2007) write: Continuously through time, the brain is processing and integrating sensory information from the world, somatovisceral information from the body, and prior knowledge about objects and situations to produce an affective state that is bound to a particular situational meaning, as well as a disposition to act in a particular way. As a result, core affective feelings and construals of the psychological situation very likely are perceptually categorized and experienced as a single unified percept, much like color, depth, and shape are experienced together in object perception. Building on this percept, a mental representation of emotion may be an example of what Edelman (1989) calls "the remembered present". (p. 14)

19. Barrett et al. (2007) write: "The central idea is that a mental representation of emotion on a particular occasion is a continuously changing stream of consciousness in which core affect continuously evolves, interacts with, and mutually constrains construals of the psychological situation" (p. 13).

20. This affect could be modulated by social schema as well. For example, if you are in a cultural location where men frequently hold hands to signify friendship, rather than sexual or romantic attachment, the affect attending this observation would be quite different.

21. If narrative processing describes how predictions depend on dynamic concatenations of semantically rich and variable sequences delineated by agentive relationality, self-reference, (and other factors), then narrative processing might be ongoing.

If narrative processing is ongoing, then perhaps it manifests in different ways situationally. For example, in a semantically rich, dynamic situation, narrative processing might attend first and foremost to presence. However, when present situation is semantically rich, but not agentively rich (as when one is doing an intellectually challenging non-narrative task like writing an essay alone), narrative processing may be suppressed. When the present is not semantically rich and/or dynamic (i.e., lack of arousal and neutral/nondynamical valence), the Default Mode Network (DMN) is recruited.

We associate the DMN with higher order goal-directed processing, as well as fantasy, daydreaming, and the like. I find these, as thus presented, difficult to reconcile, and certainly we'll learn to think of the DMN truly as a network of interrelated processes rather than as a 'closed circuit.' But what if the DMN's coherence is linked to narrative processing? That is, what if goal-directed processing and fantasy aren't so different, because goal-directed processing takes on narrative forms (what will happen when, how that will refigure my status or the status of x) and fantasy is narrativization of goals and fears.

In this model, the DMN clicks on when present demands for narrative processing are low. So, vacillations in demand for narrative processing help explain changes in modalities of cognition.

22. This view has linkages to Attention Schema Theory, the notion of 'For-Me-ness,' and other higher order binding problems, covered in the next chapter.

REFERENCES

Bakker, I., van der Voordt, T., Vink, P., & de Boon, J. (2014). Pleasure, Arousal, Dominance: Mehrabian and Russell revisited. *Current Psychology*, *33*(3), 405–421. https://doi.org/10.1007/s12144-014-9219-4.

Bar, M. (2007). The proactive brain: Using analogies and associations to generate predictions. *Trends in Cognitive Sciences*, *11*(7), 280–289. https://doi.org/10.1016/j.tics.2007.05.005

Bar M. The proactive brain: memory for predictions. Philos Trans R Soc Lond B Biol Sci. 2009 May 12;364(1521):1235–43. https://doi.org/10.1098/rstb.2008.0310. PMID: 19528004; PMCID: PMC2666710.

Barrett, L. F. & Mesquita, B. The Unconscious Mind. Perspect Psychol Sci. 2007 Jan;   3(1):73–9.   https://doi.org/10.1111/j.1745-6916.2008.00064.x. PMID: 18584056; PMCID: PMC2440575.

Barrett, L. F. (2016). The theory of constructed emotion: An active inference account of interoception and categorization. *Social Cognitive and Affective Neuroscience*, nsw154. https://doi.org/10.1093/scan/nsw154.

Barrett, L. F. (2017). *How Emotions Are Made: The Secret Life of the Brain.* Houghton Mifflin Harcourt.

Barrett, L. F., Mesquita, B., Ochsner, K. N., & Gross, J. J. (2007). The Experience of Emotion. *Annual Review of Psychology, 58*(1), 373–403. https://doi.org/10.1146/annurev.psych.58.110405.085709.

Barrett LF, Bar M. See it with feeling: affective predictions during object perception. Philos Trans R Soc Lond B Biol Sci. 2009 May 12;364(1521):1325–34. https://doi.org/10.1098/rstb.2008.0312. PMID: 19528014; PMCID: PMC2666711.

Bower, G. H. (1983). Affect and cognition. *Philosophical Transactions of the Royal Society of London. B, Biological Sciences, 302*(1110), 387–402.

Brown, S., Gao, X., Tisdelle, L., Eickhoff, S. B., & Liotti, M. (2011). Naturalizing aesthetics: *Brain areas for aesthetic appraisal across sensory modalities. NeuroImage, 58*(1), 250–258. https://doi.org/10.1016/j.neuroimage.2011.06.012

Citron, F. M. M., Gray, M. A., Critchley, H. D., Weekes, B. S., & Ferstl, E. C. (2014). Emotional valence and arousal affect reading in an interactive way: Neuroimaging evidence for an approach-withdrawal framework. *Neuropsychologia, 56*, 79–89. https://doi.org/10.1016/j.neuropsychologia.2014.01.002.

Critchley, H. D., & Garfinkel, S. N. (2017). Interoception and emotion. *Current Opinion in Psychology, 17*, 7–14. https://doi.org/10.1016/j.copsyc.2017.04.020.

Cromwell, H. C., & Panksepp, J. (2011). Rethinking the cognitive revolution from a neural perspective: How overuse/misuse of the term 'cognition' and the neglect of affective controls in behavioral neuroscience could be delaying progress in understanding the BrainMind. *Neuroscience & Biobehavioral Reviews, 35*(9), 2026–2035. https://doi.org/10.1016/j.neubiorev.2011.02.008.

Damasio, A. R. (1996). The somatic marker hypothesis and the possible functions of the prefrontal cortex. *Philosophical Transactions of the Royal Society of London. Series B: Biological Sciences, 351*(1346), 1413–1420.

De Sousa, R. (1990). *The rationality of emotion.* MIT Press.

De Sousa, R. (2006). Against Emotional Modularity. *Canadian Journal of Philosophy, 36*(sup 1), 29–50. https://doi.org/10.1353/cjp.2007.0034.

Duncan S, Barrett LF. Affect is a form of cognition: A neurobiological analysis. Cogn Emot. 2007 Sep;21(6):1184–1211. https://doi.org/10.1080/02699930701437931. PMID: 18509504; PMCID: PMC2396787.

Ellsworth, P. C., & Scherer, K. R. (n.d.). Appraisal processes in emotion. In *Handbook of affective sciences, 572,* V595.

Faucher, L., & Tappolet, C. (2007). Introduction: Modularity and the Nature of Emotions. *Canadian Journal of Philosophy.*

Forgas, J. P. (2001). The Affect Infusion Model (AIM): An integrative theory of mood effects on cognition and judgments. In L. L. Martin & G. L. Clore (Eds.), *Theories of mood and cognition: A user's guidebook* (pp. 99–134). Lawrence Erlbaum Associates Publishers.

Forgas, J. P. (2008). Affect and cognition. *Perspectives on Psychological Science, 3*(2), 94–101.

Gallivan JP, Bowman NA, Chapman CS, Wolpert DM, Flanagan JR. The sequential encoding of competing action goals involves dynamic restructuring of motor plans in working memory. J Neurophysiol. 2016 Jun 1;115(6):3113–22. https://doi.org/10.1152/jn.00951.2015. Epub 2016 Mar 30. PMID: 27030738; PMCID: PMC4946594.

Goldberg, M. E., Bisley, J. W., Powell, K. D., & Gottlieb, J. (2006). Saccades, salience and attention: the role of the lateral intraparietal area in visual behavior. *Progress in Brain Research, 155*, 157–175.

Goldie, Peter (2000). The Emotions: A Philosophical Exploration. Oxford, GB: Oxford University Press.

Hogan, P. C. (1997). Literary Universals. *Poetics Today, 18*(2), 223–249. JSTOR. https://doi.org/10.2307/1773433.

Hogan, P. C. (2011). *Affective Narratology: The Emotional Structure of Stories.* University of Nebraska Press.

Jones, K. (2006). Quick and Smart? Modularity and the Pro-Emotion Consensus. Canadian Journal of Philosophy, 36(sup1), 2–27. https://doi.org/10.1353/cjp.2007.0031

LeDoux, J. E., & Brown, R. (2017). A higher-order theory of emotional consciousness. *Proceedings of the National Academy of Sciences, 114*(10), E2016–E2025. https://doi.org/10.1073/pnas.1619316114.

Mesquita, B., & Leu, J. (2007). The cultural psychology of emotion. In S. Kitayama & D. Cohen (Eds.), Handbook of cultural psychology (pp. 734–759). The Guilford Press.

Parvizi, J. (2009). Corticocentric myopia: Old bias in new cognitive sciences. *Trends in Cognitive Sciences, 13*(8), 354–359. https://doi.org/10.1016/j.tics.2009.04.008

Pessoa, L. (2008). On the relationship between emotion and cognition. *Nature Reviews Neuroscience, 9*(2), 148–158. https://doi.org/10.1038/nrn2317.

Pessoa, L. (2013). *The cognitive-emotional brain: From interactions to integration.* The MIT Press.

Power, M. & Dalegleish, T. (1997). Cognition and Emotion: From Order to Disorder. England: The Psychology Press.

Prinz, J. J. (2004). *Gut Reactions: A Perceptual Theory of Emotion.* Oxford University Press.

Prinz, J. J. (2006). Is Emotion a Form of Perception? *Canadian Journal of Philosophy, 36*(sup1), 137–160. https://doi.org/10.1353/cjp.2007.0035.

Robinson, M. D., & Clore, G. L. (2002). Episodic and semantic knowledge in emotional self-report: Evidence for two judgment processes. *Journal of Personality and Social Psychology, 83*(1), 198–215. https://doi.org/10.1037//0022-3514.83.1.198.

Roesch, M., Calu, D., et. al. Neural Correlates of Variations in Event Processing during Learning in Basolateral Amygdala Journal of Neuroscience 17 February 2010, 30 (7) 2464–2471; https://doi.org/10.1523/JNEUROSCI.5781-09.2010

Saxe, R., & Houlihan, S. D. (2017). Formalizing emotion concepts within a Bayesian model of theory of mind. *Current Opinion in Psychology, 17*, 15–21. https://doi.org/10.1016/j.copsyc.2017.04.019

Scherer, K. R. Emotions are emergent processes: they require a dynamic computational architecture. Philos Trans R Soc Lond B Biol Sci. 2009 Dec 12;364(1535):3459–74. https://doi.org/10.1098/rstb.2009.0141. PMID: 19884141; PMCID: PMC2781886.

Seth, A. K. (2013). Interoceptive inference, emotion, and the embodied self. *Trends in Cognitive Sciences, 17*(11), 565–573. https://doi.org/10.1016/j.tics.2013.09.007.

Seth, A. K., & Critchley, H. D. (2013). Extending predictive processing to the body: Emotion as interoceptive inference. *Behavioral and Brain Sciences, 36*(03), 227–228. https://doi.org/10.1017/S0140525X12002270.

Seth, A. K., Suzuki, K., & Critchley, H. D. (2012). An Interoceptive Predictive Coding Model of Conscious Presence. *Frontiers in Psychology, 2*. https://doi.org/10.3389/fpsyg.2011.00395.

Sternberg, M. "Universals of Narrative and Their Cognitivist Fortunes (I)." *Poetics Today* 24.2 (2003): 297–395.

Tappolet, C. (2000). *Emotions et valeurs* (1re éd). Presses universitaires de France.

Vandekerckhove, M., & Panksepp, J. (2009). The flow of anoetic to noetic and autonoetic consciousness: *A vision of unknowing (anoetic) and knowing (noetic) consciousness in the remembrance of things past and imagined futures. Consciousness and Cognition, 18*(4), 1018–1028. https://doi.org/10.1016/j.concog.2009.08.002

Vandekerckhove, M., Bulnes, L. C., & Panksepp, J. (2014). The Emergence of Primary Anoetic Consciousness in Episodic Memory. Frontiers in Behavioral Neuroscience, 7. https://doi.org/10.3389/fnbeh.2013.00210

Velleman, J. D. (2003). Narrative Explanation. *The Philosophical Review, 112*(1), 1–25. JSTOR. www.jstor.org/stable/3595560.

Velleman, J.D. *Self to Self: Selected Essays.* 1. publ, Cambridge Univ. Press, 2006.

CHAPTER 8

Narrativity in Higher Order Cognition

Previous chapters have argued for a form of narrative processing to supplement research describing the role of narrative in personal identity, communication, and larger sociocultural networks. Narrative processing is ongoing meaning-directed generation and processing of emergent temporal structures consisting of related value-dynamic sequences involving value-dynamic selected agents, mediated by socio-cultural contexts. Low level narrative processing gives the phenomenology of some experiences a weakly narrative character, and it stimulates and is shaped by further cognitive processing. The previous two chapters made the case for weak narrativity in affect and cognition, locating narrativity in realms of cognitive processing far different from the autobiographical, social, and textual forms of narrative that have dominated discussions. Weak narrativity emerges via the combination of bottom-up and top-down processes in a 'reverberating causality' (see Chap. 7, Sect. 7.6).

This final chapter considers 'higher order' cognitive processes that (top-down) imbue experiences with elements of weak narrativity, and higher order qualities of experience which are shaped (bottom-up) by the weakly narrative qualities of our experiences. Higher order qualities include an ongoing sense of continuity, the deployment of knowledge garnered from prior experiences to make sense of present experiences, learning from present experiences, selfhood, autobiographical memory, and social cognition.

© The Author(s), under exclusive license to Springer Nature
Switzerland AG 2023
B. Miller, *Narrativity in Cognition*,
https://doi.org/10.1007/978-3-031-40349-1_8

This chapter thus shares with 'small story' research in discourse studies and work in narrative hermeneutics a view of narrative as an iterative, provisional, ongoing form of processing that continuously frames experiences within sociocultural values while imprinting sociocultural values into perception, reflection, and discourse (see Meretoja 2018; de Fina and Georgakopoulou 2011; Bamberg 2012; Brockmeier and Meretoja 2014; Georgakopoulou 2007). As Meretoja writes, "we are constituted through a continuous process of reinterpretation [that] ... rarely—if ever—leads to a single life story ... [but instead] emphasizes the processuality and performativity of narrative interpretation ... 'narrative' should be understood less as a noun than as an activity" (2022, pp. 280–1).

The emphasis here, on how weak narrativity emerges in individual cognition, complements the social, interactive generation and circulation of narratives studied in discourse studies. To complete the portrait of the manifold through which seemingly individual cognitive processes generate narrativity, this chapter emphasizes higher order cognitive functions that give individuals a sense of unity and continuity through time.

Some researchers acknowledge a role for narrativity in cognition. For example, Hassabis and Maguire (2007), in the chart reproduced below, define narrative as one of nine component processes implicated in a variety of cognitive functions (Fig. 8.1).

The isolation of narrative as a discrete process ("a story structure formed by the unfolding of a sequence of events") differs significantly from the more pervasive model of dynamic and relational valuing and temporal marking I've described as weak narrativity, and which is

Table I. Mapping of component processes to cognitive functions[a]

	Scene construction	Subjective time	Self	Autonoetic consciousness	Narrative	Familiarity	Visual imagery	Prospective planning	Task monitoring
Episodic memory recall	Y	Y	Y	Y	Y	Y	Y	N	Y
Episodic future thinking	Y	Y	Y	Y	Y	Y	Y	Y	Y
Navigation	Y	N	D	N	N	D	Y	Y	Y
Imagination	Y	N	N	N	D	D	Y	N	Y
Default network	Y	N	Y	D	D	D	D	N	U
Viewer replay	Y	N	N	N	Y	Y	Y	N	Y
Vivid dreaming	Y	N	D	N	Y	D	Y	N	U
Theory of mind	D	N	Y	N	N	D	D	D	D

Abbreviations: Y, yes – process is involved in that cognitive function; N, no – process is not involved in that cognitive function; D, depends – process involvement depends on the precise nature of the task and the content operated on; U, unknown – unclear if process is involved in that cognitive function.
[a]Processes are labelled along the top and cognitive functions down the left hand side.

Fig. 8.1 Mapping of component processes to cognitive functions (rpt. from Hassabis and Maguire 2007)

implicated in many of the other component processes. This grouping of processes points, in particular, to problems around unity (scene construction), intentionality (prospective planning), and self (subjective time, self, familiarity, autonoetic consciousness) that provide a bridge between weak, unreflective narrativity and the highly narrative reflections of autobiographical memory and selfhood.

8.1   UNITY

To explore connections between weak narrativity and more reflective cognitive functions, we'll begin with considering how weak narrativity might contribute to the phenomenology of our conscious experiences of ourselves. Part of the argument for weak narrativity is that it helps explain the narrative features we associate with experiences when we recall or report them.

These features include temporal boundaries set by patterns of equilibrium-disequilibrium-equilibrium, peak and end/fact experiences, spatial and agentive boundaries set by relational valuations, and sequential bindings driven by relations (typically causal) but heavily mediated by context (see Chaps. 6 and 7). Emergent narrativity is provisional and fragmentary, rather than closed form and formulaic.

In this model valuation is crucial and contingent upon a variety of experiences and knowledges. It is indistinguishable from perception and emotion, and it is derived in part from the subject's goals. That is, emergent narrativity seems to be part of the subject's grasping of experience as it unfolds, and it is part of the 'seeming' of experiences. This condition points to the implication of narrative processing in some key features of consciousness that might appear to have nothing to do with narrativity: phenomenality, unity, and selfhood.

Regarding phenomenal, subjective experience, the affective, embodied valuations characterized in theories reviewed in earlier chapters have parts to play as explanans in robust explanations. That is, the mysterious causes and mechanisms of "what it's like" to experience are linked to the phenomenology of weak narrativity insofar as it is grounded in emotion and prediction. The working through of these forms of processing is not a matter of abstracted calculation performed by a disembodied homunculus but is rather a visceral going through of experience with necessarily phenomenal properties. Dynamic, relational valuing is a form of knowing integral to experiencing. Because of valuation's affective, ecological, and predictive character, the 'what' of phenomenological features of experience might be considered from this perspective: How might the subjective peculiarities of an experience be related to a view of knowing that entails unfolding, dynamic, affective, relational valuing and predictive processing?

When the phenomenal aspect of consciousness is conceived in this manner, the nature of unity and selfhood appear to be driven by these processing features. The apparent unity of consciousness provides a vexing problem for scientists who recognize the distributed nature of cognitive processes. Unity, according to Tim Bayne's 2010 model, reflects the 'mereological' (i.e., part to whole) nature of any particular experience as a conscious state subsumed by the larger phenomenal state of the subject. That is, unity is a phenomenal feature of consciousness that results from the seamless switching between different processing faculties in the brain, and as such reflects only part of experience at any given moment.

On the view advanced here, the unity of consciousness is deeply related to ongoing dynamic valuation processes. Because these processes are relational and dynamic, unity is experienced as part of the synthetic operations that dominate attention. But it is intuitively possible that multiple, competing valuation processes can be ongoing simultaneously, as when one attends to present events while, 'in the back of one's mind,' as the phrase goes, one simulates and evaluates a past or anticipated event. Several theories of cognitive processes are conducive with this perspective. For example, Global Workspace Theory (see Chap. 5, Sect. 5.1) describes ongoing parallel distributed processing at a sub-personal level as well as conscious experience dominated by global broadcasting of whatever is presently most salient.

In a related view, Attention Schema Theory (see Chap. 6, Sect. 6.2) describes awareness as a partial model of our attention. In this view, the unity of consciousness reflects the salience-based apportionment of attention. We are endowed with limited capacity for attending, and the experience of phenomenal unity is similar to current descriptions of the unity of the visual field. In vision, the visual field includes space surrounding the focal area. Partial unity comes from this consistent structure. Moreover, visual unity is produced by saccades which assist in filling out the sense of a unified visual field, and the field is filled in via internal cognitive processes (rather than with additional perceptual data). This permits an experience of visual unity without an overload of perceptual data, and it allows the synthesis of data to occur in conjunction with construction.

Phenomenal unity is an especially challenging problem because it is multimodal and streaming. That is, the fact that experience feels unified seems contradictory to the different sensory inputs we receive and the changeability of these inputs through time. The 'seeming' of conscious experience is particularistic and an irreducible combination of qualities associated with vision, hearing, proprioception, internal reflection, and other factors. However, if the lesson of cognitive-emotional and predictive processing is that experience is constructed in part from valuation, then phenomenal unity is created by dynamics of attentional selection as the subject makes sense of the most salient valuation dynamic confronting the subject.

Moreover, if we think of attention as a means of amplifying or specifying valuation as well as being intrinsically related to salience (i.e., if attention is a limited resource most likely devoted to tracking salient value dynamisms for maximizing predictive efficacy), then the phenomenology of the subject's experiences is structured by the various types of valuation (see Chaps. 6 and 7) associated with the emotional, predictive, and embodied processes of cognition.

Within this model, the temporal extension produced by ongoing prediction is partly constitutive of unity. That is, a sense of unity is produced out of the modeling and parsing that accounts for and predicts change, limiting the salient agents and objects synthesized in any particular instant in the phenomenal field. Predictive modeling is not a discrete analytic process like the core sampling used by scientists to study various materials. Rather, it suffuses the unfolding of present time and *is* part of the experience.

That is, while prediction error minimization applies to object recognition, it also applies to change. Expected change confirms models of experience, while unexpected change challenges those models and stimulates additional processing to render the change coherent. So, the error minimization process of predictive modeling operates not outside of time, but while time and experience are unfolding, and therefore manifests as predictions about past, present, and future simultaneously. As the research on event segmentation demonstrates (see Chap. 6, Sect. 6.4), this dynamic coherence is not unstructured: contingent, meaningful temporal strands emerge in our experiences. In other words, the emergent temporal structures of narrative processing. The transitions between these strands, then, involve reorientation that feels part of experiential unity.

Also, phenomenal unity is likely correlated to affective tone. The constituents of a seemingly unified general affective tone differ from one another. On the one hand, emotional mood shapes the subject's affective posture toward a particular situation, and vice versa. On the other hand, the valuation of constituents of experience and their relations are both contributors to and shaped by affective tone.

These co-relations suggest a key aspect of how the meaningfulness associated with some temporal extension emerges: perceptual experiences and self-experiences are overlapping. In fact, individual valuations are synthesized into, and are shaped by, their relation to the experiencing subject.

8.2   FOR-ME-NESS

The models of cognition reviewed in earlier chapters—the predictive processing model (PPM), the cognitive-emotional model, and the embodied model—are characterized by dynamic valuation, which entails self-referential elements. In the case of the PPM, the experiencing is characterized by a 'making familiar or unfamiliar' of features of experience. In the case of the cognitive-emotional model, it involves hedonic feelings such as threat (at the charging attacker) or anticipated pleasure (at the arrival of an inviting plate of food at a favorite restaurant). It also involves more complex feelings derived from longer term evaluations of particulars or types manifested in experience and from socially and personally oriented schema. Finally, the embodied cognitive framework builds upon the notion of experience as an ecology of affordances—that is, what is experienced is determined by potential actions of the subject on its various affordances.

In each case, the phenomenology involves how valuation foregrounds a relation between features of experience and the subject, between some 'not-me' and 'me.' These self-oriented phenomenal properties of valuation are described in philosophy of mind in terms of 'for-me-ness.' Dan Zahavi and Uriah Kriegel, originators of this term, claim that "all conscious states' phenomenal character involves for-me-ness as an experiential constituent" (Zahavi and Kriegel 2015, p. 37). Zahavi and Kriegel do not view 'for-me-ness' as "a self-standing quale" (p. 38). This is due to its nature: "for-me-ness is not in the first instance an aspect of *what* is experienced but of *how* it is experienced; not an object of experience, but a constitutive manner of experiencing" (p. 38). Zahavi and Kriegel contrast their position to the views of Jesse Prinz and Fred Dretske, who differently point to the way experience is always *about* something and that the phenomenology of experience entails either a form of introspection (Dretske) or simply the quale presented to the subject (Prinz). Prinz believes "we always experience the world from a perspective or point of view" (p. 38), but sees this as a metaphysical fact, rather than as phenomenological (p. 39).

The view of a phenomenology of valuation advanced here seems to correspond partly to Zahavi and Kriegel's view of a 'manner' or 'how' of experiencing. Whereas they argue that "there is lemon-taste-for-me-ness, mint-smell-for-me-ness, and many other types of phenomenal character," the view advanced here sees valuation as intrinsic to, rather than a supplement of, perception (p. 38). However, this difference might involve the subject's ability to maintain some consciousness of the signatures of her own experiential historical and current context in ongoing valuation of the utility, valence, and familiarity of elements of experience.

The nexus of valuation and for-me-ness from a narrative processing perspective bears upon the experience of having a perspective. Perspective is at the heart of why some theorists have viewed narrative as essential to experience (see Chap. 2, Sect. 2.3 and Chap. 3, Sects. 3.3 and 3.4) and to our complex capacity for Theory of Mind. Yet the emergence of perspective can be located in basic cognitive processes.

8.3   SELF-SPECIFICATION AND THE MINIMAL SELF

A number of studies shed light on how basic cognitive operations produce a minimal experience of self that forms the basis of a hierarchical model of selfhood. Christoff et al. (2011) describe reafferent-efferent circuits (including sensorimotor integration, homeostatic processes, and cognitive control, including emotion regulation) that "specify the self as a bodily agent," specifically by continually producing the distinction between self and not-self (p. 105). As opposed to common views that self-feelings are suppressed during focus-intensive tasks, they hypothesize that self-specification is integral to experience: "such tasks can be expected to enhance the self-experience of being a cognitive–affective agent" (p. 109). Indeed, agency is phenomenologically experienced within the faculties of attention and self-regulation demanded by such tasks:

> the self-experience of being an emotional agent that these processes elicit would occur at the level of affect and action tendencies [26], whereas this bodily level would be subsumed by the self-experience of being a cognitive–affective agent in deliberate emotion regulation, analogous to the way the self-experience of being a cognitive agent also subsumes the self-experience of being an embodied agent in attention-demanding cognitive tasks. (p. 110)

Affect is integral to self-specification. While Christoff et al.'s model describes how affect generates the experience of a self-agent, other research notes that emotional attitudes toward memories mark the designation of self-and not-self:

> during the recall of field (first person perspective) memories [researchers found] ... a higher degree of subjective emotionality, (sic) associated with those memories in comparison to those that are retrieved from a third person ("theatrical" or "disembodied" perspective (Northoff et al. 2006). This argument echoes previous suggestions that 'the boundary between self and not-self is one's emotional attitude about an object or thought' (Barressi, 2002, qtd. in Northoff et al. 2006, p. 453). (Markowitsch and Stanilou 2011, p. 21)

These dynamics are closely related to theories that describe an inchoate self, a pre-reflective self-awareness, an illusion produced at the center of narrative gravity, a virtual selfhood, and finally a minimal selfhood.

The persistence of pre-reflective self-awareness through time constitutes a disposition toward continuity basic to the organism's interface with the world, and productive of a primal self-image. In structuring experience into meaningful episodes, the subject simultaneously generates a world oriented around a perspectival center. This creates a learning mechanism that helps the subject establish relative dispositional advantages toward types of situations.

The emergence of this self-reflective mechanism consolidates self-specification into a nascent sense of self. In this model, the emergent self is caught between pre-reflective self-awareness and self-objectification. In addition, the sense of self is subject to multiple temporalities, including an experience of the present that includes memory and anticipation, episodic and situationally based dispositions, and ultimately cumulative self-valuations that amount to an emergent autobiographical self-understanding. Each of these temporalities is subject to configuration and the reciprocal influence of other temporal "levels." As a result, self-image is both continuity-oriented and highly iterative.

Embodied cognition also points to the role of temporally unfolding experiences in fostering an emergent sense of selfhood. Evan Thompson argues for two sources of a sense of continuity: our complex time sense and a pre-reflective form of self-consciousness. Pre-reflective self-awareness can be simply described as the continuous feeling of experiencing. Thompson refers to Dan Zahavi's description of this feature of consciousness as simultaneously static and dynamic: "pre-reflective self-awareness is streaming because it is constitutive of the streaming or flowing experiences themselves, not a pure and empty awareness that appears on its own. By the same token, it is standing because it is an ever-present and unchanging feature of consciousness" (2007, p. 328). The persistence of the flow of experience, in other words, marks our presence to ourselves. This aware-ness provides a fundamental sense of continuity through time, even though it is not a repository of the characteristics of self. Rather, it is the perspective around which experience is organized. Thompson notes Naomi Eilan's similar model of "perspectival awareness" in terms of this implication: "such awareness is not yet 'the capacity for detached reflec-tion on oneself' that develops along with language and conceptual think-ing, but it is enough to suggest a kind of ladder or continuum between bodily interaction with the world and developed reflectivity" (p. 20).

Other philosophers and psychologists describe the link between self-specification and selfhood in terms of illusions generated during ordinary cognitive processes. In Daniel Dennett's view, we mistake a feature of processing in consciousness as a substance. The self is "a center of narra-tive gravity," or as Susan Schneider puts it, "a kind of program that has a persistent narrative" (Dennett 1992, p. 416; Schneider 2007). Thomas Metzinger also describes the emergence of self from a feature of con-sciousness processing but based upon an embodied model. In his meta-phor of the "ego tunnel," Metzinger argues that conscious experience is "a low-dimensional projection of the inconceivably richer physical reality surrounding and sustaining us … Therefore, the ongoing process of con-scious experience is not so much an image of reality as a tunnel through reality" (2010, p. 6). This "tunnel" reflects the transparent operation of what Metzinger terms the "phenomenal self model" (PSM)–the notion that we have a virtual model of ourselves as whole. The content of the PSM is the Ego: "the Ego is a transparent mental image: You—the physi-cal person as a whole—look right through it. You do not see it. But you see with it" (2010, p. 8).

Timothy Bayne locates the self as a "'phenomenal fiction' generated by the self-representational field." He offers a

quasi-realist view of the self, according to which the self is a merely virtual entity brought into being by the *de se* structure of the phenomenal field. This view, which I dub 'virtual phenomenalism', ensures an essential con-nection between the subject of experience and the unity of consciousness: because the subject of experience is nothing but a 'phenomenal fiction' generated by the self-representational structure of the phenomenal field, there is an *a priori* guarantee that any experiences that a subject has at a given time will be phenomenally unified with each other. (2010, p. 2)

These frameworks position narrativity as an effect of continuity processes, rather than viewing continuity as in part generated by iterative, emergent weak narrativity. It is possible that the relationship is mutually constitutive: low level narrative processing contributes to a dynamic architecture of experiential flows that generate continuity experiences and resolve in higher order narrative processing. Minimal selfhood has been explicitly linked to our capacity to view our experiences as narrative. Like Hutto and Thompson, Richard Menary insists that the 'minimal self' is an embodied subject and agent. As described earlier (Chap. 3, Sect. 3.2), this embodied self is pre-narrative: "our embodied experiences, perceptions, and actions are all prior to the narrative sense of self, indeed our narratives are structured by the sequence of embodied experiences" (p. 75).

Menary sees these experiences "taken up into inner dialogue," which brings a new component of self into being—the discursively based narrator—which "emerges in terms of narratives as anchored in the pre-narrative sequence of experiences of an embodied subject" (p. 79). For Menary, the interposition of a discourse-based narrator is key to explaining the "intersubjective" nature of selfhood. He sees inner speech as key to generating self-awareness, and self, and discredits the idea that self is "an independent substance with intrinsic properties or a fictional object" (p. 79).

In these contrasting models of minimal selfhood, self is a fiction generated either from the ordinary operations of cognition or from its processing in inner speech. In both cases, self emerges in relation to narrative structures. If minimal selfhood is dependent upon weak narrativity or the narrative form of inner speech, and if these are influenced by and shapers of more abstracted, extended, and consciously wrought narrativity usually thought of as higher order capacities, then other recognized forms of selfhood may be grounded in narrativity.

8.4   Informational Sources of Valuations, Predictions, and Simulations

In the push-pull of integrated top-down/bottom-up processing, previously learned information shapes perception in a variety of ways. In turn, experiences produce new learning. How this information is processed provides a crucial linkage between the immediate, largely sub-personal experiences of perception and self-specification and the reflective, autono-etic experiences associated with autobiographical rumination and delibera-tion. How are the concepts and values that manifest in both forms of experience related and shared?

This is a profound and much debated question, and it is complicated by differences between particularistic and generalized information and ques-tions about how they co-exist and mutually shape one another. Understanding these relations is particularly challenging for the temporal features of events, which clearly draw upon generalized, conceptual infor-mation for sensemaking, but also manifest as particular, time-stamped and phenomenologically rich structures of experience. The previous two chap-ters considered how events emerge via our attentiveness to emergent dynamic, relational salience networks. Here the top-down processes that shape (and are shaped by) these dynamics are considered in more detail.

A number of intermediate structures that mediate these functions have been proposed, including frames, scripts, stories, situation models, schema, and connectionist networks (see McRae et al. (2019, p. 3)). Schemas have been subject to considerable empirical investigation, so in this section we'll review this research before considering connectionist views. According to Ghosh and Gilboa,

> Schemas are general, higher level constructs that encompass representations of the similarities or commonalities across events, rather than the specificity that makes those events unique" (p. 106). Schemas are not, however, simple networks of related concepts. Instead, they "bind multiple features that con-sistently co-occur," are hierarchically composed of sub-schemas, include chronological relationships (Schank and Abelson), and may include action plans. (Gilboa Marlatte 2017, p. 618; Ghosh, p. 109) (p. 106)

Schemas develop and evolve via interaction with new information. In the diagram below, Ghosh and Gilboa describe how episodes create a schema and, subsequently, how a new episode leads to an adapted schema (Fig. 8.2):

Note that within Ghosh and Gilboa's figure the episodes that contrib-ute to the schema differ in three key ways: first, the number of nodes changes (in episode 1, a new node is added); second, the associative con-nections between nodes change (not all individual episodes feature con-nections between all and the same nodes, and the episodes differ in terms of the strength of connections between nodes); finally, the values of par-ticular nodes change, indicating the necessary flexibility for associative connections to be made across nodes.

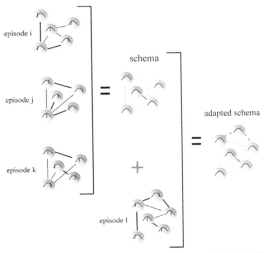

Fig. 8.2 Necessary features of scheme structure (rpt. from Ghosh and Gilboa 2014)

Fig. Necessary features of schema structure. Gray networks in the figure represent the schema as a latent neurocognitive structure of strongly interconnected nodes that could potentially be re-activated together. Colourful networks are either novel episodes or specific instantiations of the schema during a particular context of experience. The schema's *associative network structure (feature 1)* is depicted through circles, which represent schema units, and lines connecting those circles, which represent their associations. Differences in line connections and thickness indicate variability across episodes. The schema's *basis on multiple episodes (feature 2)* is illustrated through episodes i-k. Each episode differs in specificity, but all conform to the same general structure, which can be extracted as the schema. The schema's *lack of unit detail (feature 3)* is indicated by the normal distribution curve within each schema unit, which has the potential to take different values. For specific episodes or schema instantiations i-k, each unit takes a particular value on that curve. Lastly, the schema's *adaptability (feature 4)* is indicated by the inclusion of new information from episode l as green dotted lines in the adapted schema.

Schemas operate as "templates against which new information can be compared" (Ghosh and Gilboa p. 106). This may facilitate the predictive processes involved in perception. Perceptual processing with schemas likely operates through analogical recognition (what is something like, rather than exhaustive analysis of the input's properties) which activates associative networks. Bar proposes that these networks "presensitize representations of what is most likely to occur and be encountered next" (Bar 2011, p. 14). Moreover, these activated associative networks determine a "mindset," which is "a sustained (though updatable) list of needs, goals, desires, predictions, content-sensitive conventions and attitudes" (Bar 2011, p. 19). Bar provides the example of how predictive processing might engage associative networks as the subject recognizes the driver's seat of a car. The "analogies→associations→predictions" circuit activates processes that recognize other parts of a car, as well as the activity of driving.

While in this example object recognition leads to more object recognition and to action readiness, Bar notes that the model needs to account for greater temporal complexity, including "complex scenarios involving simulations and multiple elements" (p. 22). Bar's schema, in other words, "integrate[] representations from different points in time" in the cause of simulating an anticipated event, but it does not adequately explain how they are integrated (p. 23). In addition, schema models can struggle to explain how simulations can involve detailed particulars rather than general conceptions (as in the unweighted nodes in Ghosh and Gilboa's diagram). Because Bar's theory is linked to predictive processing, the stakes for explaining the origins of simulations is high, as it proves fundamental to some of the higher order cognitive processes considered later in this chapter.

One variant of schema theory addresses these temporal issues by positing the proliferation of 'schema instances,' or active copies of schemas into assemblages that integrate representations of an episode through time (Arbib 2020). In this model, schematic representations of experiences retain links to particular details. Arbib links schematic processing to the cognitive processes involved in navigation, which require maintenance of links to environmental particulars in structured temporal representations.

However, connectionist researchers offer persistent criticisms of schema theories: "the need to select among a pre-specified set of alternative structure types forces semantic representation into an ill-fitting procrustean bed" (McClelland, pp. 8–9). Connectionist models argue that "conceptual knowledge can emerge from a constrained learning process, without prior domain-specific knowledge and without requiring pre-specification of possible knowledge structures or selection among them" (p. 8). The connectionist approach focuses on the weightings between particulars as sources of identification and learning. In this sense, it seems more conducive to the view of valuation considered in the dimensional model of emotion (see Chap. 7).

One difference between schema accounts and connectionist accounts involves how they explain temporal structure. Whereas schema accounts include chronological relationships in the field of represented nodes, in connectionist accounts temporal structure is described as "an emergent property of a computational system that implicitly represents ... time in its processing" (McRae Brown Elman, p. 215). This view is compatible with the argument for emergent temporality in event processing in Chap. 6, in which valuation dynamism structures time. However, it should be stressed that such forms of temporal emergence do not preclude their *post hoc* representation.

The connectionist critique of schema theory raises additional questions around the relation of schema (which are dynamic, but general) to several forms of fixed, but specific information structures: narratives, event gists, and episodic memories. Recent research supports the idea that "a given experience may have multiple representations, each advantageous in a different scenario" (i.e., in different forms of cognitive processing) (Schlichting et al. 2015, p. 7). Gilboa and Marlatte propose a regular process of splitting of detailed 'gist' extraction and schematization of experiences (Fig. 8.3):

Gists are abstracted elements of narrative. Ghosh and Gilboa, citing Moscovitch, define gists as 'high-level story elements that are central and critical to the overall plot'; they 'contain multiple units and their interrelationships,' and 'refer to a specific event … not based on multiple episodes' (p. 110). Ghosh and Gilboa's definition, drawn from Thorndyke, contrasts gists with unimportant story details.

Narratives, in this model, are:

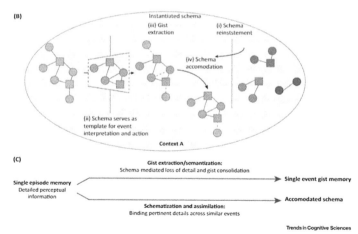

Figure 1. Hypothetical Functional Neuroanatomical Model of Memory Schemas. (A) Memory schemas are coactivated long-term representations in the posterior neocortex [e.g., retrosplenial cortex (RSPL), middle temporal gyrus (MTG)/superior temporal sulcus (STS), anterior temporal lobe (ATL), temporoparietal junction (TPJ)]

Fig. 8.3 Hypothetical Functional Neuroanatomical Model of Memory Schemas (rpt. from Gilboa Marlatte, p. 620; note: a brain diagram at the top of this figure is not included)

series of actions and events that unfold over time, according to causal principles. As such, to be considered a narrative, both an associative network structure and chronological organization are necessary. Unlike schemas, however, in which units are lacking in detail, narratives are specific in that each unit, or event, occurs in a particular way. Similarly, narratives are fixed, rather than adaptable. Further distinguishing them from schemas, narratives can be encoded in an episode, rather than being composed of commonalities extracted from multiple episodes. (Ghosh Gilboa, p. 110)

In this definition, narratives embody the complexity schemas fail to encompass via particulars. As the previous chapter considered, the organization of particulars into meaningful, rememberable structures depends on a variety of factors, including temporal structures emerging from patterns of dynamic, relational valuation. Schema that facilitate an understanding of complex events and that foster effective predictive simulations may be organized around processing patterns rather than the analogy-> association->prediction circuit. That is, we process experience into chunked event structures via schema that create boundary definitions at crucial break points (such as, as mentioned above, equilibrium-disequilibrium-equilibrium patterns, or action-fact structures).

Narratives depend deeply upon schematic network elements. For example, in Elman and McRae's connectionist figuration of event processing network architecture, perception is attuned to 'Agents, Actions, Patients, Instruments, Contexts, and Recipients,' providing evidence of the selection and sequencing processing based on relational, dynamic valuation that figures into event definition (see Chap. 6). I speculate further that these general schematic categories have either situation-specific variants or embedded subschema that attune the subject to experiencing certain situations in terms of weak narrativity.

To summarize, current research on schema, while underdeveloped regarding the relation between schemas and narratives, suggests the following: narratives are schema-dependent, emergent in experiential processing, component to gist processing, and refined in memory processes.

Gists appear to be vital to another function which is vexing for schema theory: processing ill-defined problems via scenario simulation. In "ill-defined problems," there is "no specific script or solution path that can be applied" (Sheldon et al. 2011, p. 2). For ill-defined, or "open-ended" problems, because there's no solution to store semantically, "it [is] likely that solutions to such problems…rely on an event simulation strategy" (p. 2). Sheldon and colleagues cite findings (reviewed in Chap. 6) that episodic memory is used to imagine future events to hypothesize that episodic memory processes are implicated in solving ill-defined problems (*ibid.*, 8), particularly because of the flexibility and "relational binding" capabilities of episodic memory. The mechanisms that initiate and perform these simulations are speculative but might include analogical processing at the beginning to identify similar problems from the past, the associated solutions to which would provide material from which solution simulations might be built (p. 8). Beatty, Morgan, and Wise emphasize that narrative simulations of 'counterfactual' events and structured around outcomes help reveal the contingency (and therefore meaning) of actual events. Additionally, problem-solving via simulation works by creating a phenomenology of feeling associated with particular scenarios, allowing us to 'pre-feel' possible experiences (Schacter et al. 2015).

Event simulation requires that subjects conceive of an outcome derived from beginning and ending value conditions of selected actors. Presumably, the repertoire of potential value conditions has certain primitives (including conditions of power in relation to the perceiving subject—see Chap. 7, Sect. 7.9) as well as culturally mediated conditions available in schema for these agents. The outcomes, too, may have primitives and schema ready for analogical processing. However, the processing of their dynamism and relationality (and the dynamics of their relations) requires a capacity for complex time-extended imagining: the ability to coordinate multiple agents and contextual factors into a meaningful sequence, resulting in an event (or chain of events). For a more detailed argument, (see Chap. 6).

The phenomenology associated with simulation (as a 'pre-feeling' of possible experiences) reflects how valuation involves a primitive concatenation of affective, embodied, and anticipatory value elements. Gists derive from high salience elements in the experiential field. Refining these elements into gists after experience must involve some selection and binding of these values via associative linkages to other experiences and schema. That is, gists are complexes of valuative elements—rather than simple unvalued particulars—with deep links to the outcome structures of narratives, and which are refined via (and which in turn contribute to) schemas or connectionist networks. More simply put, particulars from our experiences have emergent meanings that shape our general understanding while aligning our memories into flexible narrative patterns. Our reflective experiences of self and others necessarily bear the traces of gists in the schema we bring to bear on experience and the narrative processing we employ to recollect and anticipate it.

8.5   SELF, EPISODIC AUTOBIOGRAPHICAL MEMORY, AND SOCIAL COGNITION

Having considered how intermediary processing might involve narrative features, we will now turn to how weakly narrative cognition might interact with more strongly narrative aspects of selfhood, consciousness, and social cognition.

In "Narrative Modes of Consciousness and Selfhood" Keith Oatley synthesizes different approaches to narrative and selfhood. He proposes that people possess "narrative consciousness" in the form of a "unified narrative agent" (p. 378). He "explore[s] [following David Velleman] the idea of a conscious, unified self, based on functional properties of narrative" (p. 380). Oatley's views resonate with ideas traced earlier in this and other chapters. Specifically, narrative qualities, including action plans based upon goals and intentions, emotions as forms of self-feedback, and coherence based upon meaning are critical to the emergence of a central organizing agency, a self (pp. 383–4). These qualities, moreover, permit communication of our own mental states with others, enabling us to receive and process like communications, and to formulate theories of others' states of mind and self while unconsciously, and sometimes consciously, refining our own (pp. 385–6). Thus, we construct a self analogously to a novelist constructing a character, but "improvising as we go along" (p. 386). This self is "embodied ... [and] accomplishes things in the world and interacts with others whom we assume are constituted in a way that is much like our self" (p. 386).

Oatley views selfhood in terms of a multiplicity of both 'low-level' processes and higher order personal and social processes. First, consciousness has four aspects: "simple awareness, the stream of inner consciousness, conscious thought as it may affect decisions and actions, [and] consciousness of self-with-other" (p. 377). These aspects roughly anticipate the sections that follow. Second, Oatley proposes multiple roles for emotions: as a "primary form of Helmholzian consciousness, ... [as] frames or scripts for inter-individual relationships, ... [as] caused by disruptions of action or expectancy" and as the basis, when combined with language, for "social cognition … based on narrative-like simulations" (p. 390). Third, narrative capacities are developmental. Finally, 'modern narratizing consciousness' is the product of historical changes in human interaction wrought by economic, political, and technological developments. Overall, Oatley's claims are grounded in the narrative quality of simulation.

In the previous section and the previous two chapters, we considered how more recent research into 'low-level' and intermediary processes might contribute to a sense of weak narrativity in experience. Recent work on episodic autobiographical memory (EAM) has shed some light on the possible relations between various notions of selfhood while illuminating mechanisms by which narrative structures form, circulate, and interact with semantic knowledge. The next section reviews some of this research before considering the development of narrative capacities in childhood and the role of narrative in folk psychology.

8.6   SELFHOODS AND EPISODIC AUTOBIOGRAPHICAL MEMORY

How might recent research into memory inform theories about the narrativity of self? Markowitsch and Stanilou (2011) review the many different notions of self described in cognitive research: "narrative self," "self as containing conceptual knowledge of one's own personality traits," "self as… agent," "core self," "proto-self," and "feeling self" (p. 24). Amid this multiplicity, they seem to agree with Northoff's et al. (2006) assessment that it is unclear whether these are relevant only within specific cognitive functions (including memory) or whether there can be a unified theory of self. Several authors they cite (Feinberg and Keenan 2005; Panksepp 1998; Damasio 1999; Gallagher 2000) offer hierarchical notions of nested forms of self.

Autobiographical memory serves selfhood in its global forms—supporting a sense of personal identity within (and in relation to) social groups and the values and experiences that bind them. Autobiographical memory contributes to the time-extended, contextually complex idea of an ever-developing 'life story.'

The relation between episodic memory and autobiographical memory, then, is crucial to understanding how weak narrativity in general experience and reflective notions of narrative selfhood might be linked. Yet autobiographical memory is connected to semantic processes that also seem fundamental to selfhood. Martin Conway (2005) describe 'autobiograph-ical knowledge' as distinctive from episodic memories (p. 589).

Autobiographical knowledge consists of context-free "conceptual, generic, and schematic knowledge about one's life" (p. 589). By contrast, episodic memories are 'experience-near' "psychological or cognitive sum-maries of experience ... derive[d] from mental models of 'online' experi-ence configured in ... the episodic buffer" (p. 589). According to this model, autobiographical knowledge manifests in a hierarchy capped by "overarching lifetime periods or themes" with an intermediate level of "repeated categories of events (i.e., every Thanksgiving) or temporally extended events (e.g., a picnic or vacation)" (Holland and Kensinger 2010, p. 4).

At the bottom of this hierarchy, autobiographical memories provide episodic referents for autobiographical knowledge. Among episodic mem-ories, autobiographical memories are reinforced and retained because of their relevance to autobiographical knowledge and goals, as well as because of their emotional nature: "When we are cued to retrieve an autobio-graphical memory, we begin our search at the intermediate, general level and then move to retrieving more specific information" (p. 4). Autobiographical memory retrieval is *reconstructive.*

Thus, autobiographical functions are distributed along a three-tiered hierarchy of autobiographical knowledge, intermediate knowledge, and autobiographical memories. The structure of these processes provides some indication of the nature of our 'life stories.' Global and intermediate level "personal narratives" are by their nature dynamic, incorporating par-ticularly important events—especially emotional events—through "enhanced rehearsal" (p. 19). Life narratives are continuously subject to reconstruction and supplementation, particularly in relation to "interme-diate level" understandings, though sometimes via particularly impactful "flashbulb memories."

This model is reminiscent of some of the issues we considered regard-ing the interaction of schema with perceptual data in event processing. (see Chap. 6). Yet here, the transition between recollected events and self-schema is mediated, and indeed conducted, by salient types of events, extended events, and particularly impactful individual events. In other words, memory reconstruction is initiated from knowledge of past experi-ences that, whether cumulatively or because of their extension or salience, have been preserved as more abstract summaries likely characterized by strong valuations. As discussed earlier (see Chaps. 6 and 7), the "whats" of events are refined in the course of relational weighting and temporal bounding, processes that draw upon valuations of various kinds (affordances, peak-end and equilibrium-disequilibrium-equilibrium patterns, identification and familiarity, etc.). Thus, this intermediate-level knowledge includes valuative elements. Valuation also characterizes autobiographical knowledge in which overarching themes and time periods reflect a sense of one's present relation to the past, and particularly to who one was in the past.

This is a key source of our commonsense notion of selfhood: rather than being a fixed substance, it is the ongoing self-evaluative processing by the subject of the self in present experiences in relation to past experiences, and vice versa.

This dynamism is partly due to the dynamism of a subject's immediate, intermediate-term, and long-term goals. Which goals have priority, particularly regarding attentional resources, provides a key index of self which the subject can introspect. These goals, as well as judgments about past and future likelihood of achieving them, are crucial, and not necessarily implicated in narrative processing. In addition, these self-generated self-valuations are (obviously) socially mediated. By considering one's own goals and achievement in relation to others', one calibrates one's own self-valuations.

Again, these forms of autobiographical knowledge about the self are not necessarily produced narratively. Yet, it is worthwhile to distinguish them from a commonsense understanding of traits. Whereas traits are propositional, goal-based valuations are temporal. As a result, the latter envisions selfhood in terms of ongoing comparison of the present to the past. Present experiences, in other words, contribute to self-evaluation in terms of relative valuations of current self-states versus self-states in past similar experiences. This modifies other metrics of self-valuation. To give a simple example, if one is a slow and messy knitter in relation to one's knitting group, this negative valuation may be attentuated by comparing one's current knitting achievements to past achievements. Of course, self-valuation also occurs in terms of present self-states in relation to projected future self-states. So one's present knitting accomplishment might, for example, be devalued if one is continuously fantasizing about future knitting accomplishments after attending a pricey knitting seminar. In both of these forms of temporal comparison inchoate narratives may support self-valuation (in the first example, a positive self-valuation based upon progress; in the second example, a complex self-valuation that diminishes self-value in the present but in anticipation of a future higher self-valuation).

Such time-extended self-valuation provides a useful feedback loop which enables the subject to modulate behavior, especially in social contexts. Yet comparative valuation also powerfully feeds into ideas about self. For example, if one makes a joke at a work event that is met with snubs, one may draw conclusions about the appropriate behavior expected at this and like functions and moderate one's comportment accordingly. Yet if one finds a co-worker then successfully making jokes, one's self-valuation, either globally or regarding one's status in this social milieu, may change (i.e., in this example, one reflects 'maybe the response is not a result of the context; rather, it's about my ability to be funny'). The point is partly that self-valuation shapes how we encounter experiences at (perhaps unobserved) set levels. These are revealed when experiences provide feedback that leads us to modulate them. In this way a nascent sense of self-consciousness emerges.

Time-extended, relationally-sensitive self-valuation is thus component to experiences of selfhood. Autobiographical knowledge of the features of the self can be flexible. Rather than offering a fixed set of traits around which autobiographical narratives are shaped, our selves are embedded in small life stories that can be contingent, iterative, and malleable.

This source of malleability requires some rethinking of approaches to narrative identity. When we consider models of the narrative self which posit narrative construction as an essential activity for generating meaning and coherence, we find, in contrast to much of the established research, that narrative construction is in part facilitated by the self-valuations emerging from the weakly narrative nature of experience. Most models do not recognize this feature, but rather attend to another important feature of narrativity—how high-level narratives or narrator functions shape immediate experiences.

Some theories, such as Rubin et al. (2003), hold that narrative both plays an important role in autobiographical memory and can be non-linguistic. For this view, narrative processing might play an important role in connecting various processing "levels" of consciousness. For example, consider the model of "flows across multiple levels of consciousness" Markowitsch and Stanilou attribute to Davies (1996), among others:

> multiple levels of consciousness and unconsciousness, in an ongoing state of interactive articulation as past experience infuses the present and present

> experience evokes state-dependent memories of formative interactive pre-
> sentations. Not an onion, which must be carefully peeled, or an archaeologi-
> cal site to be meticulously unearthed and reconstructed in its original form,
> but a child's kaleidoscope in which each glance through the pinhole of a
> moment in time provides a unique view...: determined by way of infinite
> pathways of interconnectedness. (p. 197)

As the discussion of event segmentation (Chap. 6), episodic memory
(Chap. 5, Sect. 5.2 and Chap. 6, Sect. 6.5), and the intersections of episodic and autobiographical memory have emphasized, however, the
"moment in time" view of these images is reductive. Bounded temporal
extensions, segmented into basic 'chunks' of experience, subject to revision and rehearsal, are emergent 'primitives' of our experiences for which
Davis, Markowitsch, and Stanilou's "infinite pathways of interconnected-
ness" must account. The position I've argued is that, rather than temporal
markers becoming simply semantic facts incorporated into schema (though
they are likely processed in this manner), they are inextricably shaped by
the cognitive-emotional and relational forms of valuation that allow for
the priming and prediction of subsequent experiences.

Such a view requires that EAM, and particularly the ability to mentally
time travel, not be dependent on language. According to Markowitsch
and Stanilou, although "language and mental time travel might have co-
evolved,... mental time traveling might have been rooted in a form of
embodied cognition" (p. 26).

Narrative may have another relation to episodic memories as well.
Milivojevic, Varadinov et al. (2016) hypothesize that

> narratives may provide a general context, unrestricted by space and time,
> which can be used to organize episodic memories into networks of related
> events. However, it is not clear how narrative contexts are represented in the
> brain. Here, we test the novel hypothesis that the formation of narrative-
> based contextual representation in humans relies on the same hippocampal
> mechanisms that enable formation of spatiotemporal contexts in rodents.
> (p. 12412)

So it is possible that the "higher order" organization of episodic memories
draws on the same processing mechanisms involved in event
segmentation.

As we continue to revise our understanding of how the hippocampal
region facilitates future simulation, predictive processing, and affective

cognition, we may clarify how narrative processing occurs, and perhaps develop a novel taxonomy of types of interrelated forms of narrative processing distinguished by the role intention, iteration and rehearsal, language, and experience nearness and distance play in forms of cognition we have described.

The model of (higher order) narrative I am proposing, then, is an iterative processing logic that draws upon and informs weak narrativity in experience. Strong narrativity may emerge in various forms in relation to this processing and may involve processes of narrative rehearsal that shape particular accounts of episodes and larger 'stories' of experience mutually.

Theories of memory, self, and narrative development in childhood provide some support for this idea. In the model of the emergence of autobiographical memory offered by Nelson and Fivush, "narrative structure and content" develops around ages 3–5, after the establishment of a "core self" and in feedback with the emergence of increasingly autonomous temporal concepts, complex language concepts, self-representation, and theory of mind. It co-develops roughly with the establishment of episodic memory and overlaps with the establishment of autobiographical memory.[1]

So, if the ability to form episodic memories is related to the emergence of a theoretical weak narrativity in experience, then these malleable narrative forms help drive autobiographical self-understanding.

One key area of interest for researchers that involves "higher order" cognition is how narratives operate in social cognition. This chapter concludes by considering how narrative processing might be crucial to an essential way we navigate the social world: through "theory of mind."

8.7   Social Cognition and Narrative

Hasson, Furman et al. (2008) note a deep correlation between brain regions involved in social cognition and episodic memory formation for narratives.[2] Viewing narrative as a practice for making inferences about targeted social agents' beliefs, motivations and values is part of a debate over the workings of folk psychology. In a review of this debate, Hutto and McGivern (who advocate a narrative processing account of theory of mind) contrast "theory theory" with their narrative practice hypothesis (NPH). "Theory theory" involves having a general set of ideas about mind and its exterior signs providing the basis for our folk psychology, whereas the narrative practice hypothesis postulates that the consumption and creation of narratives provide this basis. Folk psychology, in the NPH, involves a simulation of experience from the perspective of another in a narrative logic, which enables *ad hoc* particulars, situations, and contexts to be combined into meaningful form. For Hutto and McGivern, "theory theory" struggles to explain how its general principles are practically realized in particulars.

Standard "theory theory" is propositional. However, Hutto and McGivern review a version promoted by Maibom (2009) as "model theory," in which the centrality of practice (that is, realization in particulars) is recognized (Hutto and McGivern, rpt. from Maibom (p. 361)). "Model theory" evokes definitional concerns about narrative as a "thing" or a form of practice: "this massively softer way of construing theory theory," Maibom (2009) argues, "accounts *not just as well as, but better than*, narrativity theory for the fact that our folk psychological explanations appear to contain, or form part of, narratives" (Maibom 2009, p. 361, emphasis added). Model theory, then, points to how narrative forms can emerge from diverse forms of practice which themselves deploy models that render a narrative character in experience. That is, instead of narrativity deriving entirely from consumed, artifactual narratives or consciously created narratives, narrativity inheres in or emerges from the sensemaking process.

This view fits well with Dewhurst's (2017) speculation that if we adopt a predictive processing framework we'll need to develop "a hybrid theory that includes elements of both theory-theory and simulation theory," which might include "narratives and social norms," including folk psychological narratives operating "as a form of cognitive scaffolding" (p. 9). Thus, Dewhurst does not see folk psychology as impossible to "reconcile with predictive processing," though he believes we need a "novel conceptual taxonomy that more accurately reflects the structure of cognition and allows us to move beyond the limitations of folk psychological discourse" (p. 11).

In the previous two chapters, some perceptions driven by affective, relational, and dynamic valuations with emergent temporal boundaries are characterized by "weak narrativity." This model constitutes one attempt to add to our conceptual repertoire.[3] If the simulation processes characteristic of predictive processing depend upon weak narrativity (see Chap. 6), then perhaps the capacity to simulate another's mindset has related origins (see Hutto and McGivern; also Stueber 2012).

The limitation of this view, according to Hutto and McGivern (citing Medina 2013; Moran 1994), is that simulation theory lacks the 'hot' character of the phenomenology of happening characteristic of theory of mind.

For Hutto and McGivern, traditional accounts of "narrative understanding" and "simulation" lack the feeling of being viscerally moved—that is, the feeling of active engagement. Citing Medina, they argue that "what drives our hot narrative engagements is neither self-projective simulation, nor simulating or pretending to believe a set of propositions; rather, 'the central difference between emotionally engaged and emotionally disengaged imagination has to do with the mode of imagining, not with its content'". Hutto and McGivern's point resonates with research by Hassabis and Maguire that scene construction, rather than self-projection, links episodic memory with "other cognitive functions such as episodic future thinking, navigation, and theory of mind" (2016, p. 299).

Drawing upon conventional elements of literary narrative, Medina believes "mode of imaging" determines the "hot" character of theory of mind. I'm not convinced this is sustainable—instead, I believe these resources ("figuration, allusion, rhythm, repetition, assonance, and dissonance") in the arts create a 'hot' character in artistic artifacts (including the visual arts and music) that simulates the (generally) more weakly hot character of our experiences. Rather, as Hutto and McGivern seem to suggest, this hot character is in large part wrought by the enactive and other valuative elements of both real-time and imagined experiences.

One way of explaining this is to consider what sensitivities are developed through long experience with processing narratives: "by developing our narrative understanding through [consuming narratives] ... we become sensitive to a variety of possible perspectives that may be adopted on events, including—especially—cognitive, emotional, and evaluative perspectives that may diverge from our own" (n.p.).

Of course, our apprehension of another's "perspective" via narrative involves a complex synthesis of overt characterization (whether from a narrator's, the character's, or another's perspective) and inferences about the principles, sense of self or self-narrative, 'hot' nature (or phenomenology), and priors that inform particular reactions to particular events. In other words, even in the consumption of artifactual narratives, perspective involves a great deal of inferential reasoning about the interior dynamics of another that result in particular and—if the inference is successful—relatively predictable valuations of experience. In this, as in the discussions of episodic memory and schema, as well as the discussion of self, this involves modeling that helps predict patterns of valuation.

In Theory of Mind, then, we seek to understand the valuative predilections that comprise the givenness of experience for another. As many theorists have noted, TOM provides a ready means of social learning that helps us contextualize, evaluate, and revalue our own values. It is crucial to self-reflection.

In engaging in this inferential process in non-narrative contexts, particularly banal social experiences, we may in part experience it as a set of propositions that make up our understanding of another. For example, note the valuative aspects of the following: "Tom does not like cats, and he is a fan of avant-garde jazz and expensive wine." We might develop more abstract ideas about the other's character from these facts—Tom is a 'highbrow' and maybe a snob—from which we might create, associatively, speculative propositions ("Tom probably only dates highly educated people"). We may also develop a set of causally related insights: "Tom has allergies, and maybe this explains why he doesn't like cats." Yet as a model of Tom, this is sterile, "cool" stuff.

However, if we evaluate Tom narratively (instead of propositionally)— "he flirted with but ultimately snubbed my friend Kelly" or "he confessed that he grew up impoverished in a house with alcoholic parents and more than 20 cats," then our engagement may become warmer—we may have visions of Tom's life that connect to our understanding of Tom in the present day.

Tom's supposed propositional characteristics are now placed into relational, real-time valuative contexts. And in this form, we may be more likely to simulate Tom's experiences or an encounter with him. In other words, processing what we learn about Tom's experiences and actions in narrative terms engages our emotional faculties and leads to a greater sense of engaging his perspective. This cues our future responses to him, though our understanding is subject to alteration via new knowledge, experiences, or exposure to other people's perspectives on him. Theory of mind is greatly enhanced by 'hot' weakly narrative simulation.

Theory of mind reflects social processes that may happen automatically, but have an important link to highly reflective forms of narrative that provide a form of explanation that uses contingent particulars to explain the nature of events and the actors that produce them. We reviewed how the logic of narrative affords explanation of heterogenous elements in a variety of disciplines in Chap. 2. As John Beatty memorably puts the matter, "Narratives tell us, and sometimes in a manner that not only represents the world but makes sense of it, by leading us from the contingent past to outcomes that are contingent upon their past" (p. 41).

This chapter has considered multiple ways narrative might play a role in a variety of forms of "higher order" cognitive processing. Viewing narrative from a processing perspective, based upon dynamic valuations, allows us to speculate about a more or less vital role for narrative in our experiences, our identities, and our social intuitions.

NOTES

1. Note, though, that complex language representation and narrative structure and content are reciprocally influential. The theory I'm advancing is not that language does not support narrative representation. However, it remains necessary to account for how complex language facility shapes capacities for narrative structure and content.
2. They note that "given that much of what we encounter and value on a daily basis is fundamentally social, these findings highlight the important role that social cognitive processes play in episodic memory formation" (p. 458).
3. There are others. For example, Lisa Quadt's notion of Embodied Social Inference sees embodied cognition as crucial to social cognition.

REFERENCES

Arbib, M. A. (2020). From spatial navigation via visual construction to episodic memory and imagination. *Biological Cybernetics, 114*(2), 139–167. https://doi.org/10.1007/s00422-020-00829-7

Bamberg, M. G. W. (1997). *Positioning Between Structure and Performance.* 5.

Bamberg, M. & Georgakopoulou, A. (2008). Small stories as a new perspective in narrative and identity analysis, *28*(3), 377–396. https://doi.org/10.1515/TEXT.2008.018.

Bamberg, M. (2012). Narrative analysis. In H. Cooper, P. M. Camic, D. L. Long, A. T. Panter, D. Rindskopf, & K. J. Sher (Eds.), *APA handbook of research methods in psychology, Vol. 2. Research designs: Quantitative, qualitative, neuropsychological, and biological* (pp. 85–102). American Psychological Association. https://doi.org/10.1037/13620-006.

Bar, M. (2007). The proactive brain: Using analogies and associations to generate predictions. *Trends in Cognitive Sciences, 11*(7), 280–289. https://doi.org/10.1016/j.tics.2007.05.005.

Bar, M. (2011). The proactive brain. *Predictions in the brain: Using our past to generate a future,* 13–26.

Bayne, T. (2010). *The unity of consciousness.* New York: Oxford University Press.

Bayne, T., Hohwy, J., & Owen, A. M. (2016). Are There Levels of Consciousness? *Trends in Cognitive Sciences, 20*(6), 405–413. https://doi.org/10.1016/j. tics.2016.03.009.

Beatty, J. (2017). Narrative possibility and narrative explanation. *Studies in History and Philosophy of Science Part A, 62,* 31–41. https://doi.org/10.1016/j. shpsa.2017.03.001.

Brockmeier, J., & Meretoja, H. (2014). Understanding narrative hermeneutics. *Storyworlds: A Journal of Narrative Studies, 6*(2), 1–27.

Christoff K, Cosmelli D, Legrand D, Thompson E. Specifying the self for cognitive neuroscience. Trends Cogn Sci. 2011 Mar; 15(3):104–12. https://doi. org/10.1016/j.tics.2011.01.001. Epub 2011 Feb 1. PMID: 21288760.

Conway, M. A. (2005). Memory and the self. *Journal of Memory and Language,* 53(4), 594–628.

Damasio, A. (1999). The Feeling of What Happens: Body and Emotion in the Making of Consciousness. Harcourt College Publishers.

Davies, J. M. (1996). Linking the "pre-analytic" with the postclassical: Integration, dissociation, and the multiplicity of unconscious process. *Contemporary Psychoanalysis, 32*(4), 553–576.

Davis, J. B. (2009). Identity and Individual Economic Agents: A Narrative Approach. *Review of Social Economy, 67*(1), 71–94. https://doi. org/10.2307/41288440.

Dennett, D. C. (1992). The self as a center of narrative gravity. In F. Kessel, P. Cole, & D. Johnson (Eds.), *Self and Consciousness: Multiple Perspectives.* Hillsdale, NJ: Erlbaum. *Philosophia, 15,* 275–288, 1986.

De Fina, A., & Georgakopoulou, A. (2011). *Analyzing Narrative: Discourse and Sociolinguistic Perspectives.* Cambridge: Cambridge University Press. https:// doi.org/10.1017/CBO9781139051255.

Dewhurst, J. (2017). Folk Psychology and the Bayesian Brain. In T. Metzinger & W. Wiese (Eds.), *Philosophy and Predictive Processing.* Frankfurt am Main: MIND Group.

Eilan, N. "Consciousness, self-consciousness and communication." *Reading Merleau-Ponty.* Routledge, 2007. 130–150.

Elman, J. L., & McRae, K. (2019). A model of event knowledge. *Psychological Review, 126*(2), 252–291. https://doi.org/10.1037/rev0000133

Feinberg, T. E., & Keenan, J. P. (2005). Where in the brain is the self?. *Consciousness and cognition, 14*(4), 661–678.

Fivush, R., & K. Nelson. "Culture and Language in the Emergence of Autobiographical Memory." *Psychological Science,* vol. 15, no. 9, Sept. 2004, pp. 573–77. *Crossref,* https://doi.org/10.1111/j.0956-7976.2004.00722.x.

Gallagher, S. (2000). Philosophical conceptions of the self: Implications for cognitive science. *Trends in Cognitive Sciences, 4*(1), 14–21.

Georgakopoulou, A. (2007). Small Stories, Interaction and Identities. https://doi.org/10.1075/sin.8.

Ghosh, V. E., & Gilboa, A. (2014). What is a memory schema? A historical perspective on current neuroscience literature. *Neuropsychologia, 53,* 104–114. https://doi.org/10.1016/j.neuropsychologia.2013.11.010.

Gilboa, A., & Marlatte, H. (2017). Neurobiology of Schemas and Schema-Mediated Memory. *Trends in Cognitive Sciences, 21*(8), 618–631. https://doi.org/10.1016/j.tics.2017.04.013.

Hassabis, D., & Maguire, E. A. (2007). Deconstructing episodic memory with construction. *Trends in Cognitive Sciences, 11*(7), 299–306. https://doi.org/10.1016/j.tics.2007.05.001

Hasson, U., Furman, O., Clark, D., Dudai, Y., & Davachi, L. (2008). Enhanced Intersubjective Correlations during Movie Viewing Correlate with Successful Episodic Encoding. *Neuron, 57*(3), 452–462. https://doi.org/10.1016/j.neuron.2007.12.009.

Holland, A. C., & Kensinger, E. A. (2010). Emotion and autobiographical memory. *Physics of Life Reviews, 7*(1), 88–131. https://doi.org/10.1016/j.plrev.2010.01.006.

Hutto, D., McGivern, P. Updating the Story of Mental Time Travel: Narrating and Engaging with Our Possible Pasts and Futures. Altshuler, R., & Sigrist, M.J. (Eds.). (2016). Time and the Philosophy of Action (1st ed.). Routledge. https://doi.org/10.4324/9781315819303.

Kriegel, U. (2014). *The sources of intentionality.* Oxford University Press.

Kriegel, U. (2016). Précis of The Varieties of Consciousness. *Rivista Internazionale Di Filosofia e Psicologia,* 240–246. https://doi.org/10.4453/rifp.2016.0023.

Maibom, H. 2009. In defence of (model) theory. *Journal of Consciousness Studies.* 16: 6–8. pp. 360–378.

Markowitsch, H. J., & Stanilou, A. (2011). Memory, autonoetic consciousness, and the self. *Consciousness and Cognition, 20*(1), 16–39. https://doi.org/10.1016/j.concog.2010.09.005.

Medina, J. 2013. "An enactivist approach to the imagination: embodied enactments and fictional emotions." 50(3): 317–335.

Meretoja, H. (2013). Philosophical underpinnings of the narrative turn in theory and fiction. *The Travelling Concepts of Narrative,* 93–117.

Meretoja, H. (2018). The ethics of storytelling. Oxford: Oxford University Press.

Meretoja, H. (2022). Life and narrative. *The Routledge Companion to Narrative Theory,* 273–285. https://doi.org/10.4324/9781003100157-26.

Milivojevic, B. et al. "Coding of Event Nodes and Narrative Context in the Hippocampus." *The Journal of Neuroscience,* vol. 36, no. 49, Dec. 2016, pp. 12412–24. *Crossref,* https://doi.org/10.1523/JNEUROSCI.2889-15.2016.

McRae, K., Brown, K. S., & Elman, J. L. (2019). Prediction-Based Learning and Processing of Event Knowledge. *Topics in Cognitive Science*, tops.12482. https://doi.org/10.1111/tops.12482.

Menary, R. (2014). *Cognitive integration: Mind and cognition unbounded.* Palgrave Macmillan.

Menary, R. (2008). Embodied Narratives. *Journal of Consciousness Studies*, *15*(6), 63–84.

Menary, R. (2010). Introduction to the special issue on 4E cognition. *Phenomenology and the Cognitive Sciences*, *9*(4), 459–463. https://doi.org/10.1007/s11097-010-9187-6.

Menary, R. (2013). Cognitive integration, enculturated cognition and the socially extended mind. *Cognitive Systems Research*, *25–26*, 26–34. https://doi.org/10.1016/j.cogsys.2013.05.002.

Metzinger, T. (2009). *The ego tunnel: The science of the mind and the myth of the self.* Basic Books (AZ).

Metzinger, T. (2010). The self-model theory of subjectivity: A brief summary with examples. *Humana Mente—Quarterly Journal of Philosophy*, *14*, 25–53.

Metzinger, T., & Wiese, W. (n.d.). *Philosophy and Predictive Processing.* 453.

Moran, R. (1994, January). The expression of feeling in imagination. *The Philosophical Review*, *103*(1), 75. Crossref, https://doi.org/10.2307/2185873

Northoff, G., Heinzel, A., de Greck, M., Bermpohl, F., Dobrowolny, H., Panksepp, J. (2006, May 15). Self-referential processing in our brain—a meta-analysis of imaging studies on the self. *Neuroimage*, *31*(1): 440–457. https://doi.org/10.1016/j.neuroimage.2005.12.002. Epub 2006 Feb 7. PMID: 16466680.

Panksepp, J. (1998). Affective Neuroscience: The Foundations of Human and Animal Emotions. Oxford University Press.

Oatley, K. (2007). Narrative Modes of Consciousness and Selfhood. In P. D. Zelazo, M. Moscovitch, & E. Thompson (Eds.), *The Cambridge Handbook of Consciousness* (pp. 375–402). Cambridge University Press. https://doi.org/10.1017/CBO9780511816789.015.

Oatley, K., Keltner, D., & Jenkins, J. M. (2006). *Understanding emotions* (2nd ed.). Blackwell Pub.

Rubin, D. C., Schrauf, R. W., & Greenberg, D. L. (2003). Belief and recollection of autobiographical memories. *Memory & Cognition*, *31*, 887–901.

Schacter, D. L., Benoit, R. G., De Brigard, F., & Szpunar, K. K. (2015). Episodic future thinking and episodic counterfactual thinking: Intersections between memory and decisions. *Neurobiology of Learning and Memory*, *117*, 14–21. https://doi.org/10.1016/j.nlm.2013.12.008

Schlichting, M. L., Mumford, J. A., & Preston, A. R. (2015). Learning-related representational changes reveal dissociable integration and separation signatures in the hippocampus and prefrontal cortex. *Nature Communications*, *6*(1), 8151. https://doi.org/10.1038/ncomms9151.

Schneider, S. (2007). Daniel Dennett on the nature of consciousness. In M. Velmans, & S. Schneider (Eds.), *The Blackwell Companion to Consciousness* (pp. 313–324). Blackwell.

Sheldon, S., McAndrews, M. P., & Moscovitch, M. (2011). Episodic memory processes mediated by the medial temporal lobes contribute to open-ended problem solving. *Neuropsychologia*, *49*(9), 2439–2447. https://doi.org/10.1016/j.neuropsychologia.2011.04.021

Stueber, K. R. (2012). Varieties of empathy, neuroscience and the narrativist challenge to the contemporary theory of mind debate. *Emotion Review*, *4*(1), 55–63.

Thompson, E. (2007). *Mind in life: Biology, phenomenology, and the sciences of mind*. Belknap Press/Harvard University Press.

Wiese, W., & Metzinger, T. (2017). Vanilla PP for philosophers: A primer on predictive processing.

Zahavi, D. (2007). Self and Other: The Limits of Narrative Understanding. *Royal Institute of Philosophy Supplement*, *60*, 179–202. Cambridge Core. https://doi.org/10.1017/S1358246107000094.

Zahavi, D. (2018). Consciousness, Self-Consciousness, Selfhood: A Reply to some Critics. *Review of Philosophy and Psychology*, *9*(3), 703–718. https://doi.org/10.1007/s13164-018-0403-6.

Zahavi, D., & Kriegel, U. (2015). For-me-ness: What it is and what it is not. In *Philosophy of mind and phenomenology* (pp. 48–66). Routledge.

CHAPTER 9

Conclusion

This book has argued that narrative processing is part of ordinary cognition, amounting to emergent 'weak narrativity.' Narrative processing is ongoing meaning-directed generation and processing of emergent temporal structures consisting of related value-dynamic sequences involving value-dynamic selected agents, mediated by socio-cultural contexts. This definition applies to processes occurring in a wide range of cognitive activities; also, elements of the definition describe aspects of discourses and experience that are properly bundled together, and for which 'narrativity' is an apt description.

Weak narrativity can be viewed as what I described in previous research as a 'functional illusion': a quality of sensemaking shaped by the cognitive history that enables it (Miller). Consider a literary example in which the 'veil' of this illusion is lifted: a passage from Robert Musil's novel *The Man Without Qualities* that describes a character who has lost his sense of experience having a narrative quality. The novel employs a third-person narrator with access to the thoughts of the protagonist, Ulrich:

> This is of course the beginning of life's notorious turning into abstraction.
> And in one of those apparently random and abstract thoughts that so often assumed importance in his life, it struck him that when one is overburdened and dreams of simplifying one's life, the basic law of this life, *the law one longs for, is nothing other than that of narrative order*, the simple order

B. Miller, *Narrativity in Cognition*,
https://doi.org/10.1007/978-3-031-40349-1_9

that enables one to say: 'First this happened and then that happened…' It is the simple sequence of events in which the overwhelmingly manifold nature of things is represented in a unidimensional order, as a mathematician would say, stringing all that has occurred in space and time on a single thread, which calms us; that celebrated 'thread of the story,' which is, it seems, the thread of life itself…

…*This is the trick the novel artificially turns to account*: Whether the wanderer is riding on the highway in pouring rain or crunching through snow and ice at ten below zero, the reader feels a cozy glow, and this would be hard to understand if this eternally dependable narrative device, which even nursemaids can rely on to keep their little charges quiet, *this tried-and-true 'foreshortening of the mind's perspective,' were not already part and parcel of life itself.…*

It now came to Ulrich that *he had lost this elementary, narrative mode of thought to which private life still clings, even though everything in public life has already ceased to be narrative* and no longer follows a thread, but instead spreads out as an infinitely interwoven surface. (pp. 708–9, emphases mine)

This passage points to the artificiality of 'narrative order' in the novel in contrast to life while noting that both involve 'foreshortening' to produce a sense of coherence. While Ulrich's vision of narrative order as a 'single thread' might seem rather reductive, the image implies selection, sequencing, and affective relief from an unaccountably complex reality. Ulrich's disillusionment at the end of the novel involves losing this narrative thread. While this turn, on the one hand, might parallel a more general sense of fragmentation in public life, it also suggests a shift from phenomenological, embodied, narrative meaning into dessicated, fossilized abstractions.

Considering narrativity in low-level cognition leads to further consideration of how we parse different forms of narrative, and why narratives can be rich sources of meaning. Weak narrativity is characteristic of the emergent, dynamic values recorded in event segmentation and episodic memory. The boundaries and internal logic of perceived events and episodic memories correspond to our definition of narrativity. In addition, narrativity characterizes the associative logic between discrete events, and it helps clarify the fuzzy boundaries between events as we understand them as they emerge and as we reflect upon them. Our ongoing narrative processing shapes, and is shaped by, our encounters with communicated narratives and narrative artifacts in a variety of social contexts.

This model of narrative processing reflects the insights of new models of cognition. Theories of predictive processing describe the way perception is built upon error-minimization-based modeling. For dynamic experiences, these models suggest perception is inextricable from anticipatory modeling. Event segmentation theories describe the emergence of boundaries at instances of prediction failure, as well as in relation to patterns of equilibriar-disequilibriar-equilibriar oscillation. Theories of embodied cognition and affective cognition implicate valuation into perceptual processes. Schemas, connectionist networks, and other models of higher order learning shape these valuation-perceptual complexes into meaningful experiential temporal bundles. As a result, experience reflects dynamic, relational valuation processes that shape awareness:

- a 'reverberating causality' between 'bottom-up,' emerging perceptions, and 'top-down' learned concepts and values;
- the accumulation of emergent meaning within a future-orientation.

Taken together, experience has emergent structure. In some cases, this structure is best characterized as weak narrativity.

The weak narrativity we perceive in our experiences forms a 'bottom-up' basis for the 'ready to hand' nature of ordinary narratives, such as our ability to describe our day. The weakly narrative character of remembered events, combined with schematic models of the progress of a day (embedded with valuations that reflect the teller's personality and social priors), makes recounting a recognizably narrative version of one's day possible without great forethought.[1]

More refined narratives are constructed via an iterative processing logic that both draws upon and informs weak narrativity in experience. Strong narrativity may emerge in various forms in relation to this processing and may involve processes of narrative rehearsal that shape particular accounts of episodes and larger 'stories' of experience mutually.

How might literary scholars draw from this study to refine concepts about narrative? For narrative theorists, there are opportunities that might emerge in the expanded study of ordinary narratives (including 'ready-to-hand' narratives), of non-artifactual 'small stories' (such as unsettled, competing histories of an ongoing conflict), and of narrativity within experiences and representations that are not narratives. There are also opportunities to consider the project of 'literary universals' as (paradoxically) expressions of the 'low level' nature of processes that imprint socio-cultural particulars upon our experiences of the world.

For literary scholars most interested in the politics of language and representation, the model of weak narrativity presented here supports

theories of the deep immanence of social values and our predisposition to
micropolitical valuations. As creatures disposed toward narrative as a form
of the most basic sensemaking, perception and cognition are inevitably
shaped by the texts, and voices, and institutions that shape us. The political powers of language and representation are grounded in their innateness.

Consider how such a viewpoint might inform a reading of Mary Oliver's
poem "Breakage." In this poem, Oliver's persona looks upon shells
dropped by gulls onto rocks by the sea:

> I go down to the edge of the sea.
> How everything shines in the morning light! The cusp of the whelk,
> the broken cupboard of the clam, the opened, blue mussels,
> moon snails, pale pink and barnacle scarred—
>
> and nothing at all whole or shut, but tattered, split,
> dropped by the gulls onto the gray rocks and all the moisture gone.
>
> It's like a schoolhouse of little words, thousands of words.
> First you figure out what each one means by itself, the jingle, the periwinkle,
> the scallop
>   full of moonlight.
>
> Then you begin, slowly, to read the whole story.

As the poem develops, the persona experiences first the particulars of
the seaside, and then compares the scene to a schoolhouse of words.
Through this image, she describes her experience of particulars in terms of
slowly revealed narrative. Oliver is teaching us how to look at a natural
scene mindfully. That is, she urges our attention to each element of the
experience individually, and either through this attention, or subsequent
to it, the 'whole story' emerges. The overt comparison of particulars to
words suggests that the tenor—the particulars—carry meaning-qualities
in their perception, just as words do. We might take this as a story of
humanization: we encounter a meaningless experience and populate it
with values. When we arrive at the 'schoolhouse' image, our minds have
transformed raw materiality into a linguistic corpus. Perhaps we move
from aestheticizing the broken shells to understanding the larger, ongoing
processes they reflect, thereby replacing an objectifying gaze with one sensitive to change, power, and context. It is a sensemaking operation.

But beneath this dynamic, there are hints that Oliver teaches us about the violence of our sensemaking, that we are, like the gulls, architects of 'breakage.' If we compare the natural images at the end of the poem to those at the beginning, we observe an *absence* of anthropomorphizing. While the opening features metaphorical terms like 'cusp' and 'cupboard,' the language of the end attends to something more like the thing-in-itself (*ding an sich*): a 'periwinkle' and a 'scallop full of moonlight.' She describes "figure[ing] out what each one means by/itself," which could refer to the space outside cognition as well as the individuality of the thing. The attention she directs toward, for example, a periwinkle involves passive, patient revelation of meaning—not the automatic associations we normally attach as we make sense of the world. To tease out the meaning of a thing is, in a sense, to seek an inhuman language.

In a final twist, though, Oliver's comparison of these non-metaphorical images to words reminds us of the tautology that all perceived objects are phenomena, not noumena. Our abstraction processes, our 'breakages,' both desiccate nature and facilitate storifying it.

The message behind these reversals is that we need to slow down in order to put up some resistance to inserting our own values into experience, artificially imputing tendentious, self-oriented narrativity to experience. Paradoxically, when we do so we discover an underlying narrative structure associated with (and here the poem is ambiguous) either the world-in-itself or our encounters with it. Stripping away reflexive narrative assignations may begin to reveal the world, but it does not necessarily remove the narrative processing essential to our sensemaking. That Oliver can open us to this underlying order through words alone is remarkable and suggests a deep and essential interplay between the narrativity of experience and the narrative form and perspective conveyed in language.

How might social scientists and natural scientists make use of these ideas? First, there is ample opportunity for empirical research testing certain concepts and for modeling of weakly narrative structures in experience as described throughout the book, but with most direct reference to ongoing cognitive research programs in Chaps. 5, 6, 7, and 8. Examples might include the study of reading as a form of sensemaking, refining how schemas or connectionist networks encode temporal extension and prime anticipation, and explaining the contribution of affect to the cognitive processes associated with event segmentation.

There is also a need to develop in some detail the relation between these ideas and narrative knowing and narrative explanation, as assessed in Chaps. 2, 3, and 4. In particular, there's opportunity to develop greater consensus about the value of narrative explanation in particularistic description and counterfactual accounting of phenomena.

In the end, this book is about the temporal elements of our ongoing sensemaking, broadly conceived. As such, it illuminates how narrative processing in various aspects of cognition processes illuminates a familiar, even hackneyed trope: we experience life as a journey; meaning as a quest forever on the cusp, rather than a destination. We have goals that may be conceived as endpoints, but when these goals are realized we understand the false promise of endings. Realized, they decline in salience. We move with and toward the promise of meaning, making 'breakages' and 'narrative order' from the seamless fabric of time and space.

NOTE

1. Such 'ready-to-hand-ness' reflects a history of social training for delivering a narrative account of one's day. This training and practice in discourse make the 'small stories' of our lives seem to emerge automatically in our minds, and it shapes how we perceive the world.

REFERENCES

Miller, B. (2013). *Self-consciousness in Modern British Fiction*. Palgrave.

Musil, R. (1965). *The man without qualities*. New York, Capricorn Books.

Oliver, M. (2017). *Devotions: the selected poems of Mary Oliver*. New York, Penguin Press, an imprint of Penguin Random House LLC.

Index[1]

NUMBERS AND SYMBOLS

4E Perspective, 106

101 Dalmatians, 83

A

Abelson, R. P., 18

Academic disciplines and narrative, 4

Addis, D. R., 140

Affect and synthesis, 172

Affect Infusion Model, 159

Affective cognition, 161

Amis, Martin, 67

Anderson, M. L., 104, 110

Andrews-Hanna, J. R., 102

Anoetic substrate, 167

Anticipatory cognition, 103

Appraisal theories of emotion, 160

Arbib, Michael, 209

Aristotle, 13

Armstrong, Paul, 62, 73, 78, 87n4, 89n20, 90n28, 90n30

Arnold, Magda, 159

Ascription, 49

Attention, 124–130

Attention Schema Theory, 125, 200

Austen, Jane, 74

Autobiographical memory, 21

Autobiographical narrative, 1, 14

Autobiographical selfhood, 219

Autonoesis, 99–100

B

Baars, B. J., 97

Bakker, I., 174, 181

Bamberg, Michael, 16, 198

Bargh, J. A., 163

Barnes, Julian, 69

Barrett, L. F., 169, 170, 172

Barsalou, Lawrence W., 64, 80, 129

Bartlett, Frederic, 18

Bauer, Patricia, 128

Bayne, Tim, 200, 206

Beatty, J., 17, 223

Bergson, Henri, 108

[1] Note: Page numbers followed by 'n' refer to notes.

B. Miller, *Narrativity in Cognition*,
https://doi.org/10.1007/978-3-031-40349-1

235

Block, Ned, 99
Bottom-up, 61
Bottom-up views, 43
Boundary parameters, 52
Bower, G. H.
    emotional congruence account, 159
Boyd, Brian, 16
Braver, T. S., 128
Brockmeier, Jens, 19, 34, 198
Brown, K. S., 210
Brown, Richard, 183
Brown, Stephen, 172
Bruineberg, J., 105
Bruner, Jerome, 14, 34, 41
Buckner, R. L., 102, 134
Burke, Michael, 62, 87n6
Burr, C., 96
Butler, Judith, 143

C
Caracciolo, Marco, 63, 64, 80, 88n12
Care, 182
Carr, David, 19
Carroll, Joseph, 16
Chabris, Simons, 133
Chatman, S., 17
Christoff, K., 204
Citron, F. M., 169, 172
Clark, Andy, 106, 110
Clay, E. R., 108
Clore, G. L., 160
Component process model of
    emotion, 160
Computationalism, 95, 112n9
Concurrent strands framework, 137
Configured wholes, 77, 78, 80
Connectionism, 210, 211
Conrad, Joseph, 69
Constructivist models of emotion, 170
Constructivist theories of
    cognition, 110

Conway, Martin, 215
Corballis, M. C., 103
Core affect, 169
Critchley, H. D., 168, 169
Cromwell, H. C., 155
Current global theories of
    cognition, 97–98
Currie, Adrian, 88n16
Currie, Gregory, 34

D
Damasio, Antonio, 160
Davis, J. B., 218
de Boon, J., 174, 181
De Fina, Anna, 198
De Sousa, Ronald
    The Rationality of Emotions, 161
Default Mode Network, 103
Definition of cognition, 95
Definitions of narrative, 4, 11–12, 66
Dehaene, Stanislas, 97
Dennett, Daniel, 15, 19, 205
Dewhurst, Joe, 220
Di Paolo, Ezequial, 88n10, 110
Discourse studies, 198
    small stories, 16
Dual process theory, 183
Duration, 109
Dutton, Dennis, 16
Dynamic valuation, 200
    See also Value dynamism

E
Eakin, Paul, 15
Easterlin, Nancy, 16
Ecological account of experience, 106
Eilan, Naomi, 108, 205
Elman, J. L., 210, 211
Embodied cognition, 107, 205
Emergent structures, 77, 85

Emotional congruence account, 159
Emotion and Perception, 163
Emplotment, 41, 42, 44, 53
Enactive cognition, 105, 110
Episodic autobiographical
    memory, 219
Episodic memory, 1, 101, 140, 215
Equilibriar dynamics, 129, 130
Evaluation in perception, 3, 157, 158
Events, boundary processing and
    selection, 46, 77
Event indexing model, 62
Event processing, 42, 124–130,
    146, 216
Event segmentation theory, 137,
    140, 142
Experientiality, 49, 59, 63

F
Faber, M., 132
Felt time, 123
Fivush, R., 22, 219
Fludernik, Monika, 16, 49, 59, 62
Folk psychology, 14, 15
Foreground and background, 50
Forgas, Joseph
    affect infusion model, 159
For-Me-Ness, 203
Friston, Karl, 104
Furman, O., 219

G
Gallese, Vittorio, 61, 76, 80
Gao, Xiaoqing, 172
Garfinkel, S. N., 168, 169
Gennari, S. P., 132
Georgakopoulou, Alexandra, 16, 198
Gerrig, Richard J., 16, 62, 81,
    87n4, 90n30
Ghosh, V. E., 210

Gibson, James, 106
Gilboa, A., 210
Gist processing, 212, 213
Global theories of cognition, 98
Global Workspace Theory, 97, 200
Goal processing, 216
Godard, Jean-Luc, 79
Goldberg, M. E., 163
    and colleagues, 163
The Golden Bowl (1904), 75
Goldie, Peter, 11
Graziano, M. S. A., 125
Greenberg, D. L., 22
Groundhog Day (1993), 72

H
Hassabis, D., 103, 199
Hasson, U., 219
Hatavara, M., 17
Heidegger, Martin, 13, 78
Herman, David, 7, 12, 16, 34, 49, 60,
    67, 80, 86–87n1
Heterogenous concatenation, 42
Higher order cognitive processes, 197
Higher order theory, 97, 183
Higher Order Theory of Emotional
    Consciousness, 183
Hogan, Patrick Colm, 157
Holland, A. C., 21, 215
Hommel, B., 133
Human development, 22
Hurley, S., 96
Husserl, Edmund, 13, 62, 78, 108
Hutto, Daniel, 15, 54, 221

I
Implicit narrativity, 54
In-event processing, 134
Intention, 33
Iser, Wolfgang, 62

J

Jacobs, Arthur M., 63, 64, 70, 83, 88n8
James, Henry, 75
James, William, 108, 120
Johnson, Mark, 18
Jongepier, F., 54
Jonze, Spike
  Her, 35

K

Kensinger, E. A., 21, 215
Kim, A. S., 140
Kintsch, W., 12
Kreiswirth, M., 17
Kriegel, Uriah, 203
Kuiken, Don, 79, 90n32

L

Labov and Waletzky, 12
Lakoff, George, 18
Lamarque, Peter, 11
Lazarus, Richard, 159
LeDoux, Joseph, 183
Lewin, Phillip, 15
Lewis, K., 147
Life-story, 2
  See also Autobiographical narrative
Little Red Riding Hood, 65
Local recurrence theory, 97
Lyotard, Jean-Francois, 13

M

MacIntyre, Alisdair, 14
Mackenzie, Catriona, 11
Maguire, E. A., 103, 199
Maibom, H., 220
Mair, Miller, 14
Mar, Raymond A., 63, 88n7, 140

'Mark of the cognitive' debate, 95
Markowitsch, H. J., 20, 214, 218
Marlatte, H., 210
McAdams, Dan, 19
McGivern, P., 221
McRae, K., 210, 211
McTaggart, J. Ellis, 108
Medina, J., 221
Memelink, J., 133
Memento (2000), 67
Memory systems, 102
Menary, Richard, 20, 43, 144, 206
Mental time travel, 15
Meretoja, Hanna, 7, 19, 40, 60, 198
Merill, N., 22
Mesquita, B., 169–171, 173, 181
Metzinger, T., 104, 106, 205
Miall, David S., 79, 90n32
Michael Dudok De Wit
  The Red Turtle, 1
Milivojevic, B., 21, 218
Minimalist theories of narrative, 11
Minimal selfhood, 206
Mink, Louis, 13
Modal and amodal representation, 129
Models of cognition, 5
Model theory, 220
Montemayor, Carlos, 122
Morgan, M. S., 17
Morsella, E., 163
Moshe Bar, 209
Multiple drafts model of cognition, 108
Multiple waves model, 163

N

Narrative artifacts, 37, 40, 54
Narrative as methodology, 19
Narrative hermeneutics, 19, 40, 60, 147, 198

Narrative identity, 217
Narrative processing, 5, 7, 37, 142, 146, 155
Narratives and experiences, 3, 10, 16, 49
Narrativity, 34
Nature of narrative, 3
Nelson, Katherine, 11, 22, 65, 128, 219
Neurocognitive Poetics Model, 63
Noesis, 99

O
Oatley, Keith, 21, 214
Object-based schema, 54
Overflow hypothesis, 99

P
Panksepp, J., 155
Perceptual cognition, 19
Perspectival awareness, 108
Pessoa, Luiz, 88n9, 163, 164
Phenomenal self model (PSM), 205
Phenomenological features of consciousness, 200
Piolino, P., 102
Power and Dagleish, 160
Prediction Failure and Event Boundaries, 137
Predictive processing, 106, 201, 220
  active inference, 104, 105, 169
Pre-narrative fodder, 144
Pride and Prejudice, 74
Prinz, Jesse
  Gut Reactions, 161
Propp, Vladimir, 12, 67
Proto-configurations, 78, 80, 81, 85, 90n31
  Whole-directed, anticipatory temporal figuration, 77

R
Radvansky, Gabriel A., 88n15
Raichle, Marc, 102
Reader response criticism, 16
Reading, 61
Reading and narrative, 4
Ready-to-hand narratives, 5
Rebel Without a Cause (1955), 74
Relational dynamism, 120, 142, 175, 182
  See also Value dynamism
Relationality, 70–73
Representation in cognition, 95
Reverberating causality, 168
Richmond, L. L., 137
Ricoeur, Paul, 41, 77, 89n17
  Oneself as Another, 147
  Time and Narrative, 13
Ritivoi, Andreas, 42
Roberts, Robert, 161
Room (2010), 72
Rubin, D. C., 22, 217
Rumination, 38
Ryan, Marie-Laure, 12, 53

S
Salience, 70–73
Salience map, 163
Scene construction, 103
Schacter, D. L., 102, 140
Schank, R. C., 18
Schectman, Marya, 15
Schema, 18, 49, 62, 210
Schema theory, 210
Scherer, Klaus, 160
Schlichting, M. L., 210
Schneider, Susan, 19, 205
Schrauf, R. W., 217
Self as illusion, 206
Selfhood, 15, 21, 206, 214
Self-valuation, 217
Semanticization, 101

Semantic memory, 101
Sensemaking, 40, 110
    accumulative sensemaking, 66
Sentinel view, 102
Sequencing, 70
Serial, parallel, independent model of
    memory, 100
Seth, Anil, 167, 170
Shipley, Thomas, 125, 130
Simulation, 64, 213
Simulation theory, 221
Situation boundaries, 175, 182
Situation modeling, 62
Skilled coping, 62
Small stories, 39, 198
Social cognition and
    narrative, 223
Social discourse, 13
Sociality and narrative, 4
Somatic marker hypothesis, 160
SPAARS model, 160
Speed, Laura J., 80
Speer, Nicole K., 62, 136
Spreng, R. N., 140
Stanilou, A., 20, 214, 218
Starr, Gabrielle, 62
Sternberg, Meir, 66, 68, 155
Stream of consciousness, 120
Structuration, 82, 147
    temporal associative networks, 77
Suddendorf, T., 103

T
Temporality, 13, 65, 124
Theories of emotion, 159
Theory of Event Coding
    (TEC), 133
Theory of mind, 19, 44
Theory theory, 219, 220
Thompson, Evan, 108, 205
Top-down, 61
Top-down views, 43, 51
Tulving, Endel, 101

Turner, Mark, 19, 50
Tversky, B., 128

U
Unity, 202
Unity and affect, 202
The Usual Suspects (1995), 82

V
Valuation, 6, 74–76, 129, 165
Valuation dynamism, 142
    and event boundaries, 134
Van Dijk, T. A., 12
Van Peer, W., 17
Varadinov, Meryl, 218
Varieties of narrative, 1
Velleman, David, 156
Vigliocco, Gabriella, 80
Virtual phenomenalism, 206

W
Watkins-Goffmann, 17
Weak narrativity, 5
Webb, T. W., 125
Weick, Karl E., 88n10
White, Hayden, 13
Wiese, W., 104, 106
Wise, M. N., 17
Wittman, Marc, 122, 123
Woolf, Virginia, 77

Y
The Yellow Wallpaper (1892), 72

Z
Zacks, J. M., 128, 137
Zahavi, Dan, 108, 203, 205
Zunshine, Lisa, 19, 88n7
Zwaan, Rolf A., 62, 82, 87n5, 88n15